D1600164

G. E. Moore

The Early Essays

G. E. Moore

The Early Essays

Edited by

Tom Regan

Temple University Press
Philadelphia

Temple University Press, Philadelphia 19122
Copyright © 1986 by Temple University. All rights reserved
Published 1986
Printed in the United States of America

The paper used in this publication meets the minimum requirements of American National Standard for Information Sciences—Permanence of Paper for Printed Library Materials, ANSI Z39.48-1984.

Library of Congress Cataloging-in-Publication Data

Moore, G. E. (George Edward), 1873–1958.
G. E. Moore: the early essays.

Includes index.
1. Philosophy. I. Regan, Tom. II. Title.
B1647.M73G2 1986 192 86-6007
ISBN 0-87722-442-0 (alk. paper)

Fred L. Mathews Library
Southwestern Michigan College
Dowagiac, MI 49047

To my teachers,
Peter Heath and David Yalden-Thomson,
who introduced me to
Moore's philosophy

Contents

Preface

During the academic year 1984–1985, it was my great pleasure to hold the position of Fellow at the National Humanities Center. I was accepted as a Fellow to work on a book-length study of the moral philosophy of G. E. Moore. That project, *Bloomsbury's Prophet: G. E. Moore and the Development of His Moral Philosophy*, is now complete. Its publication marks the first installment on my debts both to Moore and to the Center.

A second installment is the present collection of Moore's early essays. Neither the idea of forming this collection nor the time to do it would have presented themselves to me had it not been for my tenure as a Fellow. For having these and other blessings I am grateful to those who wrote in support of my application, to the members of the Selection Committee for finding merit in my plan of study, to my university, North Carolina State University, for its support of research in the humanities, and to all the members of the Center's staff for their cordial interest. It is doubtful whether there are many better places in the world for humanistic scholars to carry on their research. May the work of those of us who have had the privilege of making our temporary homes at the Center be a small but lasting repayment for the abundant opportunities we have enjoyed.

These previously published essays by Moore are collected here for the first time. They are arranged chronologically and reproduced as they originally appeared, except for a few minor emendations. For readers who wish to consult the originals, the journal page number has been included in brackets at the point in the text where the original page begins. Near his death in 1958 Moore opposed their republication. Permission to collect them at this time has been granted by Moore's literary executor, Casimir Lewy and by Moore's son, the composer Timothy Moore.

I am immensely grateful to Timothy Moore for his support of this project and to Casimir Lewy for saving me from a number of factual errors in my Introduction. If the present volume achieves its aim of helping to rekindle scholarly interest in Moore's work, I hope Timothy Moore and Casimir Lewy will accept this achievement as fair payment for their confidence and trust.

I also owe debts of gratitude to Jane Cullen and Doris Braendel of Temple University Press, for their wise counsel and moral support on this and other projects, and—as always—to my wife, Nancy.

Raleigh, N. C.
May 19th

G. E. Moore

The Early Essays

Introduction

The Moore most of us know is half the man he was. Accustomed as we are to distinguishing between the various stages of a philosopher's development, finding it natural to speak of the early Plato, for example, or the later Wittgenstein, we seem almost to suppose that Moore was never early. Or later. Moore was—well, Moore was Moore, born with a proof of the external world in his mouth.

Anyone who has made even a cursory examination of Moore's published work knows that this is the Moore of popular mythology, not the Moore of hard historical fact. The later Moore, let us agree, distinguished himself as the plain man's philosopher. But not the early Moore, not the Moore we meet up to and through *Principia Ethica.* That Moore voiced paradoxes that have taken the later Moore's breath away, energetically endorsing propositions which, as we shall note briefly below, his future self found "perfectly monstrous."

Why does the early Moore remain unknown to so many? Partly no doubt this is due to the near idolatrous stature the elder Moore enjoyed, the glow from which, associated as it was with his defense of common sense, conspired to keep the raucous philosophical exuberance of his youth in the shadows. And partly, too, we know comparatively little of the early Moore because of the later Moore's influence on a particular "school" of philosophy, ordinary language philosophy, so-called, the members of which, themselves disdainful of speculative metaphysics, helped perpetuate the fable that their hero never dabbled in that suspicious trade. But plausible as these explanations are, neither, whether taken separately or together, is quite enough. Each fails to mention the essential role Moore himself played in controlling what his successors would most likely know about his intellectual development.

In addition to dozens of reviews and a number of miscellaneous writings, including his important contributions to Paul A. Schilpp's *The Philosophy of* G. E. *Moore* (1942), Moore published three booklength studies during his lifetime: *Principia Ethica* (1903), *Ethics* (1912), and *Some Main Problems of Philosophy* (1953). A selection from three courses of lectures given at Cambridge at various times between 1925 and 1934 was edited by Casimir Lewy and published in 1966 under the title *Lectures on Philosophy*. A second posthumous volume, also edited by Lewy, appeared in 1962 under the title *Commonplace Book, 1919–1953*. It is a collection of philosophical notes from those years. Moore himself oversaw the publication of *Philosophical Studies* (1922), a collection of ten papers written between 1903 and 1921, two of which had not been published before. In the summer of 1959 there appeared a second collection of essays, *Philosophical Papers*. This contains ten papers written between 1923 and 1955, two of which were published in the collection for the first time. Moore died in October 1958, and the supervision of his book through the Press was taken over by Lewy. These collections of papers, the posthumously published books, the three books published during his lifetime, and a few of the miscellaneous writings, most notably his contributions to the Schilpp volume, form the standard Moorean corpus with which most philosophers are familiar.

Viewing this corpus in the abstract, one might naturally infer that Moore wrote nothing before 1903, the date of publication both of *Principia Ethica* and of "The Refutation of Idealism", the earliest published essay included in *Philosophical Studies*. However natural this inference might be, the conclusion bears no resemblance to reality. Moore published no fewer than ten papers between 1897 and 1903, of which only "The Refutation of Idealism" was republished. The other nine remained shelved way, gathering dust in rare back issues of the *International Journal of Ethics*, for example, or the *Proceedings of the Aristotelian Society*. Together with a paper on Kant, published in 1904, these papers form an essential part of the total Moorean corpus and afford us a glimpse of the neglected early Moore, both Moore the fledgling idealist metaphysician, for example, and Moore the leader of a revolt against the idealistic metaphysic to which he was initially so attracted. That most of us know so little about this period of Moore's philosophical development is, if I am right, in no small measure due to what Moore left out of, as well as what he put into, the collections of essays he drew together during his lifetime. We know little of the early Moore, in short, partly because the later Moore left us little of the early Moore we could easily study. The present collection of the early essays seeks to overcome this serious omission from his legacy.

It is not difficult to confirm that a fresh examination of these essays will serve to correct received opinions about Moore's philosophical apprenticeship. A. J. Ayer, for example, in his discussion of Moore's philosophical development, states that "almost all that Moore thought it necessary to say about the grand metaphysical questions of God and Immortality is contained in one short paragraph of the essay, 'A Defense of Common Sense,' which he contributed to the second volume of *Contemporary British Philosophy* in 1925."[1] Now, it is true that we find no lengthy discussion of either God or immortality in the standard Moorean corpus.

But two essays in the present collection assault Ayer's judgment. "The Value of Religion," published in 1901, is a sustained critical examination of the rationality of belief in God, and the greater part of a second essay, "Mr. McTaggart's 'Studies in Hegelian Cosmology,'" read before the Aristotelian Society in May 1902, consists of a lengthy critical examination of the belief in immortality. That Moore in his later work did not continue to explore these "grand metaphysical questions" may be affirmed. But that is no reason to deny that he did explore them earlier, and no reason to continue to neglect the arguments he offers there.

The mythological Moore, the philosopher who defended common sense as soon as he was able to speak prose, is captured with considerable elegance by G. J. Warnock in his *English Philosophy Since 1900*. Moore, he writes, "seems to have been . . . entirely without any of the motives that tend to make a metaphysican. . . . He . . .had no leanings whatever towards paradox and peculiarity of opinion. . . . He . . . did not hanker for any system on his own account. . . . He did not borrow a modish metaphysical idiom to make up for, or to conceal, his own lack of relish for any such thing."[2] Warnock's description is a variation on a familiar theme, one we find played again, for example, by Susan Stebbing, who writes that Moore "never attempted to produce anything like a philosophical system."[3] To bolster her case, Stebbing quotes a marvelous passage from Moore's "Freedom": "The region of the incompletely known is the favourite abode of a metaphysical monstrosity. In plain language, where facts are not completely understood, some short-sighted metaphysical theory is generally introduced as affording an easy road past the difficulties which stand in the way of thorough investigation." Moore, Stebbing assures us, "[was] never . . . tempted to enter this easy road."

Now, all this is, perhaps, a fair description of the later Moore.[4] It is wildly inaccurate when matched against the early Moore, however. Once we have read Moore's "The Nature of Judgment," for example, we shall never again suppose that "he had no leanings whatever towards paradox and peculiarity of opinion." "The world," Moore there maintains, is "formed of concepts," including existence, which "is itself a concept." Thus, "all that exists is . . . composed of concepts necessarily related to one another in specific manners, and likewise to the concept of existence." Even the youthful Moore knew a paradox when he expressed one, noting that "I am fully aware how paradoxical this theory must appear, and even how contemptible." But that did not prevent him from maintaining it then, in 1898, when, the descriptions of Warnock and Stebbing notwithstanding, Moore did hanker after a "system" of his own. For unlike some later critics of speculative metaphysics, Moore was not then intent upon undermining the whole metaphysical enterprise. If in "Freedom" he laments the existence of metaphysical monstrosities, he does so because they are monstrosities, not because they are metaphysical. The younger Moore aspired to move metaphysics out of the disreputable abode of the "incompletely known" into a neighborhood more in keeping with her status as the Queen of the Sciences. If we demythologize Moore, permitting him to speak for himself, we find an earnest young man with visions of replacing false metaphysical theories with a true one of his own.

But it is Moore himself, not just his commentators, who sometimes helps cultivate our ignorance of his philosophical past. In a famous passage in his "An Autobiography" he recounts his first meeting with J. M. E. McTaggart. Bertrand Russell "had invited me to tea in his rooms to meet McTaggart," Moore recalls, "and McTaggart, in the course of conversation had been led to express his well-known view that Time is unreal. This must have seemed to me then (as it still does) a perfectly monstrous proposition, and I did my best to argue against it."[5] Though this may be a true account of Moore's initial reaction to that "perfectly monstrous proposition," the inference which, by his silence, he invites us to make—namely, that he *always* regarded this proposition as "perfectly monstrous"—is not borne out by the contents of his early essays. In the first published philosophy, a contribution to a 1897 symposium entitled "In What Sense, If Any, Do Past and Future Time Exist?," for example, Moore concludes as follows: "If I need, then, . . . to give a direct answer to our question, I would say that neither Past, Present, nor Future exists, if by existence we are to mean the ascription of full Reality and not merely existence as Appearance." If this looks very like an endorsement of that "perfectly monstrous proposition," the following passage, from Moore's 1898 essay "Freedom," leaves no room for doubt.

> That time itself cannot be conceived to be fundamentally real is always admitted by Kant himself, and indeed he has attempted a proof of it. How far his proof is satisfactory, and whether, if unsatisfactory, any other proof is forthcoming, is too large a question to be fully discussed here. I can only state that the arguments by which Mr. Bradley has endeavoured to prove the unreality of Time appear to me perfectly conclusive.

Let this be a lesson to us: We do well to read these essays in their own terms and not rely for guidance about the early Moore's views on the elder Moore's stated recollections.

Failing to read these essays not only is likely to perpetuate our misunderstanding of Moore's philosophical development, it is equally likely to foster our misperception of the timing and logic of Moore's influence on others—Russell, for example. Both Moore and Russell cut their philosophical teeth on F. H. Bradley's Absolute Idealism, and though both in time renounced their allegiance to Bradley's theories, Russell has made it abundantly clear that it was Moore who blazed the trail. Moore, Russell writes,[6]

> took the lead in the rebellion, and I followed with a sense of emancipation. Bradley had argued that everything that common sense believes in

is mere appearance; we reverted to the opposite extreme, and thought that *everything* is real that common sense, uninfluenced by philosophy or theology, supposes real. With a sense of escaping from prison, we allowed ourselves to think that grass is green, that the sun and the stars would exist if no one was aware of them, and also that there is a pluralistic timeless world of Platonic ideas. The world which had been thin and logical, suddenly became rich and varied and solid.

Russell dates this rebellion against Bradley (and Hegel and Kant) as 1898, a period when Moore was working on "The Nature of Judgment." If we are to understand the rebellion's philosophical basis, therefore, it is to this paper, which offers an extended critique of Bradley's views, that we must look.

As a matter of history, this much is beyond dispute. And yet E. D. Klemke, for example, in his paper "Did G. E. Moore Refute Idealism?,"[7] after quoting the very same passage from Russell reproduced above, goes on to examine Moore's 1903 paper, "The Refutation of Idealism", a paper which examines, not Bradley's theories, but the Berkeleian thesis that *esse* is *percipi*. Bradley's views about Reality do not put in so much as an appearance in the 1903 paper on idealism. Moreover, when Klemke does refer to some of Moore's other published quarrels with idealism, the seminal 1898 paper, which does examine Bradley's views, is never mentioned.

None of this, of course, is meant to question the adequacy of Klemke's analysis of Moore's later arguments against idealism. It is meant only as an historical pointer: We are unlikely to understand the context and logic of those arguments that prompted first Moore, then Russell, to break loose of the ties that bound them to Bradleian idealism if we look for, and think we have found, the historical moment of that break in a paper published some five years *after* that break occurred. Nor, indeed, are we any more likely to understand these matters if we make rash inferences based on Russell's testimony. For Moore's mature conception of "the common sense view of the world" did not come full-blown into the world in 1898. At least as late as the 1901 paper, "The Value of Religion," we find a Moore who, unlike the Moore we encounter in his later writings, is *unable to claim to know, with certainty*, that such propositions as "This hand moves" or "I moved it" are true. Though we "cannot help believing" them, he writes, all such propositions "are possibly not true." Russell's recollection of this rebellion led by the early Moore may be, and doubtless is, veridical. But what it meant for Moore to believe in "common sense" in 1898 is demonstrably different from what it meant for him to believe in it later.

The reference to Kant in the passage from "Freedom," quoted earlier, points up a neglected area of Moorean scholarship. After announcing his intention in that paper to concentrate on Kant's view of Freedom, Moore goes on to explain that he has "chosen to deal with him at such length mainly because I think that reference to the views of the philosopher, with whom you are most in agreement, is often the clearest way of explaining your own view." It is not McTaggart's, not Bradley's, not Henry Sidgwick's views that are here singled out as those with which Moore's "are most in agreement." It is Kant's. Indeed, it is Kant's views, more than any other single philosopher's, that emerge time and time again for discussion in these early essays, not only in "Freedom," but also in "The Nature of Judgment" (1898), "Necessity" (1900), "Experience and Empiricism" (1902), and "Kant's Idealism" (1904). The distance by which Moore disassociates himself from Kant is a measure of the early Moore's philosophical growth. Whereas in 1897 it is Kant's views, especially his idealism, with which Moore's own "are most in agreement," by 1904 he is able to declare that "Kant's idealism . . . is certainly false." How this transition from disciple to critic came about is too large a chapter in Moore's intellectual history to attempt to tell here. That the transition did occur, and that its explanation is likely to be found, at least in part, in these early essays—these are the key points to be urged on this occasion. We shall never understand the unadvertised price Moore paid for his defense of common sense if we do not understand how magnetically he was initially attracted to the view that something other than the furniture of the plain man's world is what is fundamentally real.

But while it is Kant's presence that dominates, other notable philosophers—McTaggart, in particular, and, through him, Hegel—enjoy a large share of Moore's critical attention. "Identity" (1901), for example, includes a critique of Hegel's views, while McTaggart's positions are the main focus of "Mr. McTaggart's 'Studies in Hegelian Cosmology' " (1902) and "Mr. McTaggart's Ethics" (1903). These last two essays represent Moore's philosophical homage to his valued mentor. For it was McTaggart, Moore recalls, who had the greatest influence on him as a student. Not only did McTaggart produce "the impression of being immensely clever and quick in argument," he was constantly insisting on clearness, "on trying to give a precise meaning to philosophical expressions, asking the question 'What does this mean?' "[8] The later Moore, as is well known, made this same insistence on clarity an inseparable part of his philosophical character. But nowhere, perhaps, does he indulge this acquired habit more than in these two essays devoted to refuting McTaggart's views. One must assume that the teacher was flattered by the compliment paid by the student.

Hegel, Kant, McTaggart, and Bradley, each in his own way subscribed to a version of idealism. Because Moore's examinations of this metaphysical propensity grew increasingly critical as the years advanced, it would be natural to suppose that he put all his idealistic baggage behind him by 1903. It is not clear that this is true, however, as can be illustrated by considering certain well-known features of his moral philosophy.

Moore's acute disaffection with naturalism in ethics, especially as this is expressed in *Principia Ethica*, for example, arguably is related to his chronic displeasure with empiricism in philosophy generally. And that displeasure, as we see in these early essays, he first acquired from his youthful affair with the Idealists. Kant's Transcendental Deduction, for example, Moore writes in "The Nature of Judgment", contains a perfectly valid answer to Hume's scepticism, and to empiricism in general." Moreover, and relatedly, when, in *Principia*, Moore classifies goodness as a non-natural property, it is difficult to ignore the shadows idealism still casts on his thought. "It is not goodness," he declares, "but only the things or qualities which are good, which can exist in time—can have duration, and begin and cease to exist."[9] Does this mean that there is no such thing as goodness? Moore seems clearly to think that there is, just as he seems clearly to think that there are numbers. However, to believe in the reality of things which, by their very nature, do not exist in time, is to embrace some of the spirit, if not every letter, of Idealism. Is it possible, then, for Moore to have it both ways, denying idealism on the one hand and, on the other, affirming an ethic which seems to rest on what appear to be idealistic presuppositions? Again, if there is a compelling answer to be found, it is unlikely that we shall find it without consulting the early essays, even those containing no explicit reference to ethical questions.

In my view the rewards of giving these essays a close re-examination are much greater than these brief introductory remarks can show. The moral philosophy we find in *Principia*, for example, embodies Moore's answers to questions he had earlier considered in papers published before 1903. Read in this light, *Principia* may be seen as a step along the way to the mature development of his views in and about ethics. I have attempted to tell this story in *Bloomsbury's Prophet: G. E. Moore and the Development of His Moral Philosophy*.[10] That story involves a close study of Moore's neglected views about belief in God, including the views we find in "The Value of Religion." But it also involves a fresh examination of the other points of emphasis mentioned in the preceding—Moore's early affinities with Bradley, for example, and the influence of Kant and McTaggart. How compelling my account of the development of Moore's moral philosophy is, and how persuasive my explanation of its powerful influence on the Bloomsbury Group happens to be, are here less important than recognizing the pivotal role Moore's pre-*Principia* writings must come to play for subsequent Moorean scholarship, not only relative to his views in ethics but elsewhere as well—his views in epistemology, for example.

It is unclear what Moore, if he were alive, would think of the present collection of his essays. That he himself did not anthologize them and withheld his permission to have them collected by others suggests that he had lost whatever enthusiasm for them he at one time may have felt. From remarks he makes in his "An Autobiography," moreover, we know something of his opinion of "Freedom." Though he had not looked at it "for a long time," he states that he "[has] no doubt that it [is] absolutely worthless."[11] Perhaps Moore would make the same harsh judgment about most, if not all, of the essays collected here, though even the elder Moore, writing in 1942, after noting that he is "sure that ['The Nature of Judgment'] must have been full of confusions," does allow that "I think there was probably some good in it."[12] Like most of us, Moore may have felt that there were few sins as irredeemable as those of his youth. And these essays *are* the product of his youth: he was only twenty-four when "Freedom" was written, just twenty-nine when *Principia* first appeared. Moreover, this work was accomplished after only two years of formal study in philosophy (1894–1896). Whatever we may think of the lasting significance of these essays, Moore's raw talent surely was prodigious.

Suppose we assume that Moore would raise an eyebrow if

asked to look at these essays again. I do not think we should let this deter us. What we owe to our predecessors is our best effort to understand what light they have left us, and how they acquired it. And what we owe to our successors is our dedication to ease the burdens of their scholarship, when we can. This collection should meet these obligations, first, because it presents us with a fuller, more realistic view of Moore, one that should help us correct past and present misperceptions of the man and his philosophy, both those misperceptions fathered by his commentators and those encouraged by Moore himself. And, second, the ready availability of these early essays should also help move Moorean scholarship up a notch or two in the future. That is all the present collection would hope. Or presume. Certainly we show the later Moore no disrespect by allowing the early Moore the opportunity to speak again, freed from the not inconsiderable weight of his own future reputation, this time to a new and, one hopes, wider audience. In this way we might even soften the paradox that, despite his immense influence on others and the uncommon esteem in which he was held—indeed, no doubt in no small measure because of this—Moore remains "the unknown philosopher."[13]

NOTES

1. A. J. Ayer, *Russell and Moore: The Analytical Heritage* (Cambridge, Mass.: Harvard University Press, 1971), p. 138.

2. G. J. Warnock, *English Philosophy Since 1900* (London: Oxford University Press, 1959), p. 12.

3. L. Susan Stebbing, "Moore's Influence," in Paul Arthur Schilpp, ed., *The Philosophy of* G. E. *Moore* (New York: Tudor, 1952), p. 520.

4. Others might challenge the received opinion. See, for example, A. C. Ewing, "Moore and Metaphysics," in A. Ambrose and M. Lazerowitz, eds., G. E. *Moore: Essays in Retrospect* (London: George Allen and Unwin, 1970), pp. 139–159.

5. "An Autobiography," in Schilpp, ed., *The Philosophy of* G. E. *Moore*, pp. 13–14.

6. Bertrand Russell, "My Mental Development," in Paul Arthur Schilpp, ed., *The Philosophy of Bertrand Russell* (New York: Harper, 1963), p. 12.

7. E. D. Klemke, "Did G. E. Moore Refute Idealism?," in E. D. Klemke, ed., *Studies in the Philosophy of* G. E. *Moore* (Chicago: Quadrangle, 1969), pp. 3–24.

8. "An Autobiography," p. 18.

9. G. E. Moore, *Principia Ethica* (Cambridge, Eng.: Cambridge University Press, 1960), pp. 110–111.

10. Tom Regan, *Bloomsbury's Prophet:* G. E. *Moore and the Development of His Moral Philosophy* (Philadelphia: Temple University Press, 1987).

11. "An Autobiography," p. 21.

12. *Ibid.*, p. 22.

13. The characterization is J. N. Findlay's in his "Some Neglected Issues in the Philosophy of G. E. Moore," in Ambrose and Lazerowitz, eds., G. *E. Moore: Essays in Retrospect*, p. 64. Though, for reasons advanced in the foregoing, Findlay's characterization is accurate for the most part, there are notable exceptions. Gilbert Ryle offers a lively and, I think, insightful review of some of Moore's early essays, and Philip Petit a more thorough exegesis of some major themes found in most of the papers. See, respectively, "G. E. Moore's 'The Nature of Judgment,'" in G. *E. Moore: Essays in Retrospect*, pp. 89–101, and "The Early Philosophy of G. E. Moore," *Philosophical Forum* 4 (Winter 1972–1973): 260–298.

1

In What Sense, If Any, Do Past and Future Time Exist?

Mr. Hodgson's answer to this question appears to be that both past and future time do exist in the sense that both would be present to a conscious being whose cognitive capacities were perfect. I do not know if he can prove that such a conscious being exists; but I see no objection to accepting this hypothetical answer as giving information about reality, if it only means that reality, if it were known as it really is, would all appear to be present: for that comes to saying that reality, as it really is, is in one long present; or, to accept Mr. Hodgson's qualification, that the distinction between past and future does not exist in the world as [236] a whole in any other sense than it exists in that part of the world which is present to us in any one of our "empirical moments".

But Mr. Hodgson seems to damage his answer very seriously when he asserts that the distinction of past and future must yet be supposed to exist in quite another sense in the consciousness of

Originally published in *Mind* n.s. 6 (April 1897): 235–240. "In What Sense, If Any, Do Past and Future Time Exist?" was a contribution to a symposium in which Bernard Bosanquet and Shadworth H. Hodgson also gave papers.

the *deus ex machina*, who is necessary to his solution of the problem. "The whole real world-process," he says, "would be to such a being the immediate object of a present experience, and that in any or every one of the successive empirical moments which would compose the history of his consciousness as an existent." His consciousness then would be an existent and would have a history; and that being so, in what sense would the past and future moments of his consciousness exist? Mr. Hodgson could only answer that they would be absolutely non-existent: "only a present content," he says, "exists *now*, or is present". And he seems to see no difficulty in this assertion. But to those who cannot, as he does, treat consciousness as exclusive of reality (though, as we have seen, he also says it is "existent"), it will appear to re-open the whole discussion. At all events it is in this very transition of consciousness from past to present and future that Lotze found the difficulty that Mr. Hodgson professes not only to have faced but to have solved. In the chapter, from the end of which Mr. Bosanquet's quotation was taken, Lotze discusses at great length the possibility of conceiving the apparent succession of events in time as really nothing but the presentation of an unsuccessive whole to consciousness; and, having admitted the possibility of this conception, he is only driven to the statement in question, by the impossibility of conceiving that events in consciousness itself (what Mr. Hodgson calls "empirical moments") should appear to be successive, when they are really not successive.

But apart from Mr. Hodgson's extraordinary assumption, which perhaps he may have justified elsewhere, but which seems to vitiate the whole of his paper and to make it very difficult to find a common ground for argument with him—the assumption, namely, that consciousness is in no sense a constituent of reality, and that, therefore, succession in consciousness, as not affecting the reality of time, needs no explanation; apart from this, I think his final view may be shown to involve an open inconsistency with his premises. "The present moment of the existence of *an* object," says he, "and the present moment of our feeling it are one and the same present moment of time." Apply this to the consciousness of his *deus ex machina*, and we get the result that the whole world-process repeats itself in every successive moment in which it is presented to that consciousness. In that case, surely, the whole world-process is simply not the whole world-process.

But there is another point in Mr. Hodgson's final conception which I think it will be well to discuss, because he accepts it from Mr. Bosanquet; so that here I find myself forced to oppose them [237] both. This point relates to the use which both propose to make of the psychological doctrine that what Mr. Hodgson calls the "empirical present moment of my experience," and Mr. Bosanquet, more tersely, "our present," "has no fixed limits". It is true that Mr. Bosanquet's main argument is not affected by this point, and that he twice expressly waives a full discussion of it; still he uses it as an objection to Lotze's statement of the problem, and his words seem to imply that there are pertinent difficulties lurking in it. I think it is as well that they should be dragged to the light, not only because they vitally affect Mr. Hodgson's proposed solution, but also because they help to make clear the general nature of time; lastly, too, because I fear I am heretical with regard to them. Mr. Bradley, at all events, so far as I understand him, is against me: "There can," he says (*Principles of Logic*, p. 53), "be no part of the succession of events so small or so great, that conceivably it might not appear as present". Now I do not wish to enter into a psychological argument, for which I am very ill equipped; but I think that at all events this statement should be guarded against the use which Mr. Bosanquet and Mr. Hodgson seem to make of it, by the following proviso: "But not if it appears as a succession". Surely the psychological doctrine is only meant to emphasise the fact that in time, as in space, there is a *minimum sensibile*? The rate of change in our consciousness can only be measured against an objective standard, and the shortest events that we can discover by introspection may turn out to occupy a considerably longer duration than, *e.g.*, one revolution of a wheel revolving at 200 per second. Moreover it may be discovered that different persons, or the same person at different periods, differ in respect of the amount of inner change which corresponds to some such fixed outer standard. But this would only mean that the *minimum sensibile* of what Kant calls the "inner sense" has a merely relative value. The case here is different from that of space, because there we have only to compare the divisions which we can discover in the content of our space-presentation, with those which science necessarily infers to be actual or possible, whereas here we have to compare the successive moments of our consciousness not only with inferred motions in space but also with the content of our presentations. Time, in short, as Kant says, is a form not only of the outer but also of the inner sense. Now, as a form of the outer sense, it is precisely similar to space in respect of its infinite divisibility; but in it, as in space, it is impossible to detect divisions below a certain degree of minuteness. When, however, time appears as form of inner sense this *minimum sensibile* of presented content corresponds exactly to the *minimum sensible* of the same content, viewed as psychical event; but it is also as necessary in the history of consciousness as in physical history to regard time as infinitely divisible. Hence I entirely concur with Mr. Hodgson when he says: "The present moment of the existence of the real [238] world-process and the empirical present moment of my experience are one and the same present moment". This is true, both with regard to the perceptions of the individual, and to the rate of change in consciousness or matter, when measured by some arbitrary unit. But, when Mr. Hodgson goes on to contradict himself by saying that "we are aware of the distinctions of earlier and later in the successive parts of the content experienced in an empirical present moment of our finite consciousness," that statement is just as false. We may know that the parts of what we experience as unsuccessive must really be successive; but it is inconceivable that we should experience as successive, what, just because we are unable to detect successive parts in our experience of it, we call "our present". The fallacy, if fallacy it is, consists in confusing inner perception with scientific knowledge of the outer world—a confusion which, since Hume, could hardly be made in the case of space, because there inner perception has not the same double bearing. It would, however, be a parallel absurdity to deny the infinite divisibility of space on the ground that the smallest perceptible point was of variable extension. Mr. Bosanquet's very words that "our present includes duration" imply that it can be measured by the same arbitrary units as physical successions. And the fact is that as soon as we perceive, and do not merely infer, any succession in our present, it ceases to be our present. To ascribe to the Absolute any power of experiencing past and future as present, would be to put its consciousness on a lower level than ours, since it would be to deprive it entirely of that power of distinguishing successive events which is a condition of our progress in knowledge.

I must, therefore, plead guilty to the charge of "mischievous pedantry," with which Mr. Hodgson confutes Lotze, and at the same time may thank him for giving us, in what he regards as a *reductio ad absurdum* of philosophic thinking, a proof of the unreality of time. The present is not real, because it can only be thought as infinitely small; and past and future cannot be real, not only because they also must be thought as infinitely divisible, but also because they wholly lack that immediacy, which, according to Mr. Bradley, is a necessary constituent in reality. But, if neither present, past, nor future is real, there is nothing real left in time as such.

At the same time, I must beg Mr. Hodgson not to condemn me too hastily. If he thinks that by such a view I am bound to maintain that I "can count without time, or think without it either," there still remains much to be said. I think I may safely leave to Mr. Bosanquet to defend himself on this count; but, for my part, I should like, in fairness, to warn Mr. Hodgson that I cannot help making a distinction between the process of thinking and the content of thought. Because I cannot think without taking some time about it, I cannot see it follows that what I think about need also be in time. Mr. Hodgson himself seems to admit [239] in various parts of his paper that the content of thought, when it, as such, has reference to time, may differ in respect of its time-relations from the thought which thinks it. And, if this be so, the mere fact that we can only think in time can never prove that everything we think of need be so, except in so far as we are thinking it.

However, in connexion with the 'reality' of universal truth, I am glad to be able for once to side with Mr. Hodgson against Mr. Bosanquet. Although I hold that the point which is made against Mr. Bosanquet, in respect of his use of the word 'always' to describe the validity of universal truth, is in part merely verbal; yet I do think there is some real objection to the use which Mr. Bosanquet makes of the notions of 'permanence' and 'continuity'. As to the former term I heartily agree to Mr. Hodgson's assertion that its 'very meaning is duration of something in time'. The latter I wish to investigate more carefully.

Mr. Bosanquet, I cannot but think, tends to confuse two meanings of continuity which it is most important to distinguish. For instance, in the passage in which he supposes a theory for the 'natural man' who has once thoroughly understood that 'nothing but the permanent can change,' he speaks as if a 'continuous nexus of phases in succession' might be identified with the 'undoubted unity in reality' constituted by the fact that 'the past causes or conditions the present, and the present the future'. He seems to suggest that such unities as the laws of nature may be the continuous element in time. And his further argument in no way invalidates this part of the supposed plain man's view. It is only directed to show that the plain man must ultimately admit this continuous element to be a higher form of reality than the successiveness, which he at first supposed could not be sacrificed without involving the destruction of the continuity. Thus Mr. Bosanquet's final conception might seem to involve that we should think adequately of reality, if we imagined every content that we have reason to think real persisting unchanged through an endless time—a conception similar to some theological notions of Eternity (Milton's 'Long Eternity,' for example) and which might seem to make it impossible for beings in such a state to recognise that they were in time (since change seems to be a *ratio cognoscendi* of time), but which would not, for that reason, preclude their really being so. Surely the continuity of time, as it is generally understood, would really be destroyed along with its successiveness; but successiveness in no way involves any difference of content in events, other than that which constitutes the difference of one moment of empty time from another. The continuity of time is its qualitative nature as immediately perceived; 'time,' as Mr. Bradley says, 'is not a mere relation'. But the continuity which we must suppose to belong to reality is not this special quality of time, which as a mere quality is as unreal as the relation of succession. A universal, such as a law of [240] nature, may perhaps be spoken of as giving continuity to its particulars, since it binds them together; but it binds them in quite a different way from that in which the successive moments of time are bound together. For instance, any two durations may share the universal notion of a union of continuity with discreteness, but the unity thus constituted can obviously not be the same as the continuity which is only one term in the universal that connects the two durations.

For this reason I think Mr. Bosanquet rather underrates the difficulty of reconciling time with reality. Time must be rejected wholly, its continuity, as well as its discreteness, if we are to form an adequate notion of reality; and this thorough-going rejection of almost all the content with which our world is filled, most seriously impairs the filling of our conception of reality. We are, I think, forced with Kant and with Lotze, to desiderate an entirely different form of Perception, which would share with Space and Time nothing but the mere immediateness of the Present, without its distinction from Past and Future, and this Reality for us remains little more than a *Ding an Sich*. As such, however, I must insist against Lotze, that it does remain knowable by us. He implies this when he speaks of a totally different form of Perception as merely possible; for, in that case, he cannot ascribe to Time that absolute necessity, which anything which we are to recognise as Real must have. By this admission he seems finally to condemn Time as merely subjective, and the whole previous course of his argument tends to prove, not that it is more than an appearance, but only that if we assume an appearance to be real, we cannot prove its unreality.

If I need, then, after the foregoing discussion, to give a direct answer to our question, I would say that neither Past, Present, nor Future exists, if by existence we are to mean the ascription of full Reality and not merely existence as Appearance. On the other hand I think we may say that there is more Reality in the Present than in Past or Future, because, though it is greatly inferior to them in extent of content, it has that co-ordinate element of immediacy which they entirely lack. Again, and lastly, I think we may distinguish in this respect between Past and Future. The Past seems to be more real than the Future, because its content is more fully constituent of the Present, whereas the Future could only claim a superiority over the Past, if it could be shown that in it Appearance would become more and more at one with Reality.

2

Freedom[1]

The present paper is selected from a much longer essay on Kant's notion of Freedom, which I hope in future to rearrange and enlarge into a treatise on the whole of his Ethical Philosophy. This fact may serve to account in part for any difficulties of transition or apparent omissions of important topics, which may occur in it. If, after allowance for this, it should still seem too obscure or ill-arranged, I can only apologise. My object in the paper is to emphasise and defend, against such other views as seem to me the most important, certain points in Kant's doctrine in which I believe him to be right; and to criticise others in which I believe him to be wrong. It is not my main object to expound Kant, but to arrive at the truth on the subjects which he discusses. I have chosen to deal with him at such length mainly because I think that reference to the views of the philosopher, with whom you are most in agreement, is often the clearest way of explaining your own view to an esoteric audience; but partly, also, because I think he has been much misunderstood.

The paper falls roughly into three divisions. In the first I

Originally published in *Mind* n.s. 7 (April 1898): 179–204.

emphasise Kant's adherence to Determinism, as that doctrine is usually understood, and state briefly the nature of that Freedom which he also affirms as not inconsistent with such Determinism (pp. 179–185). In the second I attempt to defend and explain Kant's Determinism and to dispose of the theory of 'Liberty of Indifference' (pp. 185–194). In the last I discuss what seem to me the main difficulties in Kant's doctrine of Freedom, and attempt to convict him of inconsistency, and to disprove his position on those points in which he seems to approach nearest to maintaining 'Liberty of Indifference' (pp. 194–204).

I.—In beginning a discussion of Kant's notion of 'Freedom,' which he himself considers to be essentially connected with his Ethical system, it seems most important to emphasise [180] the fact that, so far as his express statements are concerned, he accepts unconditionally the view of Determinism and rejects that of Freedom, in the only sense in which the two have been generally discussed by English thinkers. In ordinary controversies on the subject, not such absolute distinction is drawn between two kinds of 'causality,' two kinds of 'determination' ('Bestimmung'—the sense which is implied in 'Determinism'), two kinds of 'possibility,' or, finally, an 'intelligible' and an 'empirical' 'character,' as is drawn by Kant. Professor Sidgwick, indeed, puts the question in such a form that Kant's answer would probably have to be on the Libertarian side; but this result seems only to be obtained at the cost of the above-mentioned ambiguity. 'Is the self,' he says,[2] 'to which I refer my deliberate volitions a self of strictly determinate moral qualities, a definite character partly inherited, partly formed by my past actions and feelings, and by any physical influences that it may have unconsciously received; so that my voluntary action, for good or for evil, is at any moment completely caused by the determinate qualities of this character, together with my circumstances, or the external influences acting on me at the moment—including under this latter term my present bodily conditions? or is there always a possibility of my choosing to act in the manner that I now judge to be reasonable and right, whatever my previous actions and experiences may have been?'

Now to the first half of the first alternative, 'Is the self to which I refer my deliberate volitions a definite character,' etc.? Kant would be compelled to give what Professor Sidgwick considers to be the Libertarian answer of 'No,' because there seems to be implied in it the alternative of what he would call an 'intelligible character'; though even here he would be in some doubt, because it seems implied that the 'intelligible character' cannot be 'of strictly determinate moral qualities' or 'definite'. And with this presumption that Professor Sidgwick accepted his distinction, he would also probably answer 'No' to the second half, 'Is my voluntary action . . . at any moment completely caused by the determinate qualities of this character?' although, had that question come by itself, his answer would probably have been 'Yes' since the sequel shows that when Professor Sidgwick says 'completely caused' he is only thinking of what Kant calls 'natural causality' (Naturcausalität). So, too, in answer to the second question, he [181] would only say 'Yes' on the presumption that Professor Sidgwick might mean by 'possibility,' intelligible, as well as empirical, possibility. But when Professor Sidgwick goes on to exemplify the deterministic view by reference to the principle of causality as employed in the Natural Sciences; when he says (p. 62) 'that the substantial dispute relates to the completeness of the causal dependence of the volition upon the state of things at the preceding instant,' there could no longer be any doubt that only that causality was meant of which Kant had been at such pains to prove the universal validity in the *Critique of Pure Reason*; and only some reason for surprise that reference should have been made to the possibility of a self with any other than a psychological character. Professor Clifford[3] gives a statement of the doctrine of Free Will, as commonly understood, which seems so clear as to be worth quoting: 'Whenever a man exercises his will, and makes a voluntary choice of one out of various possible courses, an event occurs, whose relation to contiguous events cannot be included in a general statement applicable to all similar cases. There is something wholly capricious and arbitrary, belonging to that moment only; and *we have no right to conclude that if circumstances were exactly repeated, and the man himself absolutely unaltered, he would choose the same course.*' Now this doctrine Kant would absolutely condemn. In fact, if Determinism only means that all men's actions conform to the laws of nature, and so, with the progress of psychology, could ultimately be predicted as certainly as the motions of the planets (and this is what Professor Sidgwick seems obviously to mean, and what is usually meant by it), Kant would have no hesitation in calling himself a Determinist. 'All actions of man in appearance,' says he, 'are determined (bestimmt) by his empirical character and the other contributory causes according to the order of nature, and if we could investigate all Appearances of his choice (Willkühr) to the bottom, there would be *no single human action, which we could not foretell with certainty*,[4] and recognise as following necessarily from its preceding conditions.'[5]

[182] Freedom, according to him, is absolutely impossible, if reality is ascribed to events in space and time. 'Since the thoroughgoing connexion of all Appearances in a context of Nature is a law that admits of no exception, this must necessarily upset all Freedom, if one were determined to cling obstinately to the Reality of Appearances. Hence also those, who in this latter respect follow the common opinion, have never been able to succeed in uniting Nature and Freedom with one another.'[6] Now the dispute between Libertarians and Determinists is undoubtedly conducted in general by those who do 'follow the common opinion' of ascribing reality to what Kant calls Appearances, *i.e.* matter as treated in Physics and mind as treated in Psychology. In so far as Determinism is regarded as bringing the phenomena of Will into harmony with the results established by experimental investigation of Nature, it can only be a doctrine concerned with what

Kant calls Appearances, and as such the above quotations seem to prove his unqualified adherence to it.

It would, in fact, appear absurd to the ordinary champion of Free Will, to declare that 'actions . . . which never have happened and perhaps will not happen'[7] are yet 'necessary'; and yet it is only on this basis that Kant is prepared to defend Free Will. If this be absurd, there is no choice but Determinism. Kant, in fact, uses 'necessity' here in a totally different sense from that in which common sense usually understands it. " 'Ought' expresses a kind of necessity and connexion with reasons, which is found nowhere else in the whole of Nature.[8] . . . It is impossible that anything else ought to happen in Nature, than what in all these temporal relations actually is; indeed 'ought,' if we only look at the course of Nature, has absolutely no meaning." If you declare a future action to be 'necessary' the ordinary man would suppose you must mean 'it will happen'—that you are predicting something according to the Laws of Nature; if you do mean that 'perhaps it won't happen,' he would say that you are using terms inaccurately; you ought to have said it was only probable or possible. But meanwhile it is sufficient to point out that Kant does say this absurd thing; and that from this second meaning of 'necessity' there follows a second meaning of possibility also. Since that which according to the Laws of Nature is only possible can be called necessary, that which according to the Laws of Nature is absolutely impossible may, from Kant's point of view, be regarded as [183] 'possible'.[9] It is only on this supposition of the possibility of the impossible, that Kant could have answered 'Yes' to Professor Sidgwick's second question.

What then, if Kant is a Determinist, does he mean by that Freedom, the reality of which he asserts? The answer to this question is, I think, to be found in his discussion of Transcendental Freedom, as an Idea of Reason, in the *Critique of Pure Reason*. The result of this discussion seems to me to be that Transcendental Freedom is the relation in which the world as it really is stands to events as we know them. It is the relation of Reality to Appearance. This relation necessarily appears to us as the logical relation of reason to consequent. The reason is free cause of its consequence. But though the relation is of this kind, and Transcendental Freedom is by this aspect of its nature absolutely distinguished from empirical causality and from human volition, as it appears in psychology, which is merely one form of such causality; nevertheless it differs from the logical relation of reason and consequent, in that neither reason nor consequent is here an abstract notion, but must be considered as having existence. A mere logical reason can never, as such, be considered as actual. If we seek for an actual existence as the ground of another, we get a mere cause. But that which has Transcendental Freedom is not a mere cause because it is no part of the temporal series of events; and it is not a mere logical reason because it has all the self-subsistence which appears to belong to the given temporal series.

This 'free causality,' therefore, is not causality in the ordinary sense; and there may well seem a good case for the contention that it is not free either, on the ground that freedom has an essential reference to human volition. Kant's conclusion at the end of the *Critique of Pure Reason* should have been that Transcendental Freedom was not merely possible but actual. But this independence of the proof of 'Freedom' from the Categorical Imperative, would seem to justify a suspicion that this 'Freedom' is not freedom, since its connexion with human action is by that [184] independence certainly lessened. And, indeed, it must be admitted that there is no longer any reason for connecting the 'Intelligible Character' with the psychological character which distinguishes one individual from another. The 'Intelligible Character' is the one sufficient reason of all phenomena, whether processes of inanimate nature, or human actions. It is not proved that it is individualised in a multiplicity of souls; and it is certain that in any case it is the same in each. Our doctrine will not enable us to decide between a Monadism and a Monism, but it shows that, if there be Monads, they will be identical in so far as each exemplifies the 'Intelligible Character'. The 'Intelligible Character' cannot be used to explain why one man is different from another, so that you could say A is so and so, because his 'Intelligible Character' is of this sort; and B is different because his 'Intelligible Character' is of that sort. All differences can only be explained by referring them to different causes. But the 'Intelligible Character' is the one reason of the whole world with all its differences, and so not more the reason of one part than of another.

Kant, however, does not admit that *every separate thing* may be regarded as a result of intelligible or free causality, just as every separate thing is a result of natural causality. All he claims in his discussion of Transcendental Freedom at the end of the *Critique of Pure Reason* is that 'among natural causes there may also be *some* which have a faculty that is only intelligible'.[10] And he goes on to explain that by these he means only mankind. 'In inanimate or merely animal nature we find no reason to suppose any faculty conditioned otherwise than through sense. But man, who knows the rest of nature only through senses, gets knowledge of himself also through mere apperception . . . and is to himself partly, we must admit, a phenomenon, but partly also, namely, in view of certain faculties, a merely intelligible object.'[11] Now, setting aside the statement that man knows himself through mere apperception —a kind of knowledge of which Kant has not elsewhere explained the possibility, and which seems here temporarily to take the place of the Categorical Imperative as affording a *ratio cognoscendi* for the applicability of freedom to him—it is plain that he here regards man as on an absolutely different level from other things in respect of freedom. Man has freedom and nothing else shares it in any degree. And throughout his ethical works this attitude is maintained. Free causality is attributed [185] to man alone among the objects of experience.[12] So that, whereas natural causality applies with absolute universality—to him as well as to all other objects, freedom appears as a sort of miraculous power, whose influence may be traced in some events, but not in others. In the *Critique of Judgment* he is led partly to correct this view and to see that, if Freedom is to be brought in to explain anything at all, it must be brought in to explain everything. But, meanwhile, his restricted view of freedom makes it easier for him to establish a connexion with the vulgar notion. In the vulgar notion, too, some actions are free and some are not; and though it would not be admitted, as for Kant is necessary, that those which were free, might also, in another aspect, be seen to be completely determined by natural causality, yet the mere fact that the application of freedom is so partial, and also its especial connexion with man, assimilate the view more to that of Kant, than is possible with that here advocated, according to which freedom is universal.

II.—In the vulgar notion of freedom the most universal characteristic seems to be the absence of external constraint whether exerted to impel or to prevent. Where the immediate cause of a motion or change seems to lie in the thing which moves or changes and not in anything outside it, there, in a sense at all events, freedom is predicable. But this is a notion which is obviously not limited to human actions. Many of the movements and changes of animals and plants have their proximate cause in the things themselves; and the same might probably be said of any body in so far as it moved in accordance with Newton's second Law of Motion. It is thus we seem to talk of 'free as air,' or of the wheels of a watch moving 'freely'.

But there is an obvious defect in this wide notion, in that the limits, whether spatial or temporal, of any group we may take for our unit or thing, are always more or less arbitrary. A watch may be moving freely when its spring is driving it; but the movement of any one of its wheels is not free, because the wheel is driven by the spring or by another wheel.[13] And, again, there seems no reason why we should single out the proximate or immediate cause for such pre-eminence, nor anything to determine how far back in the past a cause ceases to be proximate. It is difficulties of this sort which seem to have gradually tended to restrict the notion of freedom to man, because in man the notion of [186] self is far more striking than elsewhere and the distinction between the internally and externally caused, therefore, *prima facie* more satisfactory. The difference between himself and anything else whatever is more constantly forced on a man's notice and more practically important to him than any other difference, and it is therefore not unnatural that the notion of freedom, in the sense of self-caused action, whether or not it is originally derived from his own experience and transferred anthropomorphically to other things, should at all events be more widely applied and less easy to dispense with in his own case, and that of other beings like him, than elsewhere.

Now the vulgar doctrine of Free Will, as 'Liberty of Indifference,' seems to be in the main an attempt to raise this distinction between self and the world entirely above the level of an arbitrary distinction. It was seen that this could not be done, if the self were regarded as a part in the causal chain of events, since it must then be subject to the infinite divisibility inherent in time, and the ultimate causal unit remain as arbitrary as any unit of time. It was therefore maintained that man's soul was an agent undetermined by previous events in time; it was the absolutely simple unity of Rational Psychology, and, as such, distinguished from all natural objects, which were always both themselves divisible into parts and also incapable of certain discrimination from an ever wider whole. Such a notion of a finite uncaused cause inevitably follows from the attempt to distinguish within the world of experience cases of purely internal and purely external causation.

And there are good reasons why the human will should have been taken as the final instance of a cause which is not also an effect. The progress made in the analysis of mental processes has been very slight in comparison with that made in physical science, (1) because of their greater complexity, (2) because experiment in psychology must be either indirect or encumbered by the fact that the observed is also the observer, and (3) because subconsciousness must be taken into account. And the region of the incompletely known is the favourite abode of a metaphysical monstrosity. In plain language, where facts are not completely understood, some short-sighted metaphysical theory is generally introduced as affording an easy road past the difficulties which stand in the way of thorough investigation. And, secondly, apart from the general difficulty of establishing exhaustive causal laws, which applies in a less degree to physical science also, and prevents certain prediction even [187] there, there seems to be a real reason, which from the nature of the case can never disappear, why human volition should produce the illusion of so-called Freedom. It is this, that in virtue of the deterministic hypothesis itself, the knowledge that a certain course of action was about to be pursued[14] must always exert some influence upon the course actually pursued, and so make the result different from what was foreseen after a consideration of all the other elements that would contribute to it. And even if the fact of this knowledge were taken into account in the calculation, and the prediction modified accordingly, the knowledge of this modification would again introduce a new element, which would require a fresh calculation, and so on *ad infinitum.* This seems to be a difficulty inherent in the double nature of the mind as subject and object—a difficulty which makes it possible to pronounce *a priori* that complete prediction of the results of mental process must always be impossible. It is a difficulty which does not apply to prediction in the physical world of space, considered, as seems necessary at present, in abstraction from the world of mind. It could only modify our view of that, if the real connexion of body and mind were fully discovered. As it is, mental processes, though obviously corresponding to physiological, and useful for their investigation, have only too much the appearance of a totally independent world from the point of view of causality and reciprocity. So that the distinction is justifiable, when we say that the results of human volition, alone among causes, must *of necessity* remain incapable of prediction. And this fact, along with the greater empirical difficulties of prediction in the case of mind, seems sufficient to account for the illusive belief that the will, at any rate, is free, though it be admitted that nothing else is. The failure to discover a cause in any particular instance, of itself encourages a belief in the uncaused; and when to mere failure is added an absolute impossibility of discovery, the case is naturally strengthened.

That the belief in uncaused volition is illusory, the progress in scientific method, with the resultant growth of empirical psychology, has rendered it more and more difficult to doubt. Yet this fact by itself would be no argument against Free Will. For, in however many instances causation were proved, though that might, perhaps, be a cause [188] of our expecting it in others, yet it would not be, by itself, any *reason* for that expectation. An inductive argument always needs, as empiricists put it, to be supplemented by the assumption of the uniformity of nature. And that this assumption is not in this case an assumption, but an *a priori* necessity, may, I think, be considered to have been sufficiently proved by Kant's argument in the Analytic. He there shows that every event must have a cause, if there is to be an objective succession in time; and such an objective succession is certainly presupposed by all our actual experience. Accordingly Kant himself fully recognises the *a priori* certainty of the Deterministic view, as was shown at the beginning of this paper;[15] and it seems inevitable to agree with him.

As for 'the immediate affirmation of consciousness in the moment of deliberate action'[16] which is asserted to stand against Determinism, great care is needed in deciding what it is that consciousness then affirms. The first thing to be noted with regard to this matter seems to be that, if such an affirmation is to apply to the Free Will controversy, it must affirm, not the possibility of my *doing* what I choose, but the possibility of my *choosing*. In fact, the controversy seems to narrow itself to the question of Free *Choice*. For it is only choice which distinguishes voluntary from non-voluntary action, and the ordinary Libertarian would hardly maintain that non-voluntary actions could be free. Thus the question is also seen to be a wider one than that which is ordinarily discussed. For since the physical possibility of the action, which is the possible object of choice, cannot be considered to be a necessary element in constituting it good or reasonable, in the sense which is fundamental for 'practical reason,' it seems hardly possible to exclude mere choices, such as that I should have the genius of Shakespeare, though, that I should have it, might be reasonably considered physically impossible. Even such a case as a choice to prevent the sun rising to-morrow can hardly be excluded from the discussion. For though, perhaps, none but a madman would make such a choice, yet his choice would prove that it can be made: and we ourselves do often choose through ignorance what is impossible in this sense; the only reason why we do not choose what we also *think* impossible, seems to be not that we cannot (either in the deterministic or libertarian sense) but that it does not seem worth while. The question, whether a choice will produce in any degree [189] the effect chosen, seems to be merely one for experience to decide, and we judge of it just as we judge of the probabilities and possibilities of events in the physical world. It does not seem to be concerned in the Free Will controversy, if the issue of that controversy be clearly stated.

Locke and Hume,[17] indeed, agree marvellously in their treatment of Liberty, both asserting that it means simply 'a power to act as we choose'. But it would seem to be for this very reason, that they are able to treat the Free Will controversy so cavalierly as they do. If the question were merely as to whether we did not sometimes do what we choose, it would, as they say, be obvious what answer we should give; but it would not, as they also say, be obvious that liberty in this sense was not contrary to 'necessity,' since the question 'Can we choose?' would still remain unanswered. They both, it is true, leave an ambiguity even on the first point, by not sufficiently considering what is implied in their notion of 'power'; but, nevertheless, when they speak of a power to act as we choose, they would appear to mean only, as Locke says,[18] that the existence or non-existence of the action is dependent upon our choice. In this part of free action, then, it may be admitted that they leave no room for anything contrary to 'necessity'; since their notion is that the action is necessitated by the choice. Locke, however, sees that the point in dispute occurs not here but in the question[19] Are we free to choose? And this question he dismisses as absurd, on the ground that it means: Can a man will, what he wills? But it does not mean this, unless his definition of freedom, as power to do what I choose, be already accepted. It would indeed be absurd to ask 'Can I choose to choose?' in the sense 'Am I free to choose which of two alternatives I will choose?' But Locke has no right to assume that this is meant by the question 'Am I free to choose?' That question may mean 'Am I the original cause of my choice?' and this he leaves undiscussed. Both Locke and Hume therefore neglect the point of the controversy by their definition of freedom. They have, however, done some service to the question, inasmuch as their treatment of it is a protest against the confusion of freedom 'to do, if I choose,' with 'freedom to choose'. Their defect is that they assume that it was an answer to the first question only, which was really wanted; and hence their contempt [190] of the dispute. As a matter of fact, I am free, in the ordinary political sense, when 'I do what I choose, *because I choose it*,' since there the immediate cause of my action lies in myself, *i.e.*, in my choice. But that is not freedom in the sense demanded by Libertarians. What they wish to maintain is that the choice itself is caused only by a self which is an uncaused entity; and this implies that, where alternatives are presented, their choice between them is wholly independent of their previous habits, disposition, etc.

The question then is: 'Does consciousness affirm, when alternatives are presented, that I can choose any of them that I think either good or bad?' which would seem to be equivalent to 'any conceivable presented alternative'. And with this we come to the last ambiguity of statement, which seems to me to stand in the way of our giving a clear answer to the question. Professor Clifford (*Lectures and Essays*, p. 327) rather ingeniously urges that, if the deliverance of my consciousness is to be 'of any use in the controversy,' it must be 'competent to assure me of the non-existence of something which by hypothesis is not in my consciousness,' *i.e.*, the subconscious mental elements which the Determinist must suppose to determine the choice. But it seems possible to surmount this objection by maintaining that it is enough if consciousness can make a positive affirmation as to what is cause of the choice, without requiring it to prove exhaustively that nothing else in the world can be. If the man of science before he enunciates a law is always bound to prove that no other elements besides those whose constant connexion with the effect has been observed by him, really contributed to it, no scientific laws have been discovered yet. If, therefore, consciousness does affirm that 'I' am the cause of the choice, that should be sufficient. But then the question arises, What can it mean by 'I'? Is it quite certain that when consciousness seems to affirm that '*I can* choose so and so,' it means more than 'it is possible that such and such a choice will take place in my mind'? If it does not mean more than this, its affirmation is not against Determinism; since, as we have tried to show above (p. 187), even on the Deterministic hypothesis, it must always be entitled to affirm the latter proposition, even if it does not always exercise its right. For by saying that such and such a choice is possible I imagine we can mean no more than that we do not know but that it will happen; and even if 'the uniformity of nature' can be proved in such a sense as to justify an assertion with regard to any event whatever [191] that it certainly will not happen, this can never be the case with regard to an event conditioned by a conscious forecast.

It seems, therefore, that the 'affirmation of consciousness' as against Determinism, disappears on the attempt to make it precise. The attempt to find a more exact meaning for the vulgar notion of freedom has thrown us back upon the conception with which we started. Instead of free action being the action of an 'uncaused self,' we have to be content with it as self-caused action: anything may be said to act freely in so far as the immediate cause of its changes lies in itself. We have now to see how this notion is connected with that explained above as derived from Kant; and to examine whether there is any justification for applying it in an exclusive sense to Will—a restriction which Kant seems to adopt in the application of his notion also. If the restriction turns out to be unjustifiable in both cases, we shall have disposed of Schopenhauer's view of the ultimate reality—a view which, according to Kuno Fischer, is also that of Kant.

It was one of Kant's great merits[20] in the *Critique of Pure Reason* to have pointed out that there is nothing absolutely 'inner' in the objects of experience, either of the outer or inner sense, either in nature or in mind. He gave the final blow to the doctrine of 'essences' and 'faculties,' as principles of explanation, by showing that advance in scientific knowledge presupposed the complete interdependence of things; that all we can know for certain about them is their relation to one another. This indeed was one of his motives to his distinction of Phenomena and Dinge an Sich, for he could not avoid the conviction, though he could not justify it, that there must be something self-subsistent somewhere. But his main point was that, if you treated natural objects as if they were self-subsistent, you could not escape the most unbearable contradictions. This was the 'natural dialectic of Reason'.

In the *Critique of Judgment* however, he began to see that he had over-emphasised the doctrine that all we can know is *mere* relations. He here recognises that a philosophy of nature must take into account the 'matter of knowledge,' as such, since it too must have some element of necessity. Thus, it is not only the categories and the pure forms of Intuition which have an *a priori* certainty; but the sense-manifold must also be of such a nature that the categories and forms of Intuition will apply to it. It must be of such a nature as to supply terms to these relations. And, [192] though the amount of the nature of objects of experience, which is thus determined *a priori*, is far from giving them a claim to be considered completely rational, it yet gives them a certain amount of inwardness and self-subsistence.

Thus, in considering the course of Nature, it becomes obvious that, though we try to explain what happens by referring it in each case to something prior in time, and so on *ad infinitum*, there is also presented another element left out of account by this method (the only one allowed by Kant in the *Pure Reason*), which also helps to explain what happens. This element is the actual qualitative nature of the events we are trying to explain. So far as mere causal connexion is concerned, there is no reason why there should be any change in the world whatever, except that which is involved in the lapse of time. Each moment of time is different from the one before it, just because it is after and the other before, and, if the world were quite without other differences, there would yet be a necessary connexion between its state at one moment and its state at the next, exactly fulfilling the type which Kant sought to prove against Hume. For the state of the world at one moment would be a different *thing* from its state at the next, in the sense in which Hume denied that you were really entitled to infer from the existence of one thing the subsequent existence of another. But, even if this were so, causation would obviously not afford a complete explanation of the course of nature. The world which did thus persist unchanged through time, would still itself be part of the reason of the course of Nature. We could not exhaust our knowledge of each successive state by saying it was such as to have been the effect of the one before and the cause of the one which followed it. It would still remain true that each state was what it was, besides being related to those before and after it; each would have a content—the content in virtue of which each was identical with that of every other; and the nature of this content would require to be taken into account in explaining each state. We can assert *a priori* not only that each state of the world must be necessarily connected with those that precede and follow it, but also that it must have some definite qualitative nature. It is not only what it is because the previous state was what it was, but also because it is what it is.

This consideration seems obvious enough, but yet it is one which is very apt to be neglected. It was recognised in the Aristotelian doctrine of 'formal' causes; but has been put out of sight by the procedure of modern science, which seeks always for efficient causes, without sufficiently considering [193] that there could be no efficiency unless there were also 'form'. It is no doubt of more practical importance to establish the relation between things than just to recognise those things; and Kant, in his desire to justify the methods of natural science, seems to have been misled, by the prominence given in it to the discovery of relations, into an unjustifiable neglect of the qualitative aspect of things. There was also, as has been pointed out above, another reason for the emphasis which he lays on relation—namely, his desire to protest against the assumption that the objects of experience were real, or *absolutely* self-subsistent. And finally, quality, so far as it is necessary, is only one: there are not, as in the case of relation, a number of different forms to justify. But, still, from a philosophical point of view, it seems to be of equal importance, and is always presupposed by science in discriminating the things between which relations are to be discovered.

Things, then, in so far as they must be terms of relations, may be said to have a self. But this degree of selfhood would not suffice to define the notion of freedom. For we are as yet not entitled *a priori* to infer in the world any differences in quality. And if there were none, as in the case above supposed, there would be no reason to suppose that the causal connexion between the successive world-states was in any way dependent on their qualities. The quality would necessarily be taken into account in explaining the series as a whole; but the causal connexion might be considered to hold between them purely as *existing*, *i.e.*, in so far as they had matter, in the Aristotelian sense, not in virtue of their form. And this, it is to be noted, is all that Kant proves for causality in the *Critique of Pure Reason*; the necessary connexion is between the existence (Dasein) of things. But, as a matter of fact, there are differences of quality in the world of experience, and whatever be the justification for it, there is connected with this difference of quality a most important addition to the notion of causality. Causality in Kant's sense would not justify any Law of Nature, and yet without these science would be impossible. There is implied in any law, that 'Like cause has like effect' and *vice versâ*; and in this conception we have, at once, the causal relation between things, conceived as depending on their qualitative nature.[21] It is no longer the thing, considered as individuated merely in time, which is necessarily connected with those preceding and following, [194] but the thing, as distinguished by a particular quality, is considered to have a necessary connexion with other things so distinguished. It is not assumed that all the qualities in the world might not be different from what they are; but it is assumed that given any one quality it has a unique causal relation with some other one, in the sense that only the thing of which it is a quality can be cause of the thing, of which that other is a quality, and only that other thing can be the effect of the first thing.

With this we seem to have arrived at the notion of a thing with a distinguishable self, having a distinct efficiency in virtue of that self. And in this conception of the course of nature there is contained the union of Determination with Freedom, in its simplest form. Each thing marked by a simple qualitative nature, is no doubt determined in that it is the effect of some other thing, and, given that other thing, it was forced to appear. But also it is itself similarly the cause of something else, and free so far as its effect depends upon its own nature. It is nothing against this, that its own nature depends in its turn upon something else; for that something else could not by itself have produced the effect which it produces. It is an essential link in the chain, and though the effect is not solely due to it, some part of the effect is due to it and to it only.

Now from the common point of view which takes the world of experience as ultimately real, this, in which every part of that world is alike free and alike determined, is the only sense of freedom, which can withstand criticism as in no way based on arbitrary distinctions. It is a sense, which would, to most, seem to be the same as that of determination. But it can, I think, be seen to underlie all common uses of freedom; and it is largely to the difficulty of distinguishing it as an irreducible aspect in mechanical causation, that there is to be attributed the mistaken attempt to show that the notion of freedom is irreducible by maintaining the existence of uncaused choice. We have now to show the connexion between this and Kant's sense of Freedom; and to consider whether he can give any justification for speaking as if his, any more than the popular sense, were to be found exhibited in special cases in the world of experience, *i.e.*, especially in human volition, and not everywhere alike.

III.—Kant's use of the term Freedom does seem justified in that it coincides with the popular one in opposing the view that the aspect of the world as causally determined is alone sufficient for its explanation. Both alike recognise that to define a thing's relations to other things is not the most that [195] can be done in knowing the world. But we have seen that Kant does not, in the *Critique of Pure Reason*, seem to allow that freedom, in the sense just explained, where it consists in recognising the part played in nature by each thing's form, is an objective notion. His failure to do so seems to be due to his confusion of this notion with the wider one of systematic unity in Nature, which involves it. It is in the same way that his notion of Freedom involves the common one, but also goes much further. According to him Freedom means not only that each part of Nature is necessarily connected with all the other parts in respect of its form as well as in respect of its existence; but also that all these different forms, considered in themselves, together with their differences and the laws of their connexion, must be taken into account in explaining the world as a whole: and since the world as a whole is an impossible conception, if the objects of experience be taken to be its ultimate constituents, since they are necessarily conceived as in the infinite forms of space and time, the complete reason of all that appears must be placed in a supersensible reality. This supersensible reality is the world as a whole, and is the reason of everything that appears; and, as such, it has Freedom. As such, too, Kant will not allow it to be *known* as more than a mere Idea; but there seems reason to think that this was only due to his failure to reconcile two different criteria of reality: so that he generally considers the being given in the context of experience essential, and since the context of experience can never offer the required completeness, such completeness must be condemned as merely regulative.

Now our question is, whether a relation, really analogous to this of the real world to the world of experience, is presented in the relation of the human will to its actions, and in that alone among the objects of experience. Kant himself distinguishes between freedom 'in the cosmological sense' (which is the one we have hitherto discussed as his) and freedom in the 'practical sense'; but he asserts that the latter is possible, only if the former be also possible.[22] In the 'Critique of Practical Reason,' he proves that 'practical Freedom' is actual, and from that infers that 'cosmological Freedom' is also actual.[23] What, then, is his account of 'practical Freedom'?

'Practical Freedom' is something which must belong to all 'reasonable' beings, as such.[24] It is defined negatively as 'the independence of our choice from compulsion through [196] impulses of sense';[25] and positively as 'a power' or 'causality' of 'reason,' 'to begin a series of events entirely of itself.'[26] 'Pure practical reason' is identified with 'pure will'; and 'will' again, up to the end of the 'Critique of Practical Reason,' seems to be identical with 'choice' (Willkühr), though in the preface to the 'Metaphysic of Morals' (p. 23), they are distinguished in a very important manner; for it is there declared that only 'choice' can be called 'free,' 'will' being concerned not with 'actions,' but only, like practical Reason, with the giving of Moral Laws.

Kant's account of the way in which we must conceive 'practical freedom' in relation to experience is as follows: Every 'cause' (Ursache) has a 'power' (Vermögen), which may be also called 'causality' (Causalität), which 'power' is necessarily connected with the subsequent appearance of a definite 'effect' (Wirkung); and the law of this connexion is called the 'character' of the cause. The transition from the 'causality' to the 'effect,' however it be conceived, is called the 'action' of the cause (Handlung). Now in 'natural causation,' the 'causality' of every cause is also an effect of some previous cause, and so on *ad infinitum*; and the 'action,' therefore, is merely a transition in time. But for every natural object, we must also suppose there to be an intelligible ground;

and there is no contradiction in thinking of this intelligible ground as cause (in another sense) of the 'causality' of the natural object. The 'causality' of the natural object would thus be effect both of some preceding natural object and also of its intelligible ground. But the intelligible ground is, as such, in no way subject to 'time-conditions,' and therefore its 'action' in producing the 'causality,' which is its appearance, is not a time-transition. It cannot therefore be said to 'begin to act' at any time, although its effect, *i.e.* the 'causality' of the natural object, has a beginning. It is thus original cause of an appearance, which is on another side also effect of a conditioned cause and in its turn cause of other appearances. It begins 'of itself' a series of events in time, without itself beginning to act.

Now, so far, except for the ambiguity of the word 'cause' as applied to an intelligible object, and except for a lack of fixity about almost all his terms, many of which are at one time distinguished, and at another used as synonyms (*e.g.* Causalität = Charakter = Handlung), there seems no reason to object to Kant's account. But it is an account which [197] would apply to any natural object whatever, and we have now to consider whether it will apply in a special sense to human volition.

I quoted above (p. 184) a passage of Kant,[27] in which he says that 'man knows himself' not only through his sense, but 'also through mere apperception, and that too in actions and inner determinations, which he cannot ascribe to the impression of the senses. He is to himself, it must be admitted, partly a phenomenon, but partly also, namely in view of certain faculties, a merely intelligible object, because his action cannot be ascribed to the receptivity of sensibility. We call these faculties Understanding and Reason.' And he goes on to say that Reason appears preeminently as the faculty of a supersensible being. We are next told that the Imperatives expressed by 'ought' make it plain that 'this Reason has a Causality, or at least that we represent it as having one'. And finally we have the following sentence: 'Now this "ought" expresses a possible action, of which the ground is nothing more than a mere conception; whereas, on the contrary, the ground of a merely natural action must always be an appearance'.

In this passage I think we have presented the full extent to which Kant's error of restricting practical freedom to reasonable beings goes, together with the confusions on which that restriction was based. One ambiguity occurs in the last sentence; and it is a very important one, since it seems to have given rise to many false notions of what Kant meant by freedom. This sentence expresses in an antithetical form the difference between 'free' and 'natural' causality—which he frequently says are the only two kinds of causation possible. The first is distinguished by this, that its ground is a mere conception; whereas the ground of the second is always a phenomenon. Now from the account given above of Transcendental Freedom it will appear in what sense I accept this description of free causality. A free cause must necessarily appear to us as a logical reason, and, so far, as 'a mere conception'; because it is not, as such, presented to us as an object of intuition. It is always a universal, and though we can know that it must also be an individual, we cannot experience it as uniting both characters. But from what Kant says in the preceding context, as well as from his general account of will elsewhere, I think it is plain that he is not thinking of 'a mere conception' in this sense. When our will is [198] singled out as having a special kind of causality, inasmuch as it can be 'determined to action by the presentation (Vorstellung) of certain laws,'[28] Kant shows what it is he is thinking of. The 'mere conception,' in the only justifiable sense for freedom, would be the laws themselves, and not the 'presentation' of the laws. Every 'conception' may be regarded from two points of view, either as a psychical existent, or from the point of view of its content; and it is this very important (and obvious) distinction which Kant appears to have neglected. If the causation exercised by the presentation of a conception were enough to justify freedom, freedom would be no more than that aspect of every mechanical process, which was distinguished above as the only precise sense assignable to freedom, on the common view which regards the objects of experience as real; and thus there would not even be an appearance of conflict between it and natural causality. For it is precisely 'presentations' to which Kant repeatedly asserts that the objects of experience are reduced, when they are viewed, as he holds they must be, as appearances. An appearance is a 'mere presentation,' and it is only between such that the causal laws will hold. There would therefore be no difference between 'an action of which the ground was no more than' the presentation of 'a conception,' and an action of which the ground 'must always be an appearance': for the presentation of anything whatever is, as such, an appearance.

Kant himself would seem to recognise this in a passage of the 'Canon of Pure Reason,' in which for that very reason he is driven to an almost direct contradiction of what he says in the context quoted above. In this passage (p. 530) he says: 'Practical Freedom can be proved through experience. For not only that which charms, *i.e.*, affects the senses directly, determines human choice, but we have a power to overcome impressions upon our sensual desiderative faculty (Begehrungsvermögen), through *presentations*[29] of what, even in a somewhat remote way, is useful or harmful; and these considerations of that which, in view of our whole state, is desirable, *i.e.*, good and useful, are based upon Reason. Hence also Reason gives laws, which are Imperatives, *i.e.*, objective *Laws of Freedom*, and which tell us, what *ought to happen*, even though perhaps it never does happen, and are distinguished in that respect from *Natural Laws*, which deal only with that *which happens*.' He then goes on to suggest that, on a wider view, what here appears as freedom, might be seen to be

[199] nature (which would, indeed, with regard to part of his statement, be certainly the case) but this, he says, is a speculative question, irrelevant just here. Finally he comes to this: 'Accordingly we know practical freedom through experience as *one among natural causes*, namely a causality of the reason in determination of the will; whereas Transcendental Freedom demands an independence of this reason itself (in view of its causal power to begin a series of appearances) from all determining causes of the sense-world, and so far appears to be contrary to the Law of Nature, and hence to all possible experience; it therefore remains problematic. But for reason in its practical use this problem is irrelevant. . . . The question with regard to Transcendental Freedom concerns solely speculative knowledge. We can set it aside as wholly irrelevant when we have to do with the practical.' Now in this passage Kant states very well what is characteristic of human volition; and his definitions of 'will' are constantly expressed in the same fashion. Will differs from other instances of natural causation, inasmuch as in it the 'idea' (to use the common English word for 'Vorstellung') of something, which is not yet real, tends to bring about the realisation of that thing; and he may be justified in saying that this process 'is based upon Reason,' since to have an idea of anything either real or imaginary, presupposes that faculty of cognition which distinguishes man from beasts, and still more from inanimate nature. Nay, more than this, in the special instance, which Kant takes to be the only truly 'moral' willing, where the idea which acts as cause, is the idea of conformity to a universal law, the content of the idea is so abstract that it may be confidently asserted that only reasonable beings are capable of having such an idea. But nevertheless the idea is even here still 'an appearance,' and, as such, separated by an impassable gulf from *the content, of which it is an idea.* And, inasmuch as it is in its character of idea, *i.e.*, as a psychical existent, that it produces an effect, the causation is still merely 'natural'. This, as we have said,

Kant in the present passage fully recognises. But it is only the more remarkable that he should speak of Reason in the same context as 'giving laws of Freedom,' as if it were Reason in the same sense, which is the source on the one hand of objectivity, and on the other hand of abstract ideas, whether true or false. In this Kant betrays the too psychological standpoint above which he seems never to have completely risen in treating epistemological questions, in spite of the enormous services which he did to epistemology, as well in the metaphysics of ethics as elsewhere. [200] He supplies, as it seems to me, more materials for a true view than any one else, and those, too, in a wonderfully forward state of preparation, but nevertheless they are still for him encumbered and confused with the irrelevant matter, from which it was his merit to set them free for others. It is perhaps impossible to dispense with the term 'rational' for what is true or objective, especially after its full adoption by Hegel; but it is extremely important to avoid confusing the 'rational' in this sense, which is the fundamental one for Kant's system, with the 'rational' in the sense of that which implies the psychological faculty of making judgments and inferences. The distinction between what is true and what is only believed (although only a 'rational' being can believe) is one which cannot be either done away or bridged over, however small be the amount of what we may be thought to really know in comparison of what we must be content to believe; and it is this distinction which is here in question. Knowing, the function of Reason, is on one side a natural function, and, as such, it is indistinguishable from believing; but, in so far as knowing *is* distinct from believing, *i.e.*, in so far as that which is known is true, there are no two words which express a difference more profound. When Kant talks of the only true morality as based upon the laws which Reason gives itself, the whole course of his work shows that he means laws which tell us *truly* what ought to be done; it is, indeed, only on this condition that he could claim universality for them.[30] In this sense 'Reason determines the Will' whenever the idea which is cause of our action, is an idea of what is truly good. But it is only in an utterly different sense that 'Reason' can be said to 'determine the Will,' whenever the idea, which causes our actions, implies the power of abstraction. And it is only in this second sense that such determination of the will can be called a 'practical freedom' which is independent of 'Transcendental Freedom'. Accordingly Kant himself, as we have said, recognises elsewhere that 'the practical conception of freedom is based upon' the 'transcendental Idea of Freedom' (p. 371); and again, speaking of freedom 'as one of the faculties which contain the cause of the appearances of our sense-world,' *i.e.*, as practical, in distinction from transcendental, freedom, he declares that we cannot hope to establish its actuality in experience, 'inasmuch as we can never infer from experience to anything *which must not be conceived at all [201] according to law of experience*' (p. 385). And this seems sufficiently to contradict his statement in the 'Canon' that 'we know practical freedom through experience as one among natural causes,' and that 'for reason in its practical use' the problem of transcendental freedom 'is irrelevant'.

Kant has therefore confused the purely natural process of human volition, with the transcendental aspect of it, which alone entitles us to ascribe to man 'practical freedom'; and it is solely on this confusion that the special place he assigns to man as a 'free' agent seems to be based. It is true that the content of the idea, which acts as cause in volition, is different from the content of any other natural cause; but that content is merely the form of the cause, and difference of form is something which in no way renders one natural cause more or less of a natural cause than any other. Indeed Kant himself seems to me to have guarded sufficiently against misapprehensions on this point by the rigour with which he rejects the attempt to conceive as prior in time, that which, if it determine the will, shows that will to be 'practically free'. In this rejection he is quite consistent. 'The action,' he says (R. V., p. 381), 'so far as it is to be imputed to thought' (Denkungsart, identified just before with 'intelligible character'), 'as its cause, nevertheless does not follow from it at all according to empirical laws, that is, so that the conditions of pure reason, but only so that the effects of pure reason in the appearance of the inner sense, *precede*.' In other words, that which is to be regarded as the condition, or, as Kant calls it, cause, of the action, in so far as that action exhibits practical freedom, *does not precede the action in time.* The action is only preceded by the consequence, or, as Kant calls it, effect, of this 'intelligible' condition; and hence the action itself may be said to 'follow from' the condition, as a conclusion follows from premises, but not to follow it in the time-order (*cf.* above, p. 196). Now, in the case of moral action, this 'effect,' which produces the action, is just the presentation of the moral law; and the intelligible condition of that effect is the moral law itself. Kant himself allows that this effect or presentation must always be present in human volition; and, what I wish to maintain, is that this is all that the analysis of human volition, as such, can ever show to be present. I have examined the confusion upon which Kant's contrary view that the law itself is somehow to be obtained by analysis of volition, that it is given by a 'pure Will' or 'practical Reason,' seems to be based; and that confusion seems sufficient to explain the view and to show that, for Kant at any rate, it was baseless. [202] It only remains to give a positive summary of the reasons against the legitimacy of any such view.

The point at issue is this: Whether 'will' can be understood at all as other than a form of 'activity'; and whether, if it be an activity, it must not be conceived as essentially conditioned by time, and therefore, in Kant's language, a mere 'appearance'. If it be a mere 'appearance' the conception of a 'pure Will' is nonsense; and 'will' cannot be ascribed as an attribute to anything real—either to God or to the Transcendental Ego.

That 'will' is a form of 'activity' has, I suppose, never been disputed. Kant himself, as we have seen, refers us, for our notion of pure Will, to the pure activity of the Ego. What is disputed is whether psychical activity, at least, may not be considered as fundamentally real. Our contention is that it cannot be so, because it is inconceivable except as taking place in time. That time itself cannot be conceived to be fundamentally real is always admitted by Kant himself, and indeed he has attempted a proof of it. How far his proof is satisfactory, and whether, if unsatisfactory, any other proof is forthcoming, is too large a question to be fully discussed here. I can only state that the arguments by which Mr. Bradley has endeavoured to prove the unreality of Time appear to me perfectly conclusive. The question which remains, then, is whether we cannot conceive a timeless activity; for it is to such that Kant must be referring us, for justification of the notion of 'pure Will'. That such a conception is very difficult to maintain appears plainly enough from the attempt of Lotze,[31] who assumes psychical activity to be the fundamental reality, and finds himself forced, in consequence, much against his will, to accept the ultimate reality of time.[32] And we have seen that Kant has nothing valid to say for it. It is a notion which would seem to rest on a combination of the notion of causal dependence between empirical things in time, with that of logical dependence. Both are necessary connexions, but in the one case between things, in the other between concepts. That the relation of reality to appearance, or the inter-relation of realities, must be conceived as that of logical necessity, changed (in a way which we cannot understand, because we have no intelligible intuition) by the fact that it there holds between things, has been maintained above. And if this relation be all that is meant by 'pure activity,' there seems no objection to the notion; [203] only 'activity' seems a misnomer for it, as great as Kant's 'causality' for the same notion, apt only to create confusion. If anything else be meant, it is to be wished it were brought forward; as it would then be possible to discuss it. Meanwhile, I must be content to let the matter rest in this result: That if the logical relation of reason to consequent, regarded as synthetic, *i.e.*, holding between real objects,[33] is to be considered as established by 'Will' and the type of its 'activity,' then pure 'Will' may indeed be the fundamental reality; but I should still protest that it would be better to keep that word for the distinct notion which it ordinarily conveys, instead of transferring it to another notion which has long had a sufficiently distinctive name of its own.

My conclusion, then, is this: That 'will' is only a special form of natural causality, or, rather, a natural causal process, where the cause is of one definite sort. It is a special form of natural causality, just as explosion of gunpowder by a match is one special form of natural causality, and explosion of dynamite by concussion is another. And, that on which I wish to insist, is that voluntary action, of whatever sort, whether autonomous or heteronomous, exhibits 'freedom,' in the sense which I have hitherto explained as essential to Kant's notion, no more and no less than gunpowder explosions or any other natural process whatever. It seems, indeed, strange that this conclusion from his doctrine should have escaped the notice both of himself and others to the extent to which it has. For he repeatedly asserts that for every 'appearance' we must suppose an intelligible ground (the Ding an Sich), and it is just this dependence of the cause of his actions on an intelligible ground (the Transcendental Ego), which he describes as constituting man's 'practical freedom'. Moreover, even the identity of the Ding an Sich and the Transcendental Ego has been suggested by him and accepted by others; though this would not be necessary to justify the inference, since the dependence on an intelligible ground is by itself sufficient for practical freedom. When this is acknowledged, 'practical' freedom disappears altogether as something intermediate between natural causality and transcendental freedom. For, as Kant himself says, nothing intermediate is possible; only two sorts of causality can be conceived at all. 'Freedom,' then, for Kant means only 'transcendental freedom,' and 'transcendental freedom' is not 'practical,' in the sense that it is inseparably connected with 'action' alone. It is true that actions are dependent on [204] 'transcendental freedom,' but that is only because it is the relation which holds between the empirical causes of those actions and the transcendental ground of such causes. Whether sensible objects produced effects, and so vindicated their right to be considered practical (as they always must), or not, they would equally be results of 'transcendental freedom'.

The degree to which Kant himself was forced to recognise the unpractical nature of his conception of Freedom, is singularly illustrated by a passage in the 'Metaphysic of Morals,' to which I have referred above (p. 196; M., p. 23). He here declares that "'Will,' which he has hitherto regarded as identical with 'pure practical Reason,' and as that which is *alone* endowed with 'Freedom, in his special sense, cannot be called either 'free' or the reverse, because it is not 'susceptible of compulsion'. This 'susceptibility of compulsion' implies subjection to natural law, and, as so subject, he declares that human 'choice' (Willkühr) may be called 'free'. He would seem, therefore, here to recognise that 'action' can only be conceived as a time-process; indeed he says that 'Will' does not refer to 'actions' (Handlungen); and it is only because he sees that he would be departing too far from the ordinary use of 'freedom,' if he disconnected it from action, that he now denies freedom to 'Will'. The fact is that his previous doctrine has already departed from the ordinary usage, further than he himself was fully aware; and hence the inconsistency, with which he now tries to patch up the discrepancy. The true way of meeting the difficulty would have been, as has been pointed out, to insist on his meaning of Freedom as the true one, and to give up the special connexion which he had hitherto asserted between it and human volition: to recognise that 'Willkühr' was a mere 'appearance,' and, therefore, not 'free,' and that, that which was free, had not even so much connexion with volition as to deserve the name of 'Will'. There would, then, have stood out clearly the problem which remains for Kantian Ethics—how to establish a valid connexion between the notion of Transcendental Freedom and that of End or Good.

NOTES

1. Read before the Aristotelian Society, 15*th November*, 1897.

2. *Methods*, p. 61 (5th edition).

3. Essay on 'Right and Wrong' in *Lectures and Essays* (1886), p. 318.

4. It will be seen (p. 187) that I myself think it necessary slightly to modify this statement.

5. R. V., p. 380, Hartenstein, ed. 1867–8. Throughout this paper R. V. stands for 'Reinen Vernunft,' P. V. for 'Praktischen Vernunft,' G. for 'Grundlegung zur Metaphysik der Sitten,' and M. for 'Metaphysik der Sitten'.

6. R. V., p. 373.

7. *Ibid.*, p. 380.

8. *Ibid.*, p. 379.

9. The words in R. V., p. 379: "Now the action must undoubtedly be *possible* under natural conditions, if it is conformed to the 'ought,' " must be understood to mean that any *actual* action, which was in accordance with 'ought,' must also have natural possibility, *i.e.*, have been capable of prediction according to natural laws: not that for any conceivable action to be moral, it must also be naturally possible. So in M. d. S., p. 18, it is obvious that the 'morally possible,' the 'permitted,' may be something which you cannot actually do.

10. P. 378.

11. P. 379.

12. Though also it belongs to any other 'reasonable beings,' if such there be. Gr., p. 237.

13. *Cf.* on this subject, P. V., p. 100 foll.

14. Unless, indeed, we are to carry out logically Professor Huxley's doctrine ("Hume," *Collected Essays*, vol. vi., p. 86) that 'there is only a verbal difference between having a sensation and knowing one has it'.

15. *Cf.* P. V. Pref., p. 12–end.

16. Sidgwick, *Methods*, p. 65.

17. Locke: Essay ii., 21, 14 foll. Hume: Treatise iv., p. 110 foll.
18. § 27.
19. § 22.
20. *E.g.*, in the 'Amphibolie,' R. V., p. 225.
21. Under 'quality' is included, for this purpose, position in space.
22. R. V., p. 371.
23. Pref., pp. 3 and 4.
24. G., p. 296.
25. R. V., p. 371; *cf.* M., p. 11.
26. R. V., p. 372; *cf.* M., p. 11.
27. R. V., p. 379.
28. G., p. 275.
29. My italics.
30. This is the ground of Kant's distinction between the Categorical Imperative, or *Objective Law*, and the mere Maxim or *Subjective Principle.*
31. *Metaphysic*, § 156.
32. See my article on 'Time' in MIND, N.S., 22, p. 240.
33. See P. V., p. 52.

3

The Nature of Judgment[1]

"Truth and falsehood," says Mr. Bradley (*Logic*, p. 2), "depend on the relation of our ideas to reality." And he immediately goes on to explain that, in this statement, "ideas" must not be understood to mean mere "states of my mind". The ideas, he says, on the relation of which to reality truth depends, are "*mere* ideas, signs of an existence other than themselves," and this aspect of them must not be confused either with their existence in my mind or with their particular character as so existent, which may be called their content. "For logic, at least," he says, " all ideas are signs" (p. 5); and "A sign is any fact that has a meaning," while "meaning consists of a part of the content (original or acquired) cut off, fixed by the mind, and considered apart from the existence of the sign" (p.4).

But Mr. Bradley himself does not remain true to this conception of the logical idea as the idea *of* something. As such, indeed, it *is* only the psychological idea, related, indeed, to that which it signifies, but only related to it. Hence he finds it necessary, later, to use "idea," not of the symbol, but of the symbolised. Ideas, as *meanings*, not as "facts, which have a meaning," "are," he says (p. 8), "the ideas we spoke of, when we said 'Without ideas no

Originally published in *Mind* n.s. 8 (April 1899): 176–193.

judgment' ". And he proceeds to show that "in predication we do not *use* the mental fact, but only the meaning"; although, where he did say "Without ideas no judgment," his words were "we cannot judge until we use ideas *as* ideas. We must have become aware that they are not realities, that they are *mere* ideas, signs of an existence other than themselves." It would seem plain, then, that there his doctrine was that we do, in predication, use the mental fact, though only as a sign; whereas here his doctrine is that we do not use the mental fact, even as a sign, but only that which it signifies. This important transition he slurs over with the phrase: "But it is better to say the idea *is* the meaning". The question is surely not of which is "better to say," but which is true.

[177] Now to Mr. Bradley's argument that "the idea in judgment is the universal meaning" I have nothing to add. It appears to me conclusive, as against those, of whom there have been too many, who have treated the idea as a mental state. But he seems to me to be infected by the same error as theirs, alike in his preliminary failure to distinguish clearly whether it is the symbol or the symbolised of which he is speaking, and in his final description of the "idea, as meaning," when he has definitely decided in its favour. "A meaning," he says, as we saw above, "consists of a part of the content (original or acquired) cut off, fixed by the mind, and considered apart from the existence of the sign." And again, "an idea, if we use idea of the meaning, is neither given nor presented, but is taken" (p. 8). If indeed "the universal meaning" were thus simply a part of the content of our own ideas, as mental states, and that, too, a part "cut off" by our own minds, it would be intelligible that "truth and falsehood" should still be said to "depend on the relation of our ideas to reality". It will be our endeavour to show, on the contrary, that the "idea used in judgment" is not a part of the content of our ideas, nor produced by any action of our minds, and that hence truth and falsehood are not dependent on the relation of *our* ideas to reality.

I shall in future use the term "concept" for what Mr. Bradley calls a "universal meaning"; since the term "idea" is plainly full of ambiguities, whereas "concept" and its German equivalent "*Begriff*" have been more nearly appropriated to the use in question. There is, indeed, a great similarity between Kant's description of his "*Begriff*," and Mr. Bradley's of his "logical idea". For Kant, too, it is the "analytical unity of consciousness" which *makes* a "*Vorstellung*" or "idea" into a "*conceptus communis*" or "*gemeinsamer Begriff*" (*R.V.*, p. 116 n.).

It is our object to protest against this description of a concept as an "abstraction" from ideas.

Mr. Bradley's doctrine, as above sketched, presupposes that, when I have an idea (*Vorstellung*) of something, that something is itself part of the content of my idea. This doctrine, for the present, I am ready to admit; my question now is whether, when I have an idea of something, that something must not *also* be regarded as something other than part of the content of my idea. The content of an idea is, Mr. Bradley tells us, what the idea is; it is "a character which is different or distinguishable from that of other" ideas, treated as mental facts. Now, before I can [178] judge at all on Mr. Bradley's theory, a part of this character must have been "cut off and fixed by the mind". But my question is, whether we can thus cut off a part of the character of our ideas, and attribute that part to something else, unless we already know, in part at least, what is the character of the idea from which we are to cut off the part in question. If not, then we have already made a judgment with regard to the character of our idea. But this judgment, again, requires, on Mr. Bradley's theory, that I should have had an idea of my idea, and should have already cut off a part of the content of that secondary idea, in order that I may make a judgment with regard to the character of the primary idea that is in question. And similarly it is quite impossible that I should know what the content of my secondary idea is, until I have made it in its turn the object of a third idea, by taking part of this tertiary content. And so on *ad infinitum*. The theory would therefore seem to demand the completion of an infinite number of psychological judgments before any judgment can be made at all. But such a completion is impossible; and therefore all judgment is likewise impossible. It follows, therefore, if we are to avoid this absurdity, that the 'idea used in judgment' must be something other than a part of the content of any idea of mine. Mr. Bradley's theory presupposes that I may have two ideas, that have a part of their content in common; but he would at the same time compel us to describe this common part of content as part of the content of some third idea. But what is gained by such a description? If the part of content of this third idea is a part only in the same sense, as the common part of the other two is a part of each, then I am offering an explanation which presupposes that which was to be explained. Whereas if the part, which is used in explanation, is a part in the only sense which will make my explanation significant, *i.e.*, an existent part, then it is difficult to see how that which belongs to one idea can also come to belong to other ideas and yet remain one and the same. In short, the idea used in judgment is indeed a 'universal meaning'; but it cannot, for that very reason, be described as part of the content of any psychological idea whatever.

These difficulties, which are of the same nature as the famous *τρίτος ἄνθρωπος* urged against the hypostasised Platonic ideas, inevitably proceed from trying to explain the concept in terms of some existent fact, whether mental or of any other nature. All such explanations do in fact presuppose the nature of the concept, as a *genus per se*, irreducible [179] to anything else. The concept is not a mental fact, nor any part of a mental fact. Identity of content is presupposed in any reasoning; and to explain the identity of content between two facts by supposing that content to be a part of the content of some third fact, must involve a vicious circle. For in order that the content of the third fact may perform this office, it must already be supposed like the contents of the other two, *i.e.*, having something in common with them, and this community of content is exactly what it was proposed to explain.

When, therefore, I say "This rose is red," I am not attributing part of the content of my idea to the rose, nor yet attributing parts of the content of my ideas of rose and red together to some third subject. What I am asserting is a specific connexion of certain concepts forming the total concept "rose" with the concepts "this" and "now" and "red"; and the judgment is true if such a connexion is existent. Similarly when I say "The chimera has three heads," the chimera is not an idea in my mind, nor any part of such idea. What I mean to assert is nothing about my mental states, but a specific connexion of concepts. If the judgment is false, that is not because my *ideas* do not correspond to reality, but because such a conjunction of concepts in not to be found among existents.

With this, then, we have approached the nature of a proposition or judgment. A proposition is composed not of words, nor yet of thoughts, but of concepts. Concepts are possible objects of thought; but that is no definition of them. It merely states that they may come into relation with a thinker; and in order that they *may* do anything, they must already *be* something. It is indifferent to their nature whether anybody thinks them or not. They are incapable of change; and the relation into which they enter with the knowing subject implies no action or reaction. It is a unique relation which can begin or cease with a change in the subject; but the concept is neither cause nor effect of such a change. The occurrence of the relation has, no doubt, its causes and effects, but these are to be found only in the subject.

It is of such entities as these that a proposition is composed. In it certain concepts stand in specific relations with one another. And our question now is, wherein a proposition differs from a concept, that it may be either true or false.

It is at first sight tempting to say that the truth of a proposition depends on its relation to reality; that any proposition [180] is true which consists of a combination of concepts that is actually to be found among existents. This explanation was indeed actually used above (p. 179), as a preliminary explanation. And it may be admitted that propositions with which this is the case are true. But if this constituted the truth of a proposition, concepts too might in themselves be true. Red would be a true concept, because there actually are red things; and conversely a chimera would be a false concept, because no such combination either has been, is, or will be (so far as we know) among existent things. But the theory must be rejected as an ultimate one, because not all true propositions have this relation to reality. For example $2 + 2 = 4$ is true, whether there exist two things or not. Moreover it may be doubted here whether even the concepts of which the proposition consists, can ever be said to exist. We should have to stretch our notion of existence beyond intelligibility, to suppose that 2 ever has been, is, or will be an existent.

It would seem, in fact, from this example, that a proposition is nothing other than a complex concept. The difference between a concept and a proposition, in virtue of which the latter alone can be called true or false, would seem to lie merely in the simplicity of the former. A proposition is a synthesis of concepts; and, just as concepts are themselves immutably what they are, so they stand in infinite relations to one another equally immutable. A proposition is constituted by any number of concepts, together with a specific relation between them; and according to the nature of this relation the proposition may be either true or false. What kind of relation makes a proposition true, what false, cannot be further defined, but must be immediately recognised.

And this description will also apply to those cases where there appears to be a reference to existence. Existence is itself a concept; it is something which we mean; and the great body of propositions, in which existence is joined to other concepts or syntheses of concepts, are simply true or false according to the relation in which it stands to them. It is not denied that this is a peculiarly important concept; that we are peculiarly anxious to know what exists. It is only maintained that existence is logically subordinate to truth; that truth cannot be defined by a reference to existence, but existence only by a reference to truth. When I say "This paper exists," I must require that this proposition be true. If it is not true, it is unimportant, and I can have no interest in it. But if it is true, it means only that the concepts, which are combined in specific relations in the [181] concept of this paper, are also combined in a specific manner with the concept of existence. That specific manner is something immediately known, like red or two. It is highly important, because we set such value upon it; but it is itself a concept. All that exists is thus composed of concepts necessarily related to one another in specific manners, and likewise to the concept of existence.

I am fully aware how paradoxical this theory must appear, and even how contemptible. But it seems to me to follow from premisses generally admitted, and to have been avoided only by lack of logical consistency. I assume Mr. Bradley's proof that the concept is necessary to truth and falsehood. I endeavour to show, what I must own appears to me perfectly obvious, that the concept can consistently be described neither as an existent, nor as part of an existent, since it is presupposed in the conception of an existent. It is similarly impossible that truth should depend on a relation to existents or to an existent, since the proposition by which it is so defined must itself be true, and the truth of this can certainly not be established, without a vicious circle, by exhibiting its dependence on an existent. Truth, however, would certainly seem to involve at least two terms, and some relation between them; falsehood involves the same; and hence it would seem to remain, that we regard truth and falsehood as properties of certain concepts, together with their relations—a whole to which we give the name of proposition.

I have appealed throughout to the rules of logic; nor, if any one rejects these, should I have much to fear from his arguments.

An appeal to the facts is useless. For, in order that a fact may be made the basis of an argument, it must first be put in the form of a proposition, and, moreover, this proposition must be supposed true; and then there must recur the dilemma, whether rules of logic are to be accepted or rejected. And these rules once accepted, would seem themselves to offer a confirmation of our theory. For all true inference must be inference from a true proposition; and that the conclusion follows from the premiss must again be a true proposition: so that here also it would appear that the nature of a true proposition is the ultimate *datum*. Nor is an appeal to the "matter" of the proposition more useful than the former appeal to the facts. It may be true that this matter is given in sensation, or in any other conceivable way. We are not concerned with its origin, but with its nature; and its nature, if it is to enter into a true proposition, must, we agree with Mr. Bradley, be the nature of a concept and no [182] other: and then the old conclusions follow. Nor, finally, is a vicious circle involved in our own attempt to establish conclusions with regard to truth, by rules of logic in which that conception is presupposed. For our conclusion is that truth is itself a simple concept; that it is logically prior to any proposition. But a vicious circle occurs only where a proposition is taken as prior to a concept, or a more complex proposition (one involving more concepts) as prior to one which is more simple. Valid logical processes would seem to be of two kinds. It is possible to start from a complex proposition and to consider what propositions are involved in it. In this case the latter must always be more simple than the former; and they may be true; although the former is false. Or it is possible to start from a more simple proposition and to deduce one that is more complex, by successive additions of concepts; which is the properly deductive procedure exhibited in the propositions of Euclid: and in this case the premiss must be true, if the conclusion is so. It may be well to state that both procedures are synthetic, in the sense that the results arrived at are different from the premisses, and merely related to them. In a vicious circle, on the other hand, the two procedures are confused. A result arrived at by the former of the two processes just described, is regarded as involving the truth of its premiss. Thus, when we say that the conceptual nature of truth is involved in logical procedure, no vicious circle is committed, since we do not thereby presuppose the truth of logical procedure. But when an existent is said to be involved in truth, a vicious circle is committed, since the proposition "Something is true," in which " Something exists" is supposed to be involved, must itself be true, if the latter is to be so.

It seems necessary, then, to regard the world as formed of concepts. These are the only objects of knowledge. They cannot be regarded fundamentally as abstractions either from things or from ideas; since both alike can, if anything is to be true of them, be composed of nothing but concepts. A thing becomes intelligible first when it is analysed into its constituent concepts. The material diversity of things, which is generally taken as starting-point, is only derived; and the identity of the concept, in several different things, which appears on that assumption as the problem of philosophy, will now, if it instead be taken as the starting-point, render the derivation easy. Two things are then seen to be differentiated by the different relations in which their common concepts stand to other concepts. The opposition [183] of concepts to existents disappears, since an existent is seen to be nothing but a concept or complex of concepts standing in a unique relation to the concept of existence. Even the description of an existent as a proposition (a true existential proposition) seems to lose its strangeness, when it is remembered that a proposition is here to be understood, not as anything subjective—an assertion or affirmation of something—but as the combination of concepts which is affirmed. For we are familiar with the idea of affirming or "positing" an existent, of knowing objects as well as propositions; and the difficulty hitherto has been to discover wherein the two processes were akin. It now appears that perception is to be regarded philosophically as the cognition of an existential proposition; and it is thus apparent how it can furnish a basis for inference, which uniformly exhibits the connexion between propositions. Conversely light is thrown on the nature of inference. For, whereas it could not be maintained that the conclusion was only connected with the premisses in my thoughts, and that an inference was nothing, if nobody was making it, great difficulty was felt as to the kind of objectivity that belonged to the terms and their relation, since existence was taken as the type of objectivity. This difficulty is removed, when it is acknowledged that the relation of premisses to conclusion is an objective relation, in the same sense as the relation of existence to what exists is objective. It is no longer necessary to hold that logical connexions must, in some obscure sense, exist, since to exist is merely to stand in a certain logical connexion.

It will be apparent how much this theory has in common with Kant's theory of perception. It differs chiefly in substituting for sensations, as the data of knowledge, concepts; and in refusing to regard the relations in which they stand as, in some obscure sense, the work of the mind. It rejects the attempt to explain "the possibility of knowledge," accepting the cognitive relation as an ultimate *datum* or presupposition; since it maintains the objections which Kant himself urged against an explanation by causality, and recognises no other kind of explanation than that by way of logical connexion with other concepts. It thus renounces the supposed unity of conception guaranteed by Idealism even in the Kantian form, and still more the boasted reduction of all differences to the harmony of "Absolute Spirit," which marks the Hegelian development. But it is important to point out that it retains the doctrine of Transcendentalism. For Kant's Transcendentalism rests on the distinction between empirical and *a priori* propositions. This is a distinction [184] which offers a striking correspondence to that between the categorical and hypothetical judgments; and since one object of this paper is to combat the view which inclines to take the categorical judgment as the typical form, and attempts in consequence to reduce the hypothetical judgment to it, it will not be out of place to discuss Kant's distinction at some length.

Kant himself offers us two marks by which an *a priori* judgment may be distinguished. 'A proposition,' he says, 'which is thought along with its necessity is an *a priori* judgment.' And it is absolutely *a priori* only if it be not deduced from any proposition, that is not itself a necessary proposition. The second mark of the a priori is strict universality. But unfortunately Kant himself seems to admit the invalidity of this as a mark; since he immediately proceeds to state that an empirical universality may hold in all cases ('for example, in the proposition: All bodies are heavy') and hence be strictly universal.[2]

It is true Kant states that this empirical universality is merely arbitrary. We ought, he says, to express our proposition in the form: 'So far as we have yet observed, there is no exception from' the rule that all bodies are heavy. But it would seem that such a qualification can only affect the truth of our proposition and not its content. It may be questioned whether we have a right to assert universality, but it is universality which we assert. The limitations which Kant points out as belonging to the proposition, can properly be expressed only in the doubt whether we have found a rule at all, not in a doubt whether there are exceptions to it. It may not be true that all bodies are heavy; but whether true or not, it is a universal proposition. There is no difference between this proposition and such as are *a priori*, in respect of universality. And Kant could hardly wish to assert that the difference lay in its truth. For this proposition, he would admit, may be true; and, if so, then it would be *a priori*. But he would not admit the suggestion that it *may* be *a priori*: he asserts that it is not so. The difference between the empirical and the *a priori*, if there is a difference, must therefore be in some other mark than this universality, which Kant nevertheless asserts to be 'by itself an infallible criterion' (*ib.*, p.35). We may next consider whether such a mark is to be found in 'necessity'.

In this investigation, too, it may be well to examine his example 'All bodies are heavy,' since this proposition might [185] seem to have a claim to necessity also, just as it is undoubtedly universal. Kant speaks of it as 'a rule borrowed from experience' (*ib.*, p. 34). By this language and by his use of 'Bodies are heavy' as convertible with it, he would seem to suggest that he would not base its empirical character solely on its extensional interpretation. If, as seems probable, he would allow 'Body is heavy' or 'Man is mortal,' to be equally empirical propositions, then it is plain that what he calls empirical may involve necessity. It is certain, at all events, that if we are to understand by empirical propositions only such as experience can justify, such a proposition as 'All bodies are heavy' cannot be regarded as empirical. It is based on the proposition 'Body is heavy,' with which, if it is to be used for purposes of inference, it must be regarded as convertible. I assume, therefore, that Kant would not have refused to regard 'Body is heavy' as an empirical proposition. It would seem certainly to come under his class of 'rules drawn from experience,' whereas 'All bodies are heavy,' regarded solely as extensional, cannot be called a rule. The use of this example would seem to lead to important results with regard to the true definition of empirical propositions.

But let us first return to 'All bodies are heavy'; since even this would seem to involve in its very meaning an assertion of necessity. If it be taken purely in extension, it must be resolved into 'This body, and that body, and that body, *ad infinitum*, are, have been and will be heavy'. It involves, therefore, the proposition 'This body is heavy'. But in any proposition of this simple categorical form the notion of substance and attribute is already involved.[3] Wherever a predicate is asserted of a subject, it is implied that the subject is a *thing*; that it is something marked by the possession of certain attributes and capable of possessing others. 'This body is heavy' presupposes, therefore, 'Body is a thing, and heaviness is a mere attribute'. For we could not convert the proposition into 'Heaviness is corporeal'. But that 'Body is a thing,' and that 'Heaviness is an attribute,' would seem to be necessary propositions. We may indeed by mistaken in supposing that they are true; but if we were ever to find that heaviness was not an attribute, we should be bound to conclude that it never had been and never would be, not that it was so once but had ceased so to be. All such judgments are truly 'thought along with their necessity'. They are as necessary as that 2+2=4. The difference between [186] the two forms of proposition lies not in that the former lacks necessity, nor even that it implies the proposition 'Heaviness exists'; for even if heaviness did not exist, the proposition would be true. The proposition means that heaviness could not be other than an attribute; and hence, if Kant's words (p. 34) are to be taken strictly, it cannot be empirical. In this respect, therefore, it is quite on a level with '2+2=4'; which also would be true even if there were no two things. The difference seems to lie rather in the nature of the concepts of which the necessary relation is predicated. 'Heaviness' can exist; it is not meaningless to say 'Heaviness exists here and now'; whereas 'attribute,' 'two,' and other like conceptions can only claim a precarious sort of existence in so far as they are necessarily related to these other notions of which alone properly existential propositions can be made.

If, therefore, we wish to find propositions involving no necessity,[4] we must descend to purely existential propositions— propositions which do not involve the notions of substance and attribute. These alone can be truly taught us by experience, if experience, 'cannot teach us that a thing could not be otherwise'

(p. 34). And even these are free from necessity, only if they are understood to assert something with regard to an actual part of actual time. They must involve necessity as soon as the distinction between 'This is' and 'This was' is disregarded. It would seem, in fact, to be a mark of the sort of existence which they predicate that it is in time. They may affirm 'This exists,' or 'This has existed,' but if they take the general form 'This is,' that must always be understood to mean no more than 'This always has been, is now, and always will be,' and can be strictly analysed into as many different judgments as time is divisible into separate moments.

If, therefore, the difference between the empirical and *a priori* lay primarily, as Kant implies, in the nature of the judgment, not in that of the concept, only existential propositions could be empirical. In order to represent even 'This body is heavy' as an empirical proposition, it would be necessary to analyse it into the form 'Heaviness and the marks of body exist here and now'. But this is certainly not its whole meaning. We must, therefore, suppose that in order to obtain a clear definition of what Kant meant by empirical propositions, we must base it upon the nature of the [187] concepts used in them. Empirical concepts are those which can exist in parts of time. This would seem to be the only manner of distinguishing them. And any proposition into which an empirical concept enters may be called empirical.

Kant himself does recognise the necessity involved in such a proposition as 'This body is heavy,' although, for reasons which will appear hereafter, he states it in a somewhat different way. The main object of his 'Analytic' is to show that any such judgment involves a 'synthesis of the manifold of sense-intuition,' which is 'necessary *a priori*' (p. 126). But he regards this synthesis rather as necessary in order to bring mere perceptions into relation with the 'unity of apperception,' than as directly involved in the empirical judgment. Moreover, in order to explain how the forms of synthesis can apply to the manifold, he introduces the inner sense as mediator, and describes the judgment as converting the psychical connexion of the presentations into an objective connexion rather than as applying the categories to a mere manifold, which cannot properly be described as psychical. Accordingly he gives as the ultimate empirical judgment, out of which the application of substance and attribute produces 'Bodies are heavy,' the subjective judgment 'When I carry a body, I feel an impression of heaviness,' instead of that given above 'Heaviness and the marks of body exist together.'[5] He does not seem to see that his subjective judgment already fully involves the category in question. A statement about my feelings is just as 'objective,' in the required sense, as a statement about what is conceived as in space.

With the above definition, therefore, it is obvious why 'Body is heavy' should be called empirical; whereas, if absence of necessity had been the mark required, it would have been difficult to find a reason. For this proposition does not only involve, like 'This body is heavy' or 'All bodies are heavy,' the necessary judgments that body is a thing, and heaviness an attribute; it asserts a relation between a 'heaviness' and 'corporeity' such as no experience can prove or disprove. If we found a body which was not heavy, that would indeed lead us to deny the truth of the proposition; but it would also entitle us at once to the opposite necessary proposition 'Body cannot be heavy'. And this is just what holds of $2+2=4$. It is perhaps inconceivable to us now that two and two should not make four; but, when numbers were first discovered, it may well have been thought that two and two made three or five. [188] Experience, no doubt, must have been the means of producing the conviction that this was not so, but that two and two made four. The necessity of a proposition, therefore, is not called in question by the fact that experience may lead you to think it true or untrue. The test of its necessity lies merely in the fact that it must be either true or untrue, and cannot be true now and untrue the next moment; whereas with an existential proposition it may be true that this exists now, and yet it will presently be untrue that it exists. The doubt about the truth of 'Body is heavy' would seem to proceed chiefly from our uncertainty as to what we mean by 'Body' and by 'heavy'. We cannot recognise instances of them with as great precision as we recognise instances of number; and hence we cannot be sure whether the truth of our proposition may not be overthrown. The proposition is arbitrary solely in this sense. There would seem no doubt that we mean by it to assert an absolute necessity; but between what precise concepts the necessary relation, of which we are certain, holds, we must leave to experience to discover.

From the foregoing analysis it would, therefore, appear that the true distinction upon which Kant's division of propositions into *a priori* and *a posteriori*, necessary and empirical, is based, is the distinction between concepts which can exist in parts of time and concepts which seem to be cut off from existence altogether, but which give rise to assertions of an absolutely necessary relation. Kant would seem to include among empirical propositions all those in which an empirical concept is used; whether the proposition asserts a necessary relation between an empirical and an *a priori* concept, or between two empirical concepts. What it is important to emphasise is that these two kinds of proposition are not distinguished by the absence of the marks which he gives for the *a priori*; they both include both necessity and strict universality. Empirical propositions would therefore include a wide range of propositions, differing very much in the meaning of their assertions. They seem to extend upwards from mere assertions of the existence of this or that, of the type 'Heaviness exists here and now'; through propositions of the usual categorical form 'This body is heavy,' which include necessary propositions in their meaning, but at the same time imply an assertion of existence; to propositions which assert existence at every time, while still retaining the element of necessity included in the last, like 'All bodies are heavy'; and finally to those propositions, upon which alone the validity of the last class can be based [189]—propositions which assert a necessary relation, without any implication of existence whatever, of the type 'Body is heavy'. The only common element in all these different classes would seem to be that they all make assertions with regard to some empirical concept, *i.e.*, a concept which can exist in an actual part of time. The second and third classes are mixed and involve necessity, because there is also included in them an assertion with regard to an *a priori* concept. To all of them Kant would seem to oppose as purely *a priori* propositions, those which make an assertion solely with regard to *a priori* concepts and which for that reason can imply no assertion of existence, since an *a priori* concept is one which cannot exist in the limited sense above explained.

The line of division, therefore, upon which Kant's Transcendentalism is based, would seem to fall between propositions involving empirical concepts and those which involve none such; and an empirical concept is to be defined, not as a concept given by experience, since all concepts are so given, but as one which can exist in an actual part of time. This division is necessary in order to include all the various kinds of propositions which Kant includes under the term empirical, many of which involve *a priori* concepts. If the division were to be based on the nature of the propositions, as such, as Kant pretends to base it, we saw that pure existential propositions alone could be thought to have a claim to form a class by themselves, as empirical propositions. These do indeed obviously form the basis of the other division; for a simple concept cannot be known as one which could exist in time, except on the ground that it has so existed, is existing, or will exist. But we have now to point out that even existential propositions have the essential mark which Kant assigns to *a priori* propositions—that they are absolutely necessary.

The distinction of time was said to be ultimate for an existential proposition. If this is so, it is obvious that necessary propositions, of the kind which Kant endeavors to establish in the Aesthetic, are involved in them. It was pointed out that a pure existential proposition could only assert the existence of a simple concept; all others involving the *a priori* concepts of substance and attribute. If now we take the existential proposition "Red exists," we have an example of the type required. It is maintained that, when I say this, my meaning is that the concept "red" and the concept "existence" stand in a specific relation both to one another and to the concept of time. I mean the "Red [190] exists now," and thereby imply a distinction from its past and future existence. And this connexion of red and existence with the moment of time I mean by "now," would seem to be as necessary as any other connexion whatever. If it is true, it is necessarily true, and if false, necessarily false. If it is true, its contradictory is as fully impossible as the contradictory of 2+2=4.

But the necessity thus involved in existential propositions does not do away with the importance of Kant's distinction between the empirical and the *a priori*. So far as he attempts to base it upon the fact that what is empirical alone is "given in experience" and may be referred to "sense," it must indeed be given up; but as against the English philosophers, who held the same view about sense-knowledge, it retains its full weight. the Transcendental Deduction contains a perfectly valid answer to Hume's scepticism, and to empiricism in general. Philosophers of this school generally tend to deny the validity of any propositions except those about existents. Kant may be said to have pointed out that in any of these propositions, which the empiricists considered to be the ultimate if not the only, data of knowledge, there was involved by the very same logic on which they relied to support their views, not only the uniform and necessary succession of time, and the geometrical properties of space, but also the principles of substance and causality. He does not, indeed, thereby prove the truth of the axioms and principles in question; but he shows that they are at least equally valid with, and more ultimate than, those upon which empiricism builds. Although, therefore, it seems no longer possible to hold, as Kant held, that a reference to existents is necessary to any proposition that is to claim the title of "knowledge," and that the truth of such propositions can alone claim *immediate* certainty; although, on the contrary, it seems that existential propositions are only a particular class of necessary proposition: yet the transcendental deduction is still important. A deduction from the "possibility of experience" does not indeed really represent the nature of Kant's argument. For the possibility of experience presupposes that we have experience, and this again means that certain existential propositions are true: but this does not involve the truth of any particular existential propositions; although its truth is involved in theirs. What Kant really shows is that space and time and the categories are involved in particular propositions; and this work is of greater value than a deduction from the possibility of experience would have been. He does not indeed recognise [191] that the propositions from which he is deducing are themselves necessary, and that there may therefore be other necessary propositions, with a like claim to certainty, not to be deduced from them. He therefore imagines himself to have exhausted the field of knowledge; whereas in fact he has only shown certain logical connexions within that field. But it is not here proposed to dispute the truth of particular existential propositions; and though, unlike Kant, we admit them to be merely assumed, we may be thankful that he has shown us what can be inferred from them.

Moreover, Kant's distinction between space and time on the one hand, and the categories on the other, also retains its value, though we can no longer describe their general difference as he did. It seems rather to be this: That time alone is sufficient for some sort of experience, since it alone seems to be involved in the simplest kind of existential proposition, *e.g.*, "Pleasure exists"; and that again time and space together will suffice to account for the possibility of other pieces of knowledge, without the use of the categories. It is necessary to make a fresh assumption of propositions such as even Hume recognised, and such as are universal in physical science, in order to find the principles of substance and accident and causality implied. In all such propositions time and space are presupposed as well, but these categories are not implied in every proposition involving time and space.

The simplest existential propositions are then to be regarded as necessary propositions of a peculiar sort. In one kind the necessary properties of time are involved; in another those of space also. But though this fact, which Kant points out, is very important against empiricists, we cannot regard it with him as establishing the truth of geometry and of the corresponding propositions about time. For existential propositions which are false, as well as those which are true, involve the same propositions about space and time. No existential proposition of any sort seems discoverable, which might not thus be false; not even the famous "cogito" is indubitable. We cannot, therefore, take the "possibility of experience," in any possible sense, as sufficient warrent for our knowledge of space and time; and we must regard the truths of geometry as independently known for true, just in the same way as some existential propositions are so known.

Similarly, those propositions which involve substance and attribute are not sufficient to establish the truth of the propositions thereby involved. The permanence of substance is [192] indeed, Kant shows us, as certain as the empirical propositions which Hume took to be alone certain. But its truth must be known independently of these, since it is involved also in false propositions of this type. It would, in fact, be true, whether any such propositions were true or not. Kant has only taught us that, if any of them are true, it must be so likewise. He failed to see that its truth may be asserted immediately on the same ground as theirs; for he was misled by the previous course of philosophy to suppose that there was something more immediately indubitable in them. Their truth is, in fact, the last thing which common sense doubts, in spite of its familiarity with erroneous perceptions. Kant's merit was in pointing out, what he himself did not recognise, that their being undoubted does not prove them to be indubitable; or rather, that the doubt which is cast on some of them proves conclusively, what common sense, in its contentment with rules that have exceptions, does not perceive, that they are highly doubtful.

Our result then is as follows: That a judgment is universally a necessary combination of concepts, equally necessary whether it be true or false. That it must be either true or false, but that its truth or falsehood cannot depend on its relation to anything else whatever, reality, for instance, or the world in space and time. For both of these must be supposed to exist, in some sense, if the truth of our judgment is to depend upon them; and then it turns out that the truth of our judgment depends not on them, but on the judgment that they, being such and such, exist. But this judgment cannot, in its turn, depend on anything else, for its truth or falsehood: its truth or its falsehood must be immediate properties of its own, not dependent upon any relation it may have to something else. And, if this be so, we have removed all reason for the supposition that the truth and falsehood of other judgments are not equally independent. For the existential judgment, which is presupposed in Kant's reference to experience or in Mr. Bradley's reference to reality, has turned out to be, as much as any other, merely a necessary combination of concepts, for the necessity of which we can seek no ground, and which cannot be explained as an attribution to 'the given'. A concept is not in any intelligible sense an 'adjective,' as if there were something substantive, more ultimate than it. For we must, if we are to be consistent, describe what appears to be most substantive as no more than a collection of such supposed adjectives: and thus, in the end, the concept turns out to be [193] the only substantive or subject, and no one concept either more or less an adjective than any other. From our description of a judgment,there must, then, disappear all reference either to our mind or to the world. Neither of these can furnish 'ground' for anything, save in so far as they are complex judgments. The nature of the judgment is more ultimate than either, and less ultimate only than the nature of its constituents—the nature of the concept or logical idea.

NOTES

1. Read before the Aristotelian Society.
2. R.V., p. 35. 'Hartenstein, ed. 1867.'
3. Cf. R.V., p. 36.
4. Even these involve the necessary properties of time; but this point may be reserved for later consideration.
5. P. 121, *cf.* also *Prol.*, p. 54 n.

4

Necessity

My primary object in this paper is to determine the *meaning* of necessity. I do not wish to discover what things are necessary; but what that predicate is which attaches to them when they are so. Nor, on the other hand, do I wish to arrive at a correct verbal definition of necessity. That the word is commonly used to signify a great number of different predicates, which do actually attach to things, appears to me quite plain. But, this being so, we shall be using the word correctly, whenever we apply it to any one of these; and a correct definition of necessity will be attained, if we enumerate all those different predicates which the word is commonly used to signify: for the only test that a word is correctly defined is common usage. The problem which I wish to solve is different from either of these. It is a problem which resembles them in its universal application. There is a solution of it not only for necessity but for everything that we can think of; and in many cases the discovery of this solution appears to me to be of fundamental importance for philosophy. The nature of this problem may perhaps be exhibited as follows: When a man says

Originally published in *Mind* n.s. 9 (July 1900): 289–304.

'A is necessary' or 'red' or 'round' or 'loud' or, whatever it may be, he may be wrong in three ways. (1) He may be using the word 'necessary' in a sense in which it is not commonly used. For instance the thought which he intends to convey may be that 'A is red'; and then, whether A is red or not, he is committing a verbal error in saying that 'A is necessary'. [290] (2) He may be using 'necessary' in one of the many senses in which other people use it, but he may be mistaken in supposing that A really has the predicate, which he rightly denotes by that word. (3) He may both be using the world correctly and also be right in supposing that A has one of the predicates which 'necessary' commonly signifies; and yet he may be wrong in a different way. For while rightly thinking that it has one of these predicates he may be mistaken in supposing that it also has some other of them. That 'A is necessary' we must grant him to be both verbally and substantially correct; and again that 'B is necessary': and yet in so far as he includes with that predicate which A really has the predicate which B really has, his statement that 'A is necessary' may be very incorrect. All this is obvious enough, and such confusions have been fully recognised as a frequent source of fallacy in reasoning. What I wish to point out is that this mistake is not a mistake about the meaning of a word, nor yet about a question of fact. The question which we must answer in order to decide whether a man is mistaken in this way is quite different from either of the two questions: Is he using this word correctly? or Has the thing in question that predicate? For there may be no doubt at all that we should answer Yes or No to either of these questions; and yet there may be much doubt as to what the predicate in question is. While never doubting that certain things have certain predicates, and that all these predicates are commonly signified by the same word, we yet may be in doubt whether there is anything in common between these various predicates and, if so, what. We may be right on both the former points and yet be wrong on this. This, then, is the question which I intend to raise, in asking what is the meaning of necessity. My main object is not to discover whether any or all propositions of the form 'A is necessary' are true or false, nor yet whether they are correctly expressed; but what their *meaning* is.

But, though this question is the one I mainly want to answer, I see no means of reaching my conclusion except by a partial discussion of both the others. Their relation to it is indeed peculiar. Logically it is presupposed in both of them: for 'A is necessary' is not true or false, unless it have some definite meaning; and, if the word 'necessary' is usually applied to certain predicates, it is predicates with some definite meaning to which it is usually applied. We might then be tempted to say: We must know exactly what it is we are talking about, before we can know whether what we say of it is true or false. And it is a fact that an exact [291] knowledge of what we are talking about will often lead us to see that what we had thought true of it is false. But the order of discovery is generally just the reverse of this. We must have judged correctly that certain collections of objects were three in number many times over, before we could know exactly what three was. And so here I must examine the cases in which things are said to be necessary, before I can discover what necessity is.

Now it would appear there are three classes of entity which are commonly called necessary. We may call a connexion necessary, or we may call a thing necessary, or we may call a proposition necessary. And there is at least one property which may be common to all these three. All three of them may be forced upon the mind. We may have the feeling of compulsion with regard to them. We may feel compelled to believe that two objects have a certain relation, or that a certain thing exists, or that a certain proposition is true. But this feeling of compulsion, though it may probably have been the origin of all our ideas of necessity, has certain properties which prevent us from identifying it with them. For it accompanies different beliefs at different times and in different persons. If we were to say that a necessary truth is one, belief in which is accompanied by a feeling of compulsion, we should have to admit that the same truth was necessary at one time and unnecessary at another, and even that the same truth might be simultaneously both necessary and unnecessary. But it is certain that necessary is often used in a sense which would exclude this possibility. Necessary truths, it would be said, are truths which are always necessary: and whether there are any such or not, we certainly mean by them something different from truths, belief in which is sometimes accompanied by a feeling of compulsion. Nor can it be said we only mean such truths as are *generally* accompanied by such a feeling. For the truths which are most commonly regarded as necessary do not now generally excite any such feeling when we believe in them. A belief in the truths of arithmetic, for example, has now become so habitual, that we obtain it with the greatest ease. And, if it be said that these beliefs are nevertheless all of such a nature that they would generally excite the feeling of compulsion, if we tried to believe the opposite, it may be admitted that this is true. Probably in most cases we should find it difficult to believe the opposite of those truths which we call necessary. They would force themselves upon us in spite of our efforts. But there is no reason to believe that any truths have this property *universally*. It [292] would be a bold assertion that no one ever had believed or would believe with ease that two and two make five. And if the statement be general only and not universal, it would apply to many more truths than are commonly thought to be necessary, as, for instance, to the existence of the sun and of the earth. It can scarcely be maintained that such facts have failed to be called necessary, solely because it was not perceived that their opposites were hard to believe. The most plausible way, then, in which it might be attempted to show that the meaning of necessity always involved a reference to the feeling of compulsion, fails at least to cover the distinction between necessary and existential truths. The most plausible expression of this theory would take the form: That is always necessary, belief in which would generally excite a feeling of compulsion, if we tried to believe its opposite. And this definition of necessity, while it is doubtful even whether it would apply to most cases of supposed necessary truths, certainly fails in that it will apply to many others as well.

It seems questionable how far this feeling of compulsion is to be identified with the impression from which Hume sought to derive the idea of necessity. But his account of how we come to think events necessarily connected certainly implies quite a different meaning of necessity, which must be carefully distinguished from this. What he says is that when a succession of two events has been repeated often enough, the mind has a habit of reproducing the idea of the second on the occurrence of the impression of the first. He does not seem to maintain that it *feels compelled* to have the idea of the second event. But unless he does mean this, where is the impression of necessity for which he was seeking? Either he must mean that there are constant successions among mental events just as there are among physical; but in that case it would seem that the succession in the mind can give rise to no idea different from that to which the physical succession might of itself give rise. Necessity in this case means merely constant succession, and Hume's reference to the habits of the mind is quite superfluous. Or else he means that the mental habit does actually compel us to think of the second event on occurrence of the first. But in this case he is illegitimately transferring to the contents of the mind that very idea of necessary connexion which he is seeking to deny to physical events. For, on his own showing, we have no title to say anything more of mental contents than that they do succeed one another in certain fixed sequences. His question is: What is the meaning of [293] saying that a prior event compels another to occur? And he cannot legitimately assume that he knows the meaning of this where the events are mental and not where they are physical. To the feeling of compulsion he might indeed have referred us, as an exclusively mental impression. But this he does not explicitly do. And the view that habits do compel the mind, not that we feel compelled by them, implies quite a different meaning of necessity, which he might just as easily have derived from the physical events themselves.

This second meaning of necessity, which Hume thus seems to imply, is in fact the very meaning that is involved in the connexion of cause and effect. We do commonly think that when some events have occurred others will necessarily follow; and when we think this, we have no idea in our minds that we are compelled to think so. We do apply the idea of necessity directly to the connexion between two events; and the only question is what is the idea that we thus apply. Hume certainly set out to answer this question, when he inquired what impression it was of which the idea 'necessity' was a copy. But in his answer he was led off into two quite different issues. His explanation is in the first place only an explanation of why we come to think it, not of *what* we think when we do think it. In order to get the latter, he would have had to introduce the feeling of compulsion: as it is, he merely assigns a cause for our belief that there are causes. And in the second place he confuses the question concerning the meaning of necessity with the question of its valid application to successions of events in time. He wishes to deny that there is any necessary connexion between events which are commonly called causes and effects: he holds that they are not necessarily related in the same sense in which two similar ideas are necessarily related. But this is to allow that necessity does mean something other than constant succession: for he does not deny that events have the relation of constant succession.

Hume has, then, certainly given no answer to the question: What is the meaning of that necessity which is commonly predicated of causes and effects? In so far as he tries to explain why we come to think of certain events as necessarily connected, he seems to imply both that there is such an idea as necessary connexion, and that it may be validly applied to certain mental events. But, on the other hand, he holds explicitly that no connexion except that of constant succession may be validly applied to events; and, in the second place, he points out a *prima facie* difference between two [294] events that are thus related and two ideas that have the relation of similarity. In so far as he appeals to this difference he may be taken as allowing that here is an idea of necessary connexion which is not identical with that of constant succession; and this idea may be that which we assert of a cause and its effect, whether it really does apply to them or not. Only by his denial that this is the case—by his assertion that there is nothing in common between the idea of a necessary truth and the idea of a causal connexion—does Hume really contribute anything to the question what the latter means.

We have it, then, suggested that there are two forms of connexion commonly called necessary, and that there is nothing in common between these two; and this view seems still to be held by those who oppose a 'real' to an 'ideal' necessity. In order to decide whether it be a true view, it will be necessary to discuss at some length each of these two forms of necessity, which are at first sight so different—the necessity of necessary truths and the necessity of real causes.

Now the line which Kant took in answering Hume was based, in part at least, on a denial that they were so different as Hume had thought. Kant pointed out that truths, which Hume had allowed to be necessary, on the ground that they were analytic, were, like the relation of cause and effect, synthetic. The truths of arithmetic were both synthetic and necessary, and, if Hume had considered this, it would have destroyed his reason for allowing no common element between ideal and real necessity. Kant, however, does still allow that there are such things as analytic truths, and that they are necessary. Though, therefore, he classes together, as having a common element, two forms of necessity, which Hume had separated, he still allows another form, which may or may not be different in meaning from this. He does not decide the question: In what sense are analytic truths necessary? No, if we take the view that the sense is different from that in which synthetic truths are necessary, there would seem to be two alternatives open. Either (1) it may be said that 'necessary' here merely means 'analytic'; that the two conceptions are identical. In this case it becomes an analytical truth that analytical truths are necessary; and no exception can be taken to the separation of this meaning of necessity from all others, if only there be any meaning in analytic truths. But, at the same time, this necessity becomes utterly unimportant. It is impossible to draw from it any inferences with regard to the truths that [295] possess it, as that they have superior certainty, or are universal and eternal. For any of these predicates can only be asserted of it on the ground of a synthetic truth. But if (2) we say that the necessity of analytic truths is not identical with their being analytic, then that they are necessary is a synthetic proposition. And only, while this synthetic proposition is necessary, can any analytic proposition be so. Even, then, if there be some special necessity attaching to analytic propositions it is secondary to that which attaches to some kinds of synthesis.

But there is much doubt whether any truths are analytic. Any proposition, it would seem, must contain at least two different terms and their relation; and, this being so, the relation may always be denied of the two terms without a contradiction. It takes two propositions to make a contradiction: the law of contradiction itself excludes the possibility of any single proposition being both true and false, or self-contradictory. And hence the definition of an analytic proposition as a proposition, the contradictory of which is self-contradictory can apply to nothing. If, on the other hand, we take the definition that it is a proposition of which the predicate is contained in the subject, then either its meaning is that the predicate is united in some way with the other predicates, which along with it define the subject: in which case the analytic proposition is an synthetic as you please; or else the predicate is simply identical with the subject. But in this latter case, where the supposed analytic proposition may be expressed in the form, A is A, we have certainly not two different terms, and therefore we have no proposition.

Moreover, the law of contradiction itself, than which nothing is commonly supposed to be more plainly analytic, is certainly synthetic. For suppose some one to hold that Not every proposition is either true or false. You cannot deny that this is a proposition, unless you are also willing to allow that the law which it contradicts is not a proposition; and he may perfectly well maintain that this is one of those propositions which is true, and the contradictory of which, your law, is false, although this is not the case with every proposition. Whereas, if you urge that it is included in the notion of a proposition that it should be either true or false, either your law becomes a pure tautology and not a proposition, or else there is something else in the notion of a proposition beside the property that it is either true or false, and then you are asserting a synthetic connexion between this property and those others.

[296] We may, then, safely assume that there is no such thing as a special necessity belonging to analytic truths, because there are no analytic truths. But I do not wish to deny that the law of contradiction is necessary. Nothing would generally be thought to be more certain or more necessary than this; and hence it will be a particularly good instance in which to examine what may be meant by calling a synthetic truth necessary.

What then is the necessity which attaches to the law of contradiction?

Now there are several other predicates which have been or are commonly associated with necessity as belonging to truths like this: eternity, for instance, absolute certainty, and universality. It may, then, turn out that necessity is identical with some one of these or with the combination of them all. If, on the other hand, we find it impossible to identify necessity with them, there will be some probability that any remaining property which may belong to the truths in question will be that which is meant by their necessity.

First, then, to consider eternity. If by this be meant that the truths in question are true at every moment of time, it cannot be a mark which distinguishes necessary from any other kinds of truths. For, universally, what is once true, is always true. Every truth is true at every moment of time; whereas, when we talk of necessary truths, we certainly mean that only some truths are necessary and that others are not. That every truth is true at every moment of time has not indeed been universally perceived; but it needs no long discussion to show that it is so. Truths which have been supposed to be exceptions are such as assert that so and so exists now, whereas it did not exist in the past or will not exist in the future; and it must, of course, be admitted that things do exist now, which neither have always existed nor will always exist. But the *truth* is not the *thing*: the truth is that the thing existed at some moment of time, which we designate conveniently as present or past or future, because we thereby point out its temporal relation to another existing thing, namely our perception of the truth. That Caesar was killed on the Ides of March, to take Hume's example, if only it be true, was, is, and will be always true: no one will deny this. And it is also true that that particular date was the present once and is not the present now; and these propositions also are eternal truths. For by 'now' nothing more is meant than a particular date, which we all can distinguish from other dates in the objective time-series, by the fact that the perceptions which fall [297] on that date have, when they fall, a peculiar quality—the feeling of presence.

But if, on the other hand, by 'eternal' truths be meant truths which are true at no moment of time, then it would seem that in the same sense all truths are true at no moment of time. This is, indeed, only a more accurate way of expressing that same property of truths, which is popularly expressed by saying that they are always true. For a truth is not to be regarded in the same way either as a particular configuration of matter which may exist at one moment and cease to exist at the next, nor yet as matter itself, when it is conceived to exist at every moment. The truth that something exists, it would seem, never does exist itself, and hence cannot be accurately said to occupy any moment of time. Accurately we should express that eternity, which is the property of all truths, by the negative statement that they are incapable of change, without thereby implying that they are capable of duration.

Eternity, then, will not distinguish the Law of Contradiction from any other truth; and yet we should be unwilling to say that it was not necessary in a sense in which some other truths may be distinguished from it. Perhaps, absolute certainty will furnish this distinguishing mark.

Now if absolute certainty be understood in a psychological sense, it will not furnish a universal mark. That we are more certain of the Law of Contradiction than of any other truth, I will admit, though it would be difficult to prove it. But then it must be admitted, on the other side, that there was a time in the history of the race when men were very certain of many, particularly the most contingent, truths, before they had even thought of the Law of Contradiction; when, therefore, they could not be certain of it at all. It is, indeed, remarkable that all the truths, which we now consider particularly necessary, are so abstract that we cannot suppose them to have been thought of or believed in till after many other truths had enjoyed a long lease of certainty. That necessary truths are, then, universally more certain than others, cannot be maintained; and if it be said that nevertheless, as soon as both are thought of, the necessary ones become at once more certain, or that they are capable of greater certainty, it is fair to suspect that this is said on the *a priori* ground that, since they are more necessary, they must be more certain. Empirical evidence of it is certainly not forthcoming. Yet no one would hesitate to say, for the lack of this, that necessary truths do differ from others. It would seem, then, that certainty, in any psychological sense, [298] can not be that which makes a necessary truth what it is. If certainty be used in any other sense, it may be discussed more conveniently, after we have considered universality.

The universal certainly would seem a more likely candidate, than either of the others, for the honour of identification with the necessary. They have been ranked together by Kant as joint marks of the *a priori*. But here again it is necessary to make a distinction of meaning. For, in the first place, a truth may be said to be universal, in the sense already considered as meant by eternal, namely that it is always true. This, we found, would not serve to distinguish any one truth from any other. We must, then, find some other meaning for universality if it is to be identified with necessity. And we have obviously got a universality of some sort, which is not this, in the Law of Contradiction. For it asserts that every proposition is either true or false; and inasmuch as it thus applies to every instance of the class 'proposition' it may be said to be universal. But this suggests a distinction which is not without importance. For what is true of every proposition is that *it* is true or false; it is not true of any proposition that every proposition is true or false; but it is this latter which is said to be necessary. The necessary, therefore, is not universal in the sense of being a property common to all the instances of a certain kind. If, then, we are to say that necessity is connected with universality, we must say it in the sense that every necessary proposition is one which asserts that some property is to be found in every instance in which some other property is found. But is this true of all necessary propositions? It would seem it is not true of arithmetical propositions, for instance, of the proposition that 5 + 7= 12. For here we assert nothing about a number of instances. There are not several instances of 5 and of 7; there is but one 5, one 7 and one 12. And yet we assert a connexion between them which is commonly held to be necessary. It is indeed true of every collection of things which number five that, if you add to them a collection which numbers seven, the whole collection will number twelve. But different collections of five things, are not different fives; and though a proposition about collections of five things may be universal in the sense in which the Law of Contradiction is universal, that is no evidence that a proposition about five itself is also. It is not, then, true that every proposition about a universal is a universal proposition. For every number is a universal in the sense that it is a property of many different collections; and yet a proposition asserting the connexions between [299] numbers makes no assertion about a number of instances. It has indeed been suggested that propositions such as the Law of Contradiction might be more properly expressed in a form analogous to arithmetical propositions; that we should say, not: Every proposition is either true or false; but: Proposition is either true or false, just as we say: Man is mortal. But there seems reason to suspect that these propositions are really universal in a sense in which arithmetical propositions are not so, and that 'proposition' is not a property of propositions in the same sense in which any number is a property of the collection of which it is predicated. For even granted that 'Man is mortal' has a meaning, how can we get from this to the proposition 'All men are mortal,' except by adding that the property of mortality is *always* connected with the other properties of humanity, wherever these latter occur? Whereas from the proposition that 7+5=12, you can arrive at the conclusion that all collections of five and seven are equal to collections of twelve, without the premiss that 7+5=12, wherever they occur; for the reason, which seems to be true though it will hardly be thought convincing, that 5 and 7 never do occur. For myself, I cannot perceive that 'Man is mortal' has any meaning at all except that 'Man is *always* mortal'; and similarly with the Law of Contradiction, since propositions do not occur in time and therefore cannot be said to be *always* either true or false, the ultimate expression of it would seem to be that *all* propositions are either true or false.

We must, therefore, say that some necessary propositions are not universal in the sense that they make an assertion about a sum of instances, whereas other necessary propositions are universal in this sense. This universality too, then, will not furnish the meaning of that necessity which belongs to necessary truths. But is there, perhaps, some third kind of universality which is common both to the propositions of Arithmetic and to the Law of Contradiction, and indeed to all propositions which have a *prima facie* claim to be considered necessary truths? There is, I think, a sense in which, not indeed strict universality, but a certain generality may be claimed for all of them. They may all be said to be propositions of a wide application; and a discussion of what exactly this wide application is will furnish my answer to the question what is meant by that necessity which may be truly ascribed to necessary truths. It will then only remain to inquire what, if anything, there is in common between this so-called 'ideal' necessity and causal or 'real' necessity.

[300] This generality of necessary truths is what I take Kant to have established in part of his diverse proofs that they are *a priori*. But whereas he expressly maintains that if you see a truth to be absolutely necessary you may infer it to be *a priori*, my contention is that you can but show it to be *a priori*, and that you then add no new or true fact about it, but only a new name, when you also dub it necessary. The theory, briefly stated, is this: That *a priori* means logically prior, and that any truth which is logically prior to some other true proposition is so far necessary; but, that

as you get more and more true propositions to which a given truth is logically prior, so you approach that region within which the given truth will be said to be absolutely necessary or *a priori*. There will, then, be only a difference of degree between necessary truths and many others, namely, a difference in the number of propositions to which they bear a certain logical relation; but there will be a difference of kind between this logical relation and any other of the notions by means of which it has been sought to give a definition of necessity. If there be any truths which have this logical relation to all other propositions, then, indeed, the application of these would be not merely wide but absolutely universal; such, it would seem, is the Law of Contradiction and, perhaps, some others: and these, perhaps, might be said to differ in kind from all others in this respect also. But into this question, which is exceedingly difficult, I do not propose to enter. It is sufficient for my purpose that there are some truths, commonly called necessary, certain axioms of geometry, for instance, which have not this absolutely universal application, but which have a very wide one: and that this, at least, may be said of all necessary truths.

The logical relation, by means of which I propose to define necessity, is one to which constant appeal is made in philosophical arguments; but the appeal is almost as frequently misused. It is said that one proposition is presupposed, or implied, or involved in another; and this argument is considered to be final. And so indeed it is, if only the proposition in question is really presupposed or implied or involved. It would seem, therefore, desirable that we should be clear about what this relation, which may be designated generally as logical priority, really is: and such clearness is essential to my definition of necessity. I propose, therefore, to try to point it out, but, without attempting to assign its exact limits, or to give an exhaustive enumeration of the various kinds of logical relation, which may all be justly [301] called by this one name. It needs, I think, only to be seen in any instance, in order to be recognised. Thus when we say: Here are two chairs, and there are two chairs, and therefore, in all, there are four chairs; it would commonly be admitted that we presuppose in our conclusion that $2 + 2 = 4$. Yet it is plain that many a man may arrive correctly at the number of objects before him, in an enormous number of instances, without envisaging the socalled abstract propositions that $2 + 2 = 4$, or $3 + 1 = 4$, or $1 + 1 + 1 + 1 = 4$. These, therefore, are different propositions from those which we commonly make about four objects, and yet they are presupposed in all of them. Similarly, when a man says: This is white, and that is black, and therefore these are different objects; we should say he implied that black and white are different. And this in itself is a common enough case. But if we go farther and say: That things which have different properties are different; this is a principle which is involved in every particular judgment of difference that we make; and we should be unable to give any reason for our judgment that the things are different, except that this and that property, which belong to them respectively, are different. These then are cases of logical priority, and we can determine whether other supposed cases are also of this nature, by considering whether they are like or unlike these. And by no means all cases of inference are of such a kind. For instance, if one says: There has been a horse here: and we ask why; his reason may be: See these hoof-prints. But that a horse made them is by no means presupposed in the fact that there are hoof-prints there. And yet the inference may be perfectly valid: both propositions may be true, and the one may follow from the other. All propositions, then, are not connected by way of logical priority; whereas some propositions are. And what universally marks a prior proposition is that it may be true, even though the particular proposition, to which it is prior, should be false. And thus a logically prior proposition is universally prior both to one false and to one true proposition. And, moreover, what Kant showed is that there are a number of propositions logically prior to almost every true 'empirical' judgment that we make; and such empirical judgments form an immense majority of all the true propositions of which we are cognisant. They cannot be true, unless the propositions they involve are true: but these may be true, even if the empirical judgments are false.

That there is, then, this class of logically prior propositions, [302] and that they approach to universality in the sense that many of them are prior to a very great number of other truths, will hardly be denied. And that they coincide to a remarkable degree with the class of 'necessary truths' seems no less evident. But moreover they seem to coincide with the class of 'most certain' propositions, in any sense of certainty which is not psychological. For any one who is looking for a perfectly certain proposition from which to deduce his system of philosophy will in general try to show that it is logically prior to all other propositions. We may take as an instance the famous '*Cogito, ergo sum*'. Here the conclusion that 'I am,' because I think, is made by way of logical priority: and it really is logically prior. How far Descartes used the same argument in defence of the proposition that he thought, I am unaware: the certainty that he primarily claimed for it is certainly a psychological one, namely that he could not doubt it. But modern idealistic descendants of his constantly claim superior certainty for the '*Cogito*' itself, on the ground that it is logically prior to other propositions. Many will say straight out that thought is presupposed in all existence and all truth, and will draw the conclusion that the existence of thought is therefore the primary certainty. Others will say, in more popular forms: You cannot deny that, whatever you think, it is implied that you do think it; and therefore the ultimate certainty is that you do think it, not that what you think is true: if you deny that you are making a statement, it is impossible to argue with you. Whether or not the statements which are thus argued to be more certain are really logically prior, is another question; but it is worth while pointing out that those who use this argument are admitting the proposition that 'Logical priority is a test of certainty' to be at least as certain as the proposition which they endeavour to establish by its means: this proposition is, at all events, logically prior to their argument.

And so, if we say that no proposition is necessary in itself, but that when we call it necessary we can only mean that it is connected in a certain way with other propositions, it may be asked: But what of this connexion? Is not that necessary in itself? I should answer: Only in the same sense as those propositions, which it makes necessary, are necessary. For every statement of the form: This is involved in that, is itself a proposition; and when we say: If you admit that, you must admit this: they are necessarily connected; we only mean: This follows from that; and the general principle that what follows from a truth is itself true [303] is necessary, because it is implied in every argument. That any one thing does follow from any other is, indeed, not always a necessary proposition: but that, if it does follow, then, if the first be true, the second is also true, is a necessary proposition. It is logically prior to any statement such as: Since this, then that. And such statements are not among the least common of truths.

We have, then, an answer both as to the meaning of necessary propositions; and also as the meaning of necessary connexion between propositions. The first are necessary when they are implied in a large number of other propositions; and as to the second, it is the proposition that the truth of what is implied follows from the truth of that which implies it, that is necessary. The connexion itself is not necessary, but the truth, that if it is there, then a true conclusion may be drawn, is necessary. It remains, then, only to consider the third class of entity which may be called necessary—the class of things and their connexion.

That, when we call a thing necessary, we mean that it is cause or effect of some other thing, is evident. The question is then of that necessity which is involved in the notion of causality. Whether there be any causes—whether from the existence of one thing you can ever validly infer the existence of another—is a different question. But that if there be a cause, it is necessarily connected with its effect, and that its effect is necessary, will not be questioned. The question is merely of what this necessity means. And my answer to it is, I fear, deplorably brief. For I entirely fail to see that there can be any relation between the two things, except that from the proposition 'The one exists' there is a valid inference to the proposition 'The other existed' or 'will exist'. If it does really follow that, since one thing exists, another has existed or will exist, what more necessary relation can be desired? The supposed 'real' necessity will, then, like the supposed 'ideal,' be reduced to logical necessity. There will, indeed, be a difference. The existence of one thing is certainly not presupposed in that of another: the relation between them is certainly not that of logical priority. If we are to infer the one from the other, it must be on the basis of the principle that whenever it is true that one thing exists, it is also true that some one other thing has existed or will exist. And this principle may itself be necessary, as logically prior to other propositions. But the particular causal inference always required not only this for its premiss, but also that some one thing does exist. In this, however, there is no reason to dispute that the necessity is logical. [304] And in maintaining that it is so, we shall only differ from Hume in that whereas he said 'A thing is an effect when we *do* infer its existence from the existence of another thing,' meaning only that our belief in the latter causes us to believe in the former, we shall have to say 'A thing is an effect, when its existence may be *validly* inferred form the existence of another thing, whether we make the inference or not'.

5

The Value of Religion[1]

It is, I think, well known that a great many people nowadays believe in God. And it is also known that many people do not believe that any God exists. Each party, the believers and the unbelievers, the Christian and the infidel, does know in general that the other party numbers many members. Some time ago there was not little public controversy between these factions. Bradlaugh and Huxley, to mention well-known names, assaulted the believers very vigorously, and Matthew Arnold did his best to arbitrate. At present the question whether God exists or not, seems to have ceased to be of public interest. Books are, no doubt, still published on both sides of the question, Huxley and Matthew Arnold are still read; but in general neither side seems very anxious to convince the other. I doubt if the Christians ever think how many infidels there are. And the infidels, on their side, have ceased to question equally the right of other people to believe and their own right to disbelieve. In general no unpleasantness arises from this great difference of opinion: you do not even know whether your neighbor is a Christian or an infidel; you see no reason to inquire, even if the question should occur to you.

Originally published in *International Journal of Ethics* 12 (Oct. 1901): 81–98.

Now there was not always such indifference on this matter: the question has been one of life and death. Perhaps I have exaggerated the present state of acquiescence. If any of you think so, then there is hope that you may take more interest than I expect in what I have to say. For I mean to re-discuss this ancient controversy; to put before you, so far as I am able, what valid arguments there are in answer to the question: Ought we to believe in God?

My utmost hope in the matter is to make clear the issues, on which our answer to this question must depend. For it seems to me that on both sides false arguments are often used, and I do not know but what, if these could be dismissed, that utter [82] difference of opinion which I have pointed out might disappear. For myself I share the opinion which, as I have said, seems from their actions to be that of most men,—the opinion that this difference between the Christian and the infidel is of little practical importance. On questions of much more importance, on moral questions, both sides agree for the most part even in opinion: and in practice they agree still more. Nevertheless, so long as many say, "There is a God," while others answer, "I see no reason for thinking that there is," it remains a possible danger that hostile action should result. This difference, I remind you again, has in the past been a large cause of violence and persecution: and so, not probably, but possibly, it may become again. Especially if the majority of Christians should once become fully aware how many people differ from them in belief and how completely, the present quiet state of things might be much altered. In any case, it is, I think, desirable that agreement should be reached, and, failing this, that each side should know at least what grounds will justify belief or disbelief. These grounds I shall try to give you.

I raise the question then: Ought we to believe in God? and I put it in this form partly because, apart from any general importance it has or lacks, this is a question which occurs to most people at one time or another, as one requiring that they personally should find an answer to it. The answer that they give will make little difference to their future conduct: they will probably become accustomed to the answer they adopt; they will take it as a matter of course and quite forget that it ever was a serious question with them. For some, however, though it makes no difference to their conduct, to their happiness it may make much. And in any case, when the question is first raised, however soon they answer it and cease to think about it, just then it is a question to which they want an answer. To help them to the right one will surely be a work of use. Arguments may appeal to those who have already raised the question of themselves; whereas they are thrown away on those whom habit has convinced of their own answer. Moreover it is those who raise the question now who will determine the habitual answer of the future.

[83] Ought we, then, to believe in God? You may say that to discuss this question is not to discuss the value of religion. Religion is a very vague word, and some may agree with Matthew Arnold that it does not imply a belief in a personal God. For my part, I disagree: I think that it is generally understood to imply this, although of course it includes much more besides. But my object is not to discuss the meaning of a word. If you think that I have used religion wrongly, I am content to apologize. The question I do wish to discuss is the value of belief in a personal God. This question, quite apart from any wider meaning of religion, is certainly a serious one for many people. When Matthew Arnold says that it *ought* not to be so, that it is not a valuable element in Christianity, perhaps I should agree with him, though Christians certainly will not. But that many people feel it to be serious, even he perhaps would not deny, although his arguments imply such a denial. At all events, this is the only question with which I am concerned: What is the value of belief in a personal God? You cannot have religion, in the sense I mean, without this belief; although, when you have this, you may also have much more in your religion.

But next I must say what I mean by a personal God. As for

personal, all that I imply by the word is easily to be understood. I should hardly have thought it necessary to point the meaning out, but for Matthew Arnold's singular obtuseness in seeing what is meant when he is called a person, and his assumption that only the metaphysical ability of bishops can understand the matter. There are two properties which must belong to a person, whatever else may belong to him besides. (1) A person must be endowed with that which we call mind as distinct from our brains and our bodies; and (2) he must also have that positive quality whereby we distinguish ourselves from other people. These two marks of personality are quite sufficient for my purpose. All of us know what is meant by these two things, although we may not know exactly wherein they consist. We think that other people have minds—that they are not mere bodies—and we know from our experience of ourselves what we mean by this difference. And also [84] we know that when we talk of another person's thoughts we do not mean our own thoughts. Two persons may think of the same thing, but each one's thought belongs to him and not to the other. We know what we mean by a thought belonging to a person from our own experience of the thoughts which belong to us: and we are never tempted to think that when you and I think of the same thing, there are not two thinkings but one thinking. That you think of it, is one fact, and that I think of it is another, whatever the difference between the two may be. And so when God thinks, that he thinks must be one fact, and not the same fact as the thinking of anybody else whatever, even if it can include these other thoughts. This property that his thoughts belong to him, as our thoughts belong to us, in a sense in which they do not belong to anybody else, a personal God must have. And he must also have that other property common to you and me, which we call mind, as distinguished from body. These two properties are surely very easy to identify, and when I say a personal God I merely mean a God possessed of these two properties, whatever others he may have besides—a God with mind or spirit, and a God with *one* mind.[2]

But God must not only be a person, he must also be a God: and by that I mean that he must be powerful, wise and good, all three in a greater degree than any one of us. *How much* more powerful and wise and good has been very differently thought in different religions. Some may even have held that he was not better but worse than themselves. But even though devil-worship deserve the title of religion I am not going to discuss it. The questions: Ought I to believe that there is but one God, and that he is a Devil? is not, I think, a serious question for many people. In any case, I must neglect it, and so far agree with Matthew Arnold that the important question concerns a God, who, though he be a person also, yet does "make for righteousness." And finally the God, belief in [85] whom concerns me, must be conceived as very greatly more powerful, more wise and better, than we ourselves, however many historical religions I may be thus excluding from discussion. That we can imagine a person all-wise, all-powerful and all-good I very much doubt, but the conception of God which I mean to discuss is one which comes as near to possessing these attributes, the attributes ascribed to God by Christianity, as any Christian is likely to imagine.

With this, then, I hope to have made plain to you, the minimum of what I mean by God. And my question is whether it is good to believe, as most religious persons do believe, that a God possessing at least these qualities, however many more he may possess, however much he may transcend anthropomorphic notions, does actually exist? Is it good to believe that such a God exists? Ought we to believe that he exists? What is the value of such a belief? This is an ethical question, and for that reason I believe it covers more completely than any other the whole ground of controversy between the believer and the unbeliever. For I admit or assume, whichever you please, that if it is true that

God exists, if he really does exist, then it is good to believe that fact. It may not perhaps be much good, but it is *pro tanto* good to know the truth. It is sufficient justification for any man's belief that what he believes is true. If a thing is true, then no one can be blamed for believing it. This, so far as I know, has never been disputed, at least in this religious controversy. At all events I do not mean to argue it. The question of fact, then, of the evidence for God's existence which has played so large a part in this controversy, is completely covered by my question. Before we can fully answer the question, Is it good to believe in God? we must first decide whether God exists; for, if he does exist, then, I take it, we may say at once that we do well to believe in him.

But my question does not only cover this inquiry; it also includes another: and in this lies its advantage. For supposing we have argued the question of fact, the question whether God exists or not, and have come to the conclusion, to which, as I shall try to show, we must ultimately come, that there is [86] not one atom of evidence, establishing the smallest probability either that God exists or yet that he does not exist: supposing, I say, that we have come to this conclusion on the factual question, there still remains another which is also covered by my ethical formula. There still remain what are called the moral reasons for belief in God. Appeals to these are very often made, and they often have great weight. But the weight they have is largely due, I think, to a confusion. Under this one head of moral reasons for belief we have two entirely different sets of arguments. One set attempts to prove from moral facts, of one sort or another, that God exists. It is argued that morality is without a basis, unless God does exist: this Matthew Arnold argues for his God, and Mr. Arthur Balfour for his. It is argued too by more humble persons that the goodness of the Christian is evidence that his belief is true. But all these arguments plainly fall only under the factual inquiry: the inquiry whether there be any evidence, moral or otherwise, establishing a probability that God exists. As for the other set of so-called "moral" arguments, they would I think lose much of their influence if they were clearly distinguished from these last. It is, in fact, contended, that whether we have any evidence for God or not, to believe in him produces good effects,—is a powerful aid to moral action. This is an argument which certainly deserves to be considered. We have, some people would urge, a right and a duty to indulge in positive belief, where the evidence alone would give us no right; and this because of its effects. It is, therefore, proper to consider how far a belief in God has the alleged effects. This inquiry is what you probably understood by my title, the "value of religion." It concerns the moral arguments for belief as such; and these must be distinguished from any moral arguments there may be for the truth of the belief. Yet, as I have said, the two lines of argument are frequently confused: and how important such confusions are in strengthening religion I can show, I think, from an obvious instance. We hear a great deal of the value of religion; it is urged that its influence on conduct is enormous. But all this is usually urged on the assumption that there is some ground for thinking it true. Yet plainly, whether [87] it be true or false, the evidence for its moral efficacy is just the same. Observation alone can assure us, whether it has good effects or not; and the results of observation will stand firm, although the belief be proved a false one. This fact, steadily held before the mind, cannot fail, I think, to be a chilling one to many supporters of religion. It does not usually occur to them that they are bestowing their enthusiastic praises on a belief, which, failing other arguments to prove its truth, *may* be a mere delusion. A mere delusion may, no doubt, have very good effects: but I think I am right in saying that earnest men are very loth to think so. If, then, it be brought home to them that religious belief is possibly mere error, they will then be apt either to cool in their praises of its excellent effects, or else to argue that its effects themselves are evidences for its truth.

Now, in the former case, their moral argument for belief is sadly weakened; and, in the latter, they have fallaciously converted it into the moral argument for God's existence—for the truth of that belief. In short, if we are fairly to consider the value of religion, we must account the possible disadvantages of belief in what may be a mere delusion, as having a certain weight against alleged advantages. Many apologists, I think, are apt to forget that they are putting in the balance on their own side of the question an assumption that their belief in God is true. Now, unless they can prove by other arguments that so it is, they ought not only to remove a part of the weight from their own scale, but actually to add it to the other. For most men would admit, as I think rightly, that a strong belief in what is possibly false, is in itself a doubtful blessing.

Well, then, I hope to have convinced you that to think clearly in this matter is important. What I have called the factual inquiry into the *truth* of religious belief must be kept quite distinct from the moral inquiry into the worth of its effects. But at the same time the factual inquiry is necessary before we can decide upon the value of religion; because the truth of a belief, although it cannot alter its effects, has in itself some ethical importance. With this we may proceed to our discussion; and first to this same factual inquiry.

[88] The question here before us is this: Have we any evidence rendering it probable that God exists? The question is a large one, and I can do no more than summarize the arguments. And yet I think this summary, though brief, may be conclusive. The conclusion I wish to establish is as I have said:—There is *no* probability that God exists. That is all: a purely negative conclusion. I am an infidel, and do not believe that God exists; and I think the evidence will justify my disbelief. But just as I think there is no evidence for his existence, I think there is also no evidence that he does not exist. I am not an atheist in one sense: I do not deny that

God exists. My arguments will only urge that there is no reason for thinking that he does; they will *not* urge that there is reason for thinking he does not. I do *not* believe that he does exist, but also I do *not* believe that he does not exist. That is the attitude I am concerned to recommend.

Is there, then, evidence that God exists? Is his existence at all probable?

We say we have evidence for a thing, when it can be inferred from another thing that we suppose established. The question of evidence for God's existence is then the question whether there are any other truths from which we can infer it. To mention evidence at all implies that other things are true beside the thing we want to prove. He who would prove by evidence that God exists must first assume that something else is true.

Now the truths from which we can start on such a proof are what we call the facts of common life—experience. We all believe that we are here, between four walls, alive and able to move; nay, more, thinking and feeling. Such are the facts of observation, from which the Natural Sciences infer their laws. In these things we all do believe; we cannot help believing them, whether we like it or not. That they are true indeed, we cannot prove. Our belief is no evidence that they are so. And so far they are just on a level with a belief that God exists: the belief also is no evidence that he exists. I believe that I exist, and some one else, I grant you, believes that God exists; and so far as these beliefs go, there is not a bit of difference between the two things that are believed. Both have an equal [89] right to be taken for true and an equal right to be taken for false. But when we come to the question of evidence and probability, then there is all the difference in the world between them. There is evidence, in plenty, that I exist and there is none that God exists.

For my existence is an object of such a nature that it can be inferred from other objects of belief. These also are, like it and

God, mere objects of belief; they cannot be proved true. But they are such that *if* any one of them be true, the others and my existence are so too. The simplest statement as that "This hand moves," involves a host of others, from which again a crowd of other simple statements, as that *I* moved it, may be deduced. And all the arguments to prove the existence of God rest upon evidence like this. The evidence is certainly as good as we can get; it is what we cannot help believing, although it may be false. To the evidence, then, I have no objection: *but*—the existence of God will not rest upon it. That I have a scar on my hand is excellent evidence of something: the scar is visible and palpable, and no doubt it had some cause. I cannot prove that these things are so; and you cannot either, except from premises equally doubtful in themselves. All of them are possibly not true. But if you grant me that the scar is there, then I maintain there is no evidence, no probability, that an angel with a burning sword came down and made it: but there is much evidence, much probability that it came about in a way that I could mention.

People take, then, the world as we think we know it, and they infer that because it is such as they and we all believe it to be, God must exist. To the facts they start from I have no objection, although we must admit they may be false: but the inference they draw from them is as absurd as the inference from my scar to that angel. There are two well-known arguments of this kind—the stock arguments of what is called Natural Theology—arguments which in one form or another are still in use. These are the arguments to a First Cause and the argument from Design. The inadequacy of both these arguments was finally pointed out a hundred years ago by Kant. With the first, as distinguished from the second, we [90] need not deal, for, even if some First Cause were necessary, it would yet remain to prove that this Cause was intelligent and good: it must be both, you remember, to come within our meaning of personal God. That this Cause is intelligent and good as well as powerful is what the argument from Design attempts to prove. The only argument, therefore, with which we have to deal is that: From the nature of the world, as it appears on observation, we can infer that it or parts of it were or are caused by a being immensely intelligent, wise or good. The answer to this is summary but sound. We assume that useful and beautiful objects we find in the world were made by man—had for their cause a being of some intelligence and goodness. By these useful and beautiful objects I mean houses and drains, hospitals and works of art—if you like, a watch—and I call it an assumption that they were made by man, in order not to overstate my case. We have as our premise, then, that certain objects, which I am far from denying to be either useful or beautiful or sometimes both, had for their cause some tolerably good people. Then, says the Natural Theologian, we may infer that anything useful or good we find in the world, that is not a work of man's designing—man himself, above all, the most useful and beautiful of all—had also for its cause a person of intelligence and goodness. This is the argument. But what reason have we for supposing that anything at all of any kind in the world was caused by a good person? Simply the assumption that certain things of one kind were caused by man. And what reason have we for this assumption? Simply and solely the fact that we can follow the series of causes back from them to the working of man. And if we are therefore going to call man their cause, we must also ascribe all other events to those which preceded them in the same way as man's work plainly preceded houses and drains. If houses and drains are the effect of man's work, then man himself and all other things, must be the effect of events in the world which preceded him, and so on *ad infinitum.* If, on the other hand, houses and drains were not caused by man, then we have no reason for supposing that anything useful or beautiful ever was caused by a good person. Either of these two alternatives [91] wrecks the theologian's argument completely. If we are to infer from the nature of an effect to the nature of a cause, we can only do so on the assumption that we can find the *complete causes* of events in the course of nature. But if every natural event has a natural cause, then unless God is a natural cause, he is not a cause of anything at all. I have put this argument in a simple instance, for the sake of clearness: but it is of universal application. It has the advantage of being a question of logic, and not of fact; no new instances can overthrow it. It is as with the law of contradiction. If you have contradicted yourself, within the meaning of logic, then you must have made some mistake, however trivial. And so, if you use this argument, in whatever form you dress it, it must be worthless since your conclusion will not follow from your premises. One of your premises must be: This is the cause of that; and the other: Every event has a cause. And your conclusion is: God is the cause of these other events; his existence alone will explain them. But your first premise assigns as the cause of one natural event, another natural event. And you cannot be sure of this, unless every natural event is caused by another natural event: otherwise the effect you began with might not have had the cause which you assign—the hospital might have been made by miracle and not made by man. Either then God must be one or more among natural events, or else you have no reason to assert that he is more like one than another, more like a man than a billiard-ball. But you have asserted him to be more like a man than a billiard-ball; and you certainly cannot show that any natural event is a personal God. Either then God is a cause in some sense utterly different from that in which man is a cause: and then we cannot infer either to his existence or his nature; or else he is a cause in the sense in which man is a cause, and then we can infer his existence but not his nature: we can infer that the events in question had a cause, but not that their cause was God. This dilemma applies in general to every argument from Design—and not only to these, but to every metaphysical argument that tries to mount from Nature and Mind to any superior Reality. All such arguments infer from the nature and existence of some or all the things that are [92] agreed to exist that something else, of a different nature, also exists. But the only known valid principle by which we can infer from the existence of one thing to the existence of something else is this same principle of causality, according to which that "something else" must be one among natural events. All these arguments must therefore involve the fallacy involved in the vulgar argument from Design. On the basis of such arguments modern philosophers are fond of offering to us, in place of a personal God, a more or less consoling Reality or Absolute. But the skeleton of any such construction is nothing more than this old fallacy. They muffle it up in garments infinitely complicated, many of which are in themselves sound stuff. But the more they muffle and the sounder the stuff, the less attractive their Absolute becomes. We have, I think, every reason to prefer the old God of Christianity. In him the artifice is more transparent, and the product, none the less, by far more beautiful.

We cannot then make a single step toward proving God's existence from the nature of the world, such as we take it to be in common life or such as Natural Science shows it. That we are here to-night, that we were not here this morning, that we came here by means of cabs or on our feet: all facts of this sort, in which we cannot help believing,—these facts, with all the implications, which Science or Philosophy can draw from them, offer us not one jot of evidence that God exists. But there are other arguments which start like this one from experience. There is the argument from general belief. I will admit at once that most people, who have existed heretofore, have believed in a God of some sort. I have, indeed, no reason to believe that there are or have been other people and still less that they have had this belief, except on the same grounds as I believe in the facts of common life. If we are not here now, there is no evidence even that most people have believed in God. The mere fact of general belief, then, is no more certain than the facts of experience: if we reject the latter as untrue, we cannot use the former as evidence for God's existence. You cannot argue, as many people do: The facts of science are merely matters of general belief, and God's existence is the [93] same; therefore the one is as certain as the other. For, unless the facts of science are true, you have no title to your statement that God's existence is a matter of general belief. But now, granting that it is a matter of general belief, does this fact establish any probability that God exists? I think it cannot. For many things which we now all admit to be errors, have in the past been matters of general belief: such, for instance, as that the sun went round the earth, which Galileo controverted. All the probability is, then, in favor of the supposition that many things which are still generally believed, will in time be recognized as errors. And what ground can we have for holding that the belief in God is not among their number? The probabilities seem all the other way. For I think it will be admitted that the belief in God has in the past derived much support from ignorance of Natural Science and from such arguments as those of Natural Theology. If, then, as I have tried to show, those arguments are fallacious, in proportion as this is recognized, the belief in God will become less general. You can therefore only hold that belief in God will persist undiminished, while other beliefs disappear, if you maintain the continued triumph of ignorance and fallacious reasoning. But a belief which persists from causes like these has surely no claim to be therefore considered true. In short, if you are to argue from general belief to truth, you must have independent grounds for thinking that the belief in question is true. If you can show a probability that it is true, then the fact of general belief may confirm that probability. But if, as I try to show in this case, there is no such probability, no evidence that God exists, then the fact of general belief is perfectly useless as evidence.

The argument from general belief must then break down, and I think I need hardly discuss at length any so-called historical proofs for God's existence. They are all from the nature of the case too obviously weak. If what they aim at is establishing the fact of miracles, then no historical proof can by any possibility show that an event, which happened, was in very truth a miracle —that it had no natural cause. That an event should have had no natural cause contradicts, as I tried to [94] show, the very grounds of historical evidence, for this is all based on inferences from effect to cause, and if a miracle is ever possible, we can never say that any particular thing was the cause of any other. But if you mean by miracle only a great and wonderful work, then that a man can perform astonishing feats is no proof either that he knows the truth or that he tells it. And, miracles apart, historical proofs can only show that somebody said something: whether what he said was true must be decided on quite other grounds.

The facts of common life, then, the facts with which natural science and history deal, afford no inference to God's existence. If a man still believes that God exists, he cannot support his belief by any appeal to facts admitted both by himself and the infidel. He must not attempt to *prove* that God probably exists; for that is impossible. He must be content to affirm that he sees as clearly that God exists as he sees that he himself does. Many people, I admit, may really have had this strong conviction. And many people may be content to justify belief upon this ground alone. They, I think, are right. Their position is quite unassailable. If you have this faith, this intuition of Gods's existence, that is enough. You may, I admit, be as certain that God exists as that you yourself exist: and no one has any right to say that you are wrong. But these are two independent facts: one is perhaps *as* certain to you as the other: but the one is *not* more likely to be true, because the other is so. The moment you use that argument, you will be wrong. You cannot argue that if you exist, God also probably exists: as you can argue that if you exist, I also probably exist. Nor can you argue that because you are so certain of God's existence, I ought to admit the slightest probability that he exists: if you do this, you are appealing to an argument similar to that from general belief. In fact, if I were the only person who could not see that God exists, and all the world agreed with you, it would be just as likely that I was right, as that you and all the world were right. It is equally likely we are right and equally likely we are wrong: but only equally. I have no more right to argue that probably God does not exist, because I cannot see he does, than you to argue that probably [95] he does exist, because you see he does. This is all I have tried to show, when I maintain there is no evidence for God's existence. It is mere faith, not proof, which justifies your statement: God exists. Your belief is right, because you cannot help believing: and my unbelief is right, because I have not got that intuition. We both are justified by mere necessity.

An appeal to faith, then,—to intuition—is the sole ground for asserting the truth of religion. That truth, if it be true, is coördinate with the facts of daily life, and cannot be inferred from them, as they can be inferred from one another. And so far it would seem that religious belief stands in the same position as our moral beliefs. These moral judgments, too, it may be said, are independent of beliefs about the world: their truth also can never be inferred from that of daily facts.

That moral truth cannot be thus inferred from any facts, is, I think, quite demonstrable. But since it is denied, I must say something on this head. The argument of Mr. Balfour's book on "The Foundations of Belief" depends in part on this denial. If, he seems to say, the view of Naturalism that all things were evolved from natural causes is true, then it is inconsistent still to hold that our beliefs in the goodness of this and the beauty of that are also true. And a similar view is implied by Matthew Arnold, who seems to hold, that unless we can verify the existence of a power not ourselves that makes for righteousness, then our belief that certain conduct is righteous and other conduct wicked, must also justly perish. But is this so? Is it inconsistent to hold that this is right and that is wrong, and at the same time to hold that we only think this right, that wrong, because in fact such beliefs have helped us to survive? Or can it be less true that right is right, even if there be no power that will reward it? The former argument refutes itself. For if it be true that beliefs were evolved, then the belief that they were so must also have been evolved. And this, according to Mr. Balfour, is a reason why we must doubt its truth. That is to say, the fact of evolution is a reason for doubting the fact of evolution. It is inconsistent to believe in the fact of evolution, if we at the same time believe in the fact of evolution. The inconsistency, we may well reply, is all the other way. It is, in [96] fact, self-contradictory to hold that the validity of a belief depends in any way upon the manner in which it was acquired. And hence the truth of our moral beliefs *must* be independent of any scientific facts. Just so, we may answer Matthew Arnold: In order to verify the fact that righteous conduct is rewarded, we must already know what righteous conduct is: and to know that it is righteous is to know we ought to do it.

There is, therefore, no more evidence for moral than for religious beliefs; and the religious believer may be tempted to say, "I have as much right to my belief that God exists, as you have to any of your moral beliefs." But this claim, it should be pointed out, refutes itself. For his assertion that he has "as much right" to believe in God is itself a moral judgment. It can only rest upon the moral principle that necessity will justify beliefs: and this principle must have a prior validity to that of any particular instances which may be brought under it. The believer is therefore admitting that there is one moral principle to which he has more right than to his belief in God. It must be true, according to him, that necessity is a moral justification, whether his belief in God is so justified or not. In fact he cannot attempt to *defend* his belief in God except by a moral judgment; and by so doing he gives up the supposed parity between moral and religious beliefs in general, although it may still be true that such parity exists between religious belief and *most* moral judgments.

It remains true, however, that if a man really cannot help believing in God, nothing can be said against him. But I very much doubt whether this is often the case. With most believers, I think, the disparity between their moral and their religious convictions is much more striking. Their religious belief gains much of its strength from the fact that they think they ought to have it. They have a direct moral feeling that it is wicked to doubt of God's existence; and without this belief, which is a strong one, their direct religious certainty would offer but a weak resistance to scepticism. For such persons the final question arises: Are they right in thinking that infidelity is wicked?

Now they can no longer urge in defence of this opinion that belief in God is good, because it is true. On the contrary it is [97] only because they believe it to be good that they hold it to be true. They must therefore rest their claim to its goodness solely upon its effects; and in the inquiry whether its effects are good, they must, as I pointed out above, carefully discount the vicious tendency to think the effects must be good, on the ground that the belief is true. They should bear in mind that the belief is possibly false; and that, if they shall decide that its effects are good, they will be committed to the theory that all this good is possibly a result of mere error.

Now whether they are or are not the better, the more strongly they believe that God exists, is no longer a matter to dogmatize upon. The manners in which religious belief may act on different minds are infinitely various. But I think there is at least good room to doubt whether it ever does much good. That there is a power who is willing and able to help you would be, no doubt, an encouraging thought. But from this, if our argument holds, our believers are in any case excluded. God cannot interfere in the course of natural events. This belief, which has played such a large part in the religions of the past, is demonstrably untrue. At most, then, the encouragement must come from the knowledge that he sympathizes with us. And this is certainly no small comfort. But how are we to get it? We are faced by this dilemma. The encouragement will only be strong in proportion to our belief. But, on the other hand, our efforts to strengthen this belief are only too likely to fail, if we do not find we get the encouragement. That this difficulty is a real one I think most people for whom the present question has been raised, will acknowledge. That consolation, for the sake of which they desire to believe, must be already felt, before they can acquire it. They desire to "see that the Lord is good," in order that they may "taste" it; but on the other hand, unless they first do taste it, they cannot get to see it. It may well be urged that it would be better to give up this fruitless endeavor; especially when we consider that in so far as they succeed, they are deliberately acquiring a belief, which, for all they know, is false.

And moreover, I agree with Matthew Arnold that a more important element in religion than this is the belief that the [98] good will triumph. If we could rest in this belief, we might surely give up the belief in God, and yet get all the comfort that we needed. But for this belief also I am afraid we have no reason. That Good will triumph as that God exists is possible but only possible. Matthew Arnold's God, too, is not, as he thought, verifiable. Naturalism, as Mr. Balfour argues, does fail to verify him. We have reason to believe that human life upon this planet will presently be extinguished. We certainly have no reason to believe the contrary; nor yet that our souls will persist and grow better after death.

But though our belief in this God fails us too, I think it may be doubted whether we may not still retain the very elements which have rendered religion most effective for good in the past. They are in fact elements which have no logical connection with the belief in God.

(I) First, there is that valuable element in religious emotion, which proceeds from the contemplation of what we think to be most truly and perfectly good. We are indeed only entitled to think of this as what ought to be; not as what is or will be. But I doubt if this emotion need lose much of its force, because its object is not real. The effects of literature show how strongly we may be moved by the contemplation of ideal objects, of which we nevertheless do not assert the existence. It may indeed be doubted whether the most effective part in all religious belief has not always been similar to that which we have in objects of imagination —a belief quite consistent with a firm conviction that they are not facts. (2) And secondly, that some good objects should be real, is indeed necessary for our comfort. But these we have in plenty. It surely might be better to give up the search for a God whose existence is and remains undemonstrable, and to divert the feelings which the religious wish to spend on him, towards those of our own kind, who though perhaps less good than we can imagine God to be, are worthy of all the affections that we can feel; and whose help and sympathy are much more certainly real. We might perhaps with advantage worship the real creature a little more, and his hypothetical Creator a good deal less.

NOTES

1. A lecture delivered for the London School of Ethics and Social Philosophy.

2. Possibly the conception of the three Persons in the Athanasian Creed negates, or adds something contradictory to, part of what I have said. But I am concerned only with the manner in which most believers habitually think of God.

6

Identity

I am very anxious it should not be thought that the subject of this paper is of merely departmental interest. What I have to say is not addressed to those who are interested in any particular science, such as logic, definition, or psychology, but to all who are interested in the question what the world is. It appears to me that if what I shall say be true, most of those theories about the nature of the world, which are of the most general interest and which attract the most disciples for the various schools of philosophy, must be either false or purely chimerical. It is not, indeed, my object to show that these important consequences follow; it is possible that they do not, and I have not space to argue that they do. But I wish it should not be *assumed* that they do not. My own view is that, whether what I say be true or false, it is certainly very important, and that is my main reason for raising the question of its truth. What I most fear, then, is not that it should be proved to be false, but that it should be admitted true without enquiry, on the ground that, though true, it is unimportant. I fear that many of the doctrines I shall put forward will

Originally published in *Proceedings of the Aristotelian Society* n.s. 1 (1900–1901): 103–127.

appear to be mere platitudes. They, or others very like them, are, I think, constantly so regarded; and yet those, who thus admit their truth, are not thereby prevented from holding other doctrines, on questions of far greater intrinsical importance, which flatly contradict these truths they admit and despise. That such a state of things is possible will scarcely be denied. For my own part I am convinced that the characteristic doctrines of most philosophers, no less where they agree than where they differ, are chiefly due to their failure to trace the consequences of admitted principles. To remember the [104] possibility that this may be so with the principles of identity, may, I hope, lend some interest to my discussion of the subject.

I will give an instance of the kind of purpose which I hope the discussion may serve. Considerable use is made now-a-days by a certain school of philosophical writers of the phrases "identity in difference" and "unity in difference." I do not know whether *as a rule* the two phrases are used in the same or in different senses; but certainly they are *often* used as if they were equivalent. The same is true, I think, of another pair of phrases, which are also much used by the same writers—namely, "individual" and "organic unity." Further, this second pair is, I believe, supposed to be connected with the first, in such a way, that if you know a thing to be an "individual" or "organic unity," you can always infer that it exhibits both "identity in difference" and "unity in difference"; and I should be very much surprised if, on examination, it did not also prove that the converse inference was very frequently made. Now I do not know that many people would regard the knowledge that they were "individuals" or that the world was an "organic unity" as having much importance in itself: although I think the phrases are vaguely impressive and convey the notion that anything to which they are applied must be of worth. But a very great derivative importance they certainly have; since the writers who use them draw conclusions by their means, which no one can regard with indifference.

Yet, what is meant by these phrases? In a sense it would seem plain that any complex thing whatever exhibits identity in difference, since it has at least two different predicates and yet is one and the same thing. But it is plain that no inferences of importance can be drawn from this fact, since the possession of complexity is compatible with almost every difference of quality we can think of. "Identity in difference" must, therefore, if it is to yield us valuable information, mean something other than mere complexity; and, as I shall show, there seem to be a great many other things it might mean. The phrase is [105] therefore ambiguous; and, though it is certain that many correct inferences can be drawn by means of ambiguous words, even where their special sense is not defined, it is no less certain that the gravest errors may be incurred by arguing that what is true of a thing to which such a word applies in one sense, is also true of that to which it applies in another. A philosopher certainly, although nothing can replace for him the power of recognising that the truths he handles are different, where they are so, and though this is perhaps his most valuable gift, cannot safely trust to that power alone if he wishes to go far, but must employ the additional safeguard of attempting to discover and fix in his mind the points wherein they differ. To a certain extent he may be helped in this task by the work of others, and to supply as much of this help as I am able, by discriminating the points of difference between truths which we express and must continue to express by the use of the word identity, is the object of this paper.

The first point to which I would call attention with regard to truths in which we assert identity is a very obvious one. It is that we may assert of two things that they have the same predicate, and yet are different from one another. Thus it is true that my coat is black, and also true that my waistcoat is black; and yet it is not true that my coat is the same as my waistcoat. This state of things does not at first sight appear to present any difficulty. It seems obvious enough that the two garments, though they have one predicate in common, yet have each of them at least one other which is not shared by its fellow. And this, it may be said, is why they can have the same predicate: they have not a complete identity of content. But to say this is to imply a philosophical proposition of the very last importance, and one upon which there has never yet been agreement. It is to say that there cannot possibly be two things exactly alike. If the reason why my two coats are different is that they have different predicates, then, supposing all their predicates were the same, as their colour is, they [106] would not be two, but only one. But is it absolutely certain that there cannot be two things exactly alike? Put in this abstract form, it does not seem certain. If so—if there may be things exactly alike, which yet are two, why should not this be the case with the blackness also? Why should the blackness of both be one and the same, and not that of each a single blackness exactly like the other? There is, in fact, a real difficulty of deciding whether, in the case where two things have the same predicate, the predicates are two or only one. There is this real difficulty underlying the question which arises in Plato with regard to his "ideas," whenever he says that they are *in* things or that things are copies of them. Can one and the same thing be in two places at once, or must there be two? The copy certainly is different both from the thing copied and from any other copy of the same. With regard to the third form in which he raises a difficulty—where, namely, he says that things partake of the idea—the difficulty is the same, if by "partake" be meant "have it as well as other qualities." But it is entirely different if by "partake" be meant "have part of the idea."

What the above discussion is designed to bring out is that, even when we assert truly that two things have the same or a common predicate, there is a serious difficulty in deciding exactly what it is that is true. Our first suggestion was that the predicate of each was in no sense different from that of the other, and that the two things differed from one another only in the sense that they had different predicates. We may label this view as that which holds that no difference except *conceptual* difference is involved in two things having the same predicate. On this view when you say there are two things, you mean that they differ conceptually only, *i.e.*, it is impossible that the difference implied in duality should be other than conceptual difference. It follows that to talk of two things exactly alike, or with no conceptual difference, is to talk sheer nonsense—mere words. But so extreme a judgment seems open to [107] suspicion. Even if there are no two things exactly alike, it seems far from self-evident that there could not be. It was then suggested that there may be; and this view I propose to label as that which holds that beside conceptual difference there is also involved in two things having the same predicate, another kind which may be called *numerical* difference. But if we thus admit a separate kind of difference, compatible with the absence of conceptual difference, it is plain that this kind of difference may separate from one another not only the things, which we have said possess a common predicate, but also the predicates of each which we have hitherto said to be one and the same predicate. And hence our first view may be wrong not only in asserting that the two things differ from one another in one sense only, but also in asserting that the predicate of the one is in no sense different from that of the other. What really is the truth about this matter?

And, first: Is there such a thing as *numerical* difference, a different kind of difference from *conceptual* difference? Philosophers have commonly enough spoken as if there were. Even if it be asserted that two things which differ in the one way always also differ in the other, this is to assert that there are both kinds of difference. Thus, in so far as Leibniz deduces his principle of the Identity of Indiscernibles from the Law of Sufficient Reason, he is admitting that numerical and conceptual difference are different things. That any two things should differ numerically without also differing conceptually cannot be a self-contradictory proposition, if it requires the Law of Sufficient Reason to prove it; and hence Leibniz is guilty of inconsistency, when he remarks that to suppose two things indiscernible is to suppose the same thing under different names.[1] Our question is, which of these two views is the right [108] one? Let us suppose that there is no such thing as numerical difference. In that case, when two things have the same predicate, the only difference between them consists in the difference between two different predicates, one of which belongs to one and the other to the other. But what are the *things* to which these different predicates belong? We predicate of the things both a common predicate, and a different predicate of each. Either then we must say that the things are the different predicates, and that it is to those that the common predicate belongs; or else we must say that the things are another pair of different predicates, to each of which one of the first pair and to both of which the common predicate belongs. But in either case the common predicate belongs to or is predicated of that which is different in each of the things. And when we say it has this relation of belonging or predication to each of two different things, we certainly may mean that it has the same relation to each of them. Accordingly our two must each be analysed into: (1) point of difference; (2) relation of predication; (3) common point; of which (2) and (3) are absolutely identical in each. But, if this is so, the things turn out to *be* merely their points of difference. Of the group (1) (2) (3), which is what we originally supposed to constitute a thing, nothing can be true except that they are three. We cannot say of (*a*) (2) (3), which is what we originally called the one thing, that *it* is different from the other (*b*)(2)(3). It is only (*a*) and (*b*) which differ from one another and are two. In fact our original supposition was that (3) could only be predicated of (*a*) and (*b*), not of anything else. And if this [109] supposition holds it is plain that anything else which we might try to predicate of the group, as such, would turn out to be predicated only of (*a*) and (*b*). We can never by any possibility get a number of predicates to combine in forming a new thing, of which, as a whole, anything can be predicated. We must start, on this theory, with two points of difference—two simple predicates having conceptual difference from one another: this is essential to there being two things at all. And then we may try to form new things, also differing from one another, by finding predicates of these points of difference. But whatever we find and however many we add, we still leave the points of difference as they were—the only things of which duality can really be predicated. For anything we predicate of them, and the relation of predication itself, may always both belong to some other point of difference, so that every property by which we may try to distinguish our new thing from the old, will merely identify part of the new thing with something else, without producing any whole, which, as a whole, differs from everything else in the world, in the way in which our original points of difference differ from one another. We can never say, "This red differs from that red, in virtue of having a different position"; or "in virtue of having a different spatial relation to this other thing"; or "as being the one I think of now, whereas that was the one I thought of then." The positions differ, the spatial relations differ, my thinking now differs from my thinking then; but it is always the same red which is at both positions, and is thought of at both times. And whenever we attempt to say anything of the red at this position, as, for instance, that it was surrounded by yellow, or that it led me to think of a soldier's coat, exactly the same must be true of the red at the position, which was surrounded by blue or led me to think of a house on fire. We are unable to distinguish the two except by their relation to other things, and by whatever relations we attempt so to distinguish them we always find we have not succeeded. We can never say, "The red I mean is [110] the one surrounded by yellow, and not the one surrounded by blue." For the one surrounded by yellow is also surrounded by blue: they are not two but one, and whatever is true of that which is surrounded by yellow is also true of that which is surrounded by blue.

All this I regard as a *reductio ad absurdum* of the theory that there is no difference but conceptual difference. If any one can avoid assuming that something may be true of a quality at one position, which is not true of the same quality at another position, then he will be entitled to assert that all difference is conceptual difference. But this will at all events not be possible for those who hold that things conceptually the same may be distinguished by their relations to other things. If any one asserts or implies that a difference between this and that can be established by the fact that this is related to one thing whereas that is related to something different, he cannot without contradiction deny numerical difference. For this and that cannot have different relations, unless the relation possessed by the one is not possessed by the other. Unless, therefore, the one has a difference from the other over and above the difference of relations, it will be true of one and the same thing that it both has and has not a given relation to something else. And for the same reason it is equally impossible to assert that it is only the whole, this thing in that relation, which differs from the whole, the same thing in this other relation. For unless this which we call the same thing is in some sense two things, it has *both* relations, and everything which is true of the thing with the one relation will also be true of the thing with the other. It cannot be true that the whole formed of the thing in one relation is different from the whole formed of it in the other, unless the thing itself is different; although that it should have the one relation might be a different truth from its having the other.

I conclude then that there is such a thing as numerical difference, different from conceptual difference. And since [111] this result has been obtained by pointing out truths in which a thing conceptually the same is said both to have and not to have a given relation to something else, we have also answered a second question, and have shown that there not only may be but are things exactly similar; and further, since the things, which turned out to be so, were instances of what we originally took to be a common predicate of two different things, it is also plain that a common predicate, in its application to one thing, may differ numerically from the same predicate in its application to another. We have therefore refuted the principle of the Identity of Indiscernibles in both the forms which Leibniz failed to distinguish. We have found both (1) that Identity is not conceptually identical with Indiscernibility; there is a difference not only in name but in fact; and (2) that things which are indiscernible are not always identical. On the other hand, we have accepted the principle frequently implied in Plato that the idea in a thing may be different from the idea in itself; and we have still to see whether there is any insurmountable objection to this view.

The view we have accepted is that in some cases where two things are truly said to have a common predicate, there exists in each a predicate exactly similar to that which exists in the other, but not numerically identical with it. And I confess I see no objections to this view, except what seem to rest on a bare denial of the difference between conceptual and numerical difference. These two exactly similar things are, I may be told, identical in content: exact similarity means identity in content. I admit that they are so. In that case, my adversary may retort, they are the same thing; there is no difference between them; they are not two but one. But this is merely to beg the point at issue. What I have urged is that many of our judgments plainly imply that there may be *two* things, things having a kind of difference which I call numerical, which yet have not another kind of difference which I call conceptual. And I explain the phrase, identity of content, as applying only [112] to two such things, which have no conceptual difference. The two things, are, I admit, in one sense the same; but that they are not therefore also *one* and the same is just what I have tried to show.

Or, again, it may be urged:—Does not this identity of content between the things consist in their both having the same predicate —a common element? But, if so, then, on your view, this common predicate would itself be two; and these two predicates would again need a common element to explain their identity of content, which would again be two, and so on *ad infinitum*. So that, if you once admit a single pair of exactly similar things, for each pair thus admitted you have to admit an infinite number of other pairs. And (it may be added) if this is not absurd enough, each pair will be entirely indistinguishable from all the others, so that you will not even be able to distinguish your first pair as your first, from those which it implies. To such an objection I should answer: (1) That the pairs will not on my view be indistinguishable. Each member will differ *numerically* from the rest, and where this is the case any two, of an infinite number, may be distinguished as this and that, since it is the very meaning of numerical difference that things which have it are thus different and need not be mistaken for one another. And (2) if this is the case, I see no absurdity in the infinite regress. There may, for all I know, be an infinite number of exactly similar things; but if we can distinguish what is true of any one, from what is true of any of the rest, I see nothing to refute me in the suggestion. It is at all events true, that, if there is not an infinite number of exactly similar things, there is an infinite number of conceptually different ones. So that, even, if the admission of an infinite implies, as some hold, a contradiction, this fact cannot be urged in favour of conceptual as against numerical difference. But (3) even if the last two objections were unanswerable, they do not touch my theory. For I do not hold that in *every* [113] case, where a common predicate is truly asserted, the predicates are two. I found myself forced to maintain that in some cases they were so. But it seems to me that, as a matter of fact, wherever two predicates are exactly similar, their relation to that which is the same in each of them, is quite different from the relation of each to that of which it is the predicate. That there may be said to be in each an identical element I admit. But this identical element appears to me to be not only the same, but also *one and the same.* Nor, in default of further objections, do I see any reason for thinking that it cannot be so.

But, lastly, it may be said: If in the case of two exactly similar things there is always also a third thing, as you have just admitted, which is *one and the same* and different from either, must there not also be a fourth related to the first and third, as the third is related to the first and second; and a fifth related to the second and third in the same way, and so on *ad infinitum*? In other words, if, as Plato would say, the similarity between two particulars is to be explained by the similarity of both to one and the same idea, must not the same explanation be given of the similarity of each to this idea? To this objection again I should reply, in the first place, that a mere infinity of numerically identical things does not appear to me to be impossible. But if, as seems to be implied in the second form of words, the objection is not to this infinity but to a definition of exact similarity which consists in saying that two things are exactly similar to one another when each is exactly similar to a third thing, then I admit that such a definition is invalid. Certainly if the relation of the idea to each of its particulars were exactly the same as their relation to one another, we could not define their relation to one another by means of their relation to it. We should have to admit that exact similarity was an unanalysable relation, and that ideas, even though there might be infinite numbers of them, were superfluous hypotheses so [114] far as it was concerned, and could not be inferred from its reality. And this objection does not, as did the last, fail altogether to touch my theory; for I did intend to *define* the relation of exact similarity between two things as involving relation to a third thing, and not merely to make the gratuitous and irrelevant assertion that, whenever two things are exactly similar, there is also such a third thing. To meet this objection, then, I must assert, what has not been made plain hitherto, that the relation between the idea and its particular is *not* the same as that of one particular to the other: that the idea is not exactly similar to its particular. And this assertion does, I admit, seem strange at first sight. If they are not exactly similar, what, it may be asked, is the difference between them? We grant you they have numerical difference, but you yourself admit that they have no conceptual difference, and what more than this can be meant by exact similarity? My answer is that something more than this *is* meant by exact similarity, namely, the fact that each of the things said so to be has a peculiar relation to a third thing, numerically but not conceptually different from them, which they have not to one another. This third thing is the Platonic idea, or, as we may now call it, the universal. And this third thing is not exactly similar to either of the particulars, just because there is no fourth thing to which it has the relation which they have to it. To this view of the case I can discover no further objection. It is true it would be desirable to have some single term to express the fact that the universal differs numerically from the particular, without differing conceptually from it, although it has not that further relation to which I have just confined the term exact similarity. The term exact similarity might, indeed, be used for this purpose. But then it would be necessary to have another term to express the additional fact that each particular is also related to the other through the universal; and since the relation of particular to particular is probably far more often [115] spoken of under this name, and is also far more often an object of discussion, it seems desirable to employ the familiar term with this complex meaning. How any term is to be used is not, however, the question in which I am mainly interested at present. The point upon which I am concerned to insist is that the relation of a particular to its universal is, in fact, different from that of a particular to a particular, which would commonly be said to be exactly similar to it, although of both pairs it is true that they differ numerically without differing conceptually. This point appears to me necessary if we once admit, as I have tried to show we must, that things do differ numerically without differing conceptually. For this theory threatened to obliterate the distinction between particulars and universals, since it denied that any distinction could be found in the fact that the particular was the universal in relation to some other or others conceptually different from it. Whereas it seems impossible to deny that universals do differ from particulars, since different things are true of them: as, for instance, that particulars certainly exist, while it is at least doubtful whether any universals do; and that universals may be predicated of particulars, while particulars cannot be predicated of universals nor yet of one another. Thus it seems certain that this red and that red do exist, but very doubtful whether redness itself does. And equally certain that this red is red; whereas undoubtedly red itself is not this red, nor this red that red. I can thus claim for my theory, that it partially unites the views of those who insist on the reality of self-identical universals, but feel themselves therefore bound to deny any difference but difference of content, with the views of those who maintain exact similarity of particulars, but feel inclined to deny that any identity, save that of each particular with itself, is involved in this.

The admission of numerical difference seems, then, to be necessary; and we have failed to find any fatal objections to it. It has, however, become plain that several important [116] consequences, not generally recognised, follow from its admission; and it will now be well to sum these up.

First, then, any two things of which one has a relation which the other has not, or of one of which something is true which is not true of the other, are numerically different from one another.

But all such pairs of things are divided into two classes, according as the pair in question also have another difference called conceptual difference or have not. It is impossible to escape the conclusion that one and the same pair may have both kinds of difference. For if it be said that by their conceptual difference is merely meant that a conceptually different universal is related to each; then each may indeed differ numerically only from the other, but must differ conceptually from the universal to which it is related. But this universal has to it a relation which it has not to the other. Accordingly by definition the universal is numerically different from it; and since it is also conceptually different, we have one and the same pair possessing both kinds of difference. To proceed: Any two universals have both numerical and conceptual difference from one another. But every particular has some one universal from which it differs numerically only. To this universal it also has a peculiar nameless relation, which the universal has not to it, and which it has not to any other particular. All particulars which have this relation to the same universal differ from one another numerically only; but they differ conceptually also from any particular which has this relation to a different universal. This nameless relation which each particular has to one, and only one, universal, is not the same as the relation of a member of a class to its class-concept; since the member of a class may differ conceptually from its class-concept, and since also two universals may both belong to the same class. But, it may be said, what is the difference between a particular and a universal, since they do not necessarily differ conceptually? The difference is that they belong to different classes: the class-concept "universal" differs from [117] the class-concept "particular." And the classes may be defined as follows: Anything is a particular which has to some other things, differing from it numerically only, the peculiar nameless relation above mentioned. Anything is a universal which has this relation to nothing else at all. Thus there may be universals having only one particular, or having no particulars whatsoever: but every particular must have a universal. The name "universal" must not therefore be understood to imply particulars, but only to note the fact, that if there be more than two things differing from one another numerically only, there is one among them having a relation to *all* the rest, which none of the rest have to it or to one another. A class-concept, on the other hand, does imply at least one *member* conceptually different from it; and if there are more, it has to *all* a relation which none of them have to it or to one another. It is, moreover, always also a universal, but may have no particulars. Great care is therefore needed in distinguishing the different relations it may have to different things in either character.

We are now in a position to say something with regard to the meaning of identity. With regard to assertions of identity in general, it seems plain that they may take two different forms. We may either assert that this is identical with that, or that this is identical with itself. The latter form is that used in the logical "Law of Identity," A is A; everything is identical with itself. Of this law Hegel complains in one place[2] that those who assert it also assert its "opposite," and immediately afterwards, that utterances in accordance with it "deserve" to be "reputed silly." I cannot take upon myself to decide whether or not he regards these charges as the same, and whether or not he means by opposite "contradictory." The instances he gives ("A planet is—a planet; Magnetism is—magnetism; Mind is—mind") seem to be justly accused of silliness. But are they untrue? I do not know that either he [118] or any of his disciples have maintained that Mind is not mind, although they may have maintained that Matter is not matter. It would seem, then, that some even of these silly instances have contradictories, which are false; and that when Hegel tells us that in asserting the Law of Identity we also assert its opposite, he only means that we must assert something else of Mind as well as the fact that it is Mind; not that we may assert it is not Mind.

Accordingly, his first complaint would seem to amount to no more than a comment on the ambiguity of the copula, pointing out that many different things may in different senses be predicated of one and the same thing; a comment which is very true, and would be very useful if those who made it, or those who heard it, could be induced thereby to remember it in practice.

But there still seems room to ask why these remarks are silly if they are true. I think, in the first place, it is because the same word happens to be used in subject and predicate. It is true, as Hegel himself remarks, that the propositional form always "promises a distinction between subject and predicate," and if a distinction is meant, it usually seems silly to use the same symbol for what is meant to be distinguished. Cases are rare in which the double meaning of a symbol is so well understood that we can calculate upon a distinction being perceived in spite of our using the same symbol. We cannot enunciate all truths in the form of puns; and, even if we could, we could not expect the joke to be appreciated in all companies. "A bull is a bull" might conceivably be the best way of expressing a judgment of the relation between such very different things as an animal and an Irish form of wit; but the difference must be very obvious, or we shall have to explain our joke. Hegel is, therefore, unfair to the Law of Identity in his choice of symbols to express its instances. Supposing we say, "Mind is something of which propositions are true which are not true of anything else whatever," it is by no means obvious that the utterance is silly, although our meaning might [119] be exactly the same as we should express under other circumstances by saying, "Mind is mind." But what is our meaning when we use such expressions? I have assumed that there must be some distinction which we are trying to express; but it is obvious, from the fact that we are ever tempted to express it by "Mind is mind," that it is a distinction which is somewhat difficult to catch. When we say, "This is identical with itself," the truth of which we are thinking seems to belong to the class of truths of which the general form is, "This is identical with that," and it seems as if in all such cases "this" and "that" must have some difference from one another, and therefore that, in this case, the thing must be different from itself in order to be identical. This, I believe, is the conclusion to which Hegel wishes to drive us; and yet it is undoubtedly this which the Law of Identity wishes to deny. We must, therefore, find a point of difference between what we mean by "This is identical with itself," and what we mean by "This is identical with that," if we are to hold that any instance of our Law does not imply its own contradictory; and yet we must maintain that any such instance asserts a relation between two different things, if we are to hold that it is not pure nonsense and can have a contradictory.

Such a point of difference may be found, in the first place, in the fact that when we say, "Mind is self-identical," we are asserting something of it which is also true of everything else; whereas when we say, "Matter is identical with mind," we are asserting something of a pair of things, which is not true of every other pair. In short our Law is: "Everything is self-identical"; it is not "Everything is identical with something else." It would thus seem, at first sight, that "Mind is mind" is as far as possible from being an instance of our Law, or an "utterance in accordance with it," since it appears to be an attempt to assert of mind something which is true of nothing else, whereas, by the very terms of the law, any instance of it must assert of something a predicate which is also true of [120] everything else. The Law of Identity asserts of everything that it belongs to a certain class: let us say, the class of subjects. An instance of the law would then be: "Mind is a subject." But, then, so are "matter" and hosts of other things. Yet we do not mean to assert that it is just like these: we feel that our assertion was meant to be unique. We want to say not only that it is a subject like other things, but *which* subject it is; and we are familiar with only one method of specification—that which asserts of a given particular the universal to which it is related. When we say, vaguely enough, but with a very definite meaning, "This exists," and we are asked "Which *this* do you mean?" the answer "The this which is red" generally proves satisfactory: we have succeeded in specifying a point wherein it differs from most other things. But when the "this" of which we are speaking is "This red" or is the universal itself, this method is no longer open to us. We cannot specify any point in which it differs from other things, because it is itself a mere point of difference. We can say of it, it is a subject, a point of difference: and we are sure that this is unambiguous. But if any one asks, "*Which* subject is it?" we can only reply, "The subject which it is," although we have thereby added nothing to our meaning. This, I take it, is how we come to say "Mind is mind." We fancy that the uniqueness of a thing ought in every case to be capable of being expressed in some predicate, because this method proves successful in most ordinary cases. But the fact is that every predicate we can assign does also belong to some other thing, though not in general to all or most; and that the only thing which gives absolute uniqueness to any proposition is the subject. Any proposition will differ from some other in respect both of its subject and its predicate; but it can differ from all others only in respect of its subject.

If then we take our meaning, when we say "Mind is mind," to be that "Mind is a subject," is it still silly? Certainly this [121] particular case of the Law of Identity may be thought so; and so, under certain circumstances, may the other: for the facts they enunciate are often obvious to every one. But the Law itself does not therefore lose its importance. For it asserts that this is true of everything; whereas every philosopher who holds that Appearance differs from Reality must assert that some things are mere predicates.

The first meaning, then, which we can give to an assertion of

Identity, is that the assertion that a thing is identical with itself is equivalent to the assertion that it is a subject. Identity is not here a relation between two things, nor does it imply any difference. The assertion that such and such a thing is a subject has been common enough in philosophy, and therefore might seem to need no explanation. Moreover, the notion "subject" is itself a subject, and therefore undefinable. I may, however, attempt to convey a notion of its meaning by specifying its relations, and by recalling the terms which have been used for it. To begin with the latter: It is, in the first place, much what Spinoza meant by Substance; and his "Attribute," too, is much what I mean by predicate. It is much what is commonly meant by "Individual," and it is what Mr. Bradley and others have called a "This." Now what is intended to be conveyed by predicating any of these terms of a thing—by saying that so and so is a Substance or a Subject, or an Individual, or a "This"—appears to be mainly that the thing so said to be is a thing of which something is true which is not true of anything else whatever. But if this be taken to mean a thing which has a predicate which nothing else has, the search for such a thing obviously becomes very difficult. Hence arises a tendency to suppose that a substance must be a thing with a very great variety of predicates; since, if you assign it enough, there is some hope that there will be no other thing of which it is true that it has all those predicates. In this way we obtain such definitions of Substance as that it is that which unites all positive predicates; [122] or of an Individual, as that it combines the greatest possible differentiation with the greatest possible unity. But all such attempts leave unexplained the fact, which they cannot but recognise, that the predicates themselves, if they are different, must each have that very property, which their combination is supposed to bestow on Substance—namely, that something is true of each, which is not true of anything else. Either they are not each unique; in which case the Substance also has lost its uniqueness: or else they are;

and then the collection of any number is no whit more so than each one singly. It is not then by its predicates that a Substance can be distinguished. Something is true of it which is not true of anything else, but this cannot mean that it has either one or any number of predicates which nothing else has. There is in fact an ambiguity in the expression, "that which is true of a thing," to point out which is all that I can do in the way of defining a subject. It is the case with any subject, not only that something is true of it, which is true of nothing else, but that everything which is true of it is true of nothing else. But this does *not* mean that it may not have the same relation to other things which something else has; it may and must have some relation to some other thing, which everything else has. What is meant is that the fact of its having that relation is not the same fact as that anything else has it. That it is a subject, for instance, is a different truth from the truth that anything else is so, although what each asserts to be true of the subject in question is exactly the same.

(1) Our first kind of "Identity," then—self-sameness or individuality—neither affirms nor denies difference. It is true that if two things are numerically different, each is an individual. But to assert that a thing is not an individual is not equivalent to asserting that it is not numerically different from some other. Numerical difference can only be asserted or denied of two individuals; individuality can be asserted or denied of one. The motive of both denials is indeed the same, [123] namely, the desire to prove that a single individual possesses both of two predicates, of which it is obvious that it possesses one. But whereas the denial of numerical difference would leave it doubtful which of the two was to be benefited, the denial of individuality makes it plain that the advantages of the transaction are not to accrue to that of which it is denied. Thus, for instance, in order to prove a Spiritualism by transferring to mind some of the predicates which appear to attach to matter, it is necessary both to deny their numerical dif-

ference (which by itself might lead to Materialism), and also to deny the individuality of matter (which by itself might lead to Agnosticism).

(2) The above combination of these two denials gives us a second sense of identity. A thing may be said to be numerically identical with another, when it is denied both to have individuality and to be numerically different from that other. An assertion of identity in this sense is obviously never true; just because an assertion of it in the first sense always is so. Neither the denial of individuality nor the denial of numerical difference is ever true. Yet both are frequently denied. The reason seems to be that we frequently wish to assert that two relations both attach to one individual. In such cases the truth that the one relation attaches to the individual is a different truth from the truth that the other attaches to it; and since the truths are different it is assumed that they have different subjects. Thus the difference between truths which consists in their asserting different relations of the same subject is confused with that which consists in their asserting the same relation of different subjects. Thus, if we say, "The red I am thinking of now is the same as that of which I was thinking then," it is easy to suppose that the identity predicated is of the same kind as when we say, "The red at this place is the same as the red at that place." In the second case, however, we are asserting that two things numerically different have the same relation to one universal (a particular tint of red), whereas [124] in the first we may be merely predicating two different relations of a single individual. When once, in this way, we have come to suppose that we can deny of a thing that it differs numerically from itself, it is comparatively easy to persuade ourselves that the denial may extend to other things.

But (3) we may deny conceptual difference of two things numerically different. We may then be said to assert that they are conceptually identical. In all such cases the assertion of identity is the assertion of a relation between two different things: identity does really imply difference. The relation asserted may, according to what was said above, be either the relation of two particulars to the same universal, or the relation of the universal to a particular, or that of a particular to a universal. All three relations are different, but all are alike in implying the denial of conceptual difference. It is plain that in such cases it is very easy to suppose that, since we assert identity in spite of numerical difference, we are also denying numerical difference. And if numerical difference could be denied in the case of conceptual identicals, there would be no objection to its denial in the case of things conceptually different, since they are not a bit more numerically different than the others. Moreover

(4) Things which are both conceptually and numerically different from one another frequently have to one another a relation which is very liable to be confused with the relation of particular to particular: I mean the relation of members of a class to one another. If a number of reds of the same tint are said to have in common the fact that they are all just that red, we are liable to suppose that a number of reds of different tints also have in common in the same way the fact that they are all red. If the first set may be said to exhibit identity of content, why not the second? And if the second, why not the series of numbers, &c.? It must, I think, be admitted that 2 and 3 are sometimes said to exhibit identity in difference for no better reason than that they are both numbers. It is thought that [125] their being numbers enters into their nature as individuals, in the same way as its redness constitutes the nature of "this red." Yet it must be insisted that 2 and 3 are *not* conceptually identical. Their relation to number is quite different from that of two particulars to their universal. Though this, therefore, is a case in which identity *is* predicated, I think the usage is one which might well be given up. The confusion caused by it is largely responsible for that conception of "concrete" or

"self-differentiating" "universal," which is so powerful an instrument for persuading to the denial of numerical difference between individuals. If the conception "number" be regarded as having to the different numbers the relation of a universal to its particulars, then, in virtue of their difference, it is called a "self-differentiating universal." Moreover, the number "two," in virtue of its relation to it, may be called a (partially) concrete universal. And further, since it is very easy to confound the class-concept with the class, why should not the whole series of numbers (if only it were not infinite!) be regarded as a self-differentiating or concrete universal? (I do not know which expression, or whether either, would be considered appropriate in this instance.) And, lastly, since here we have a group of different things, each with an intimate relation to one common concept, with regard to which the identity in difference characteristic of a concrete universal is so remarkable, why should we not, wherever we have a group of different things, each of which is related to one common concept, even if that common concept be only their membership of the group, call that group, too, a concrete universal? Hence a state is a concrete universal, a man is a concrete universal; not because states and men have some properties in common, nor even because all the parts of each is a member of a single class, but because of each of the parts of each it may be said that it is a member of the state, a part of man. Such extravagances are quite soberly committed by philosophers of reputation. But the main pity of it is that, when they have thus invested a [126] group with the title of concrete universal or individual (perhaps these are the same?), then they hark back to begin to invest the group with the properties which belong to a real universal: as that, without their relation to the universal, the particulars would not be what they are; that the group, as a whole, possesses all the attributes which its particulars have singly; that they, conversely, possess all its attributes—are microcosms to its macrocosm. By such methods it is easy to prove that the world is an individual; that all differences are transcended in it; that its capability of remaining one, in spite of them, is admirable.

But to return: (5) If two things numerically different may be conceptually the same, may not two things conceptually different be numerically the same? The answer has been already given: no two things can be numerically the same. But the question introduces us to the last meaning of identity which I intend to consider —that, namely, in which identity is predicated of complex things. The case of complex things is one in which those who are, in general, most anxious to deny that there is such a thing as numerical difference, have strenuously maintained it. Their very doctrine is that conceptual difference is compatible with numerical identity. They wish to maintain that a thing may be the same with itself (that foolish proposition, "Mind is mind"), in spite of having different predicates; and that because they hold that the subject is constituted by its predicates. The first question to be answered under this head is: Can a collection be an individual? It certainly may present points of resemblance to one. Thus we can predicate things of a number of parts, which are different truths from any that can be predicated of each by itself; as that they are so many, or that they have such a shape. Moreover, we have already admitted that one kind of complex thing, a truth, may, as a whole, be numerically different from another; and where two truths assert the same predicate of things conceptually the same, they may even be [127] conceptually identical. Complexes are then capable of being subjects, both as wholes, and also in that certain predicates attach to all their parts which do not attach to each singly. But it is very important to distinguish these cases from those in which a mere relation between the parts is asserted. Thus, when I say that my coat is black, I may be understood to assert that, if not all, yet a great number of, its parts are so. But the assertion that each one of them is black is not to be understood as an assertion of the relation of particulars to a universal, but of black particulars to other particulars. Accordingly, when it is asserted of one of them that it is black and woollen, this is not to be understood as an assertion that one individual has two predicates, but that two individuals have a certain relation. The parts of my coat, then, understood in this sense, have neither conceptual nor numerical identity. In each case it is possible to distinguish some one individual related to a conceptually different individual; and it is these relations which are asserted when all are said to be black. The assertion of identity through change, and of personal identity, always involves relations of this kind. When the same identical thing is said to persist, it is always meant that two or more particulars, conceptually identical, are continuous in time; and the change resolves itself into the fact that each of two conceptually different particulars has the same relation to each at a different time. Thus the "material identity" of a thing may be said to consist in the continuous existence of conceptually identical particulars, which have at different times the same relation to different particulars.

NOTES

1. This point does not appear to have been noticed by Mr. Russell in his intricate discussion of Leibniz's principle (*Philos. of L.*, pp. 54–56). If Leibniz is to be held to his remark, his doctrine is indistinguishable from that which Mr. Russell attributes to Mr. Bradley. In any case, the fact that he made it proves that he was not always clear as to the meaning of his principle. And the same conclusion follows from the fact that, if he allows numerical difference to differ from conceptual difference, he is also bound, in consistency with another application of the Law of Sufficient Reason, to hold that the world does not exist (*ib.*, p. 57), since there must for each thing in it be something *conceivable* differing from that thing numerically only.

2. *Smaller Logic*, § 115, Wallace's Trans., p. 214.

7

Mr. McTaggart's "Studies in Hegelian Cosmology"

This book possesses a combination of merits, which is as rare as it is valuable. Mr. McTaggart attempts to prove to us directly that the whole universe is of a certain kind; and he defines with most unusual clearness both what his conclusion is and what are the premises and arguments by which he holds it to be proved. Theology may give us conclusions even more definite and more capable of appealing to the imagination; but this advantage can only be obtained at the expense either of despicable reasoning or of fundamental assumptions, which are wholly arbitrary and accepted on authority. Philosophers, again, may reason well from self-evident premises; but they can rarely reach a conclusion more definite than that the world is "rational and righteous," and in proportion as their conclusions are important, the evidence for them is apt to be obscure. Mr. McTaggart's reasoning is inferior to none in ability; his fundamental premises are not arbitrary; his conclusions are definite; and he leaves us in no doubt as to the

Originally published in *Proceedings of the Aristotelian Society* n.s. 2 (1901–1902): 177–214.

precise nature of the evidence which he has to offer for them. I know of no philosophical work which combines these merits in an equal degree.

The question "What is the nature of the Universe?" is directly dealt with only in three chapters—II, on "Human Immortality"; III, on "the Personality of the Absolute"; and IX, on "The Further Determination of the Absolute"; and it is only with these three chapters than I propose to deal. They are in no sense historical, as the title of the book might suggest. Their only connection with Hegel, is that Mr. McTaggart considers Hegel to have discovered the greater [178] part of the arguments on which his conclusions rest, and to have said nothing inconsistent with those conclusions. But, whether Mr. McTaggart really agrees with Hegel or not, his object is to prove, quite independently, that his conclusions are true; and it may certainly be doubted whether Hegel's own work possesses any of the merits which I have attributed to Mr. McTaggart, except that his premises do not seem to be arbitrary, so far as their vagueness allows us to judge.

We have, then, in these three chapters an original attempt to answer the most important of all philosophical questions—the question what exists other than, or in addition to, the things which form the object of our everyday experience; and this attempt is executed with a very rare combination of excellencies. The conclusions at which it arrives may be briefly summarised as follows:—

Chapter II may be divided into two distinct parts. Only one of these deals with the question, "What is the nature of reality?" And it arrives at the conclusion that reality is exclusively composed of a plurality of finite persons, including ourselves. This argument is presented by Mr. McTaggart merely as part of the necessary premises for his conclusion with regard to the express subject of the chapter "Human Immortality"; and it is with Human Immortality that the second part of the chapter deals. Mr. McTaggart, as I shall try to show, understands Immortality in its ordinary meaning, though he expressly states the contrary; he means by it the duration of ourselves throughout time, and not merely, as he says, eternal or non-temporal existence. This second part, therefore, differs essentially in the nature of its conclusions from the first. The first has proved, if it proves anything, that we are real, and do not exist in time. This second part, on the other hand, tries to prove that we do exist throughout time in the same sense as we exist now, *i.e.*, according to Mr. McTaggart, only "as appearance," which, so far as I can understand it, is equivalent to saying that we do not exist [179] at all. It is, indeed, obvious that if by "our existence" be meant but one fact, and that fact be eternal and not in time, then the conclusion that we exist at any time at all, let alone "throughout time," must be false. Mr. McTaggart would, I suppose, say that the latter conclusion had a certain "relative truth," *i.e.*, was truer than to say that we exist only for a limited period of time; though it is certainly impossible to explain how that which directly contradicts an absolute truth can be sure in any sense at all. In any case, this second part of Chapter II deals, on Mr. McTaggart's view, only with what has been called Phenomenology, and thus differs essentially from the first part, to which, perhaps, the name Cosmology would be more properly confined, since it tries to tell us what the world really is, not merely what it appears to be. For those, however, who do not hold Mr. McTaggart's view that the temporal is unreal, the question of our immortality may appear quite as important as any other which Mr. McTaggart discusses. Mr. McTaggart's conclusions on this subject consist chiefly in determining what is meant by saying that *we* persist, and in arguing that such persistence, even though it omits much of what we value now, has very great value.

Chapters III and IX complete the determination of the nature of Reality. III concludes that the plurality of persons, of which Reality consists, cannot *also* form one person (a personal God); and IX decides that the sole relation between these persons consists, not in their knowing, but in their loving, one another.

On what grounds, then, does Mr. McTaggart base these important conclusions? In the first place, he considers it to have been proved by Hegel's Logic, or capable of being proved on similar lines, that the whole universe is of such a nature that it is *in* each of its parts, besides being the whole of which they are the parts, and that this can only be the case if the whole is "not only *in* the individuals, but also *for* the individuals": [180] it is in this way that Mr. McTaggart interprets the undoubted Hegelian doctrine that the universe must combine perfect unity with perfect differentiation. And to the method by which this conclusion is reached no valid objection can be raised. It is expounded and defended at full length in Mr. McTaggart's earlier book, *Studies in the Hegelian Dialectic.* Briefly, it is this: Once assume (what everybody must grant) that the whole universe has "being," it may be shown by a number of steps of rigorous logical inference, that "being" implies "a whole that is not only *in*, but *for* each of its parts," in a sense similar to that in which 2 + 2 implies 4, so that that which *is* may be inferred also to be a whole of such a nature, as certainly as a pair of pairs may be inferred to be a group of four. Now, that there *might* be an implication of such a nature cannot be denied; but what, perhaps not even Mr. McTaggart himself, and certainly nobody else, can believe is that all its steps have been exhibited in a perfectly convincing form. Mr. McTaggart himself has only published the third part of the argument (*Mind* 1897, pp. 164, 342; 1889, p. 35; 1900, p. 145); and even in that part it would be surprising to hear that anyone, on a careful examination, could declare that all, if any, of the steps appeared to possess demonstrative evidence. The ingenuity displayed in the discussion is indeed quite as great as is usually displayed by philosophers in proving their most important theses, and may therefore produce a feeling of probability in the minds of those who have the amiable disposition to accept any argument for which they can find no distinct refutation; and there can be no doubt that Mr. McTaggart will be able to display as much in the two unpublished thirds of the demonstration. Meanwhile, however, it is certain that no reasonable person can be blamed for entirely refusing assent to the conclusion that the universe is a whole, which is not only *in*, but *for* each of its parts.

But even if it were proved that the universe is a whole, which is not only *in* but *for* each of its parts, what is the exact [181] meaning of this assertion? and does it follow that these parts are conscious persons like ourselves? With regard to the latter point, Mr. McTaggart expresses a doubt, which, if it were justified, would seem to leave no probability at all to his main conclusion —that conscious persons are fundamentally real. He gives us a very complicated argument upon the point, a discussion of which will serve to throw light on the meaning and validity of the conclusion of the logic.

The data which Mr. McTaggart gives us are the following: (1) He considers himself to have proved that we, as conscious persons, are parts of a whole, which is both in and for each of us. For two persons to be conscious each both of himself and of the other, is, he holds, for each to be a part of such a whole. The validity of this doctrine I shall consider presently: what I propose to discuss now is its relation to two other assertions of Mr. McTaggart's. (2) He admits "the possibility of the existence of other ways in which the whole might be for the part—ways at present unimaginable by us" (p. 20). And (3) he tries to exclude this possibility by arguing that "our selves have characteristics which they could *not* have, *unless* they were some fundamental differentiations of reality" (pp. 21–26).

Now the combination of these three contentions seems to me to involve a very gross confusion. If, as (1) assures us, the category of the Absolute Idea—the being a whole which is in and for each of its parts—does apply to two such conscious persons, what can be the meaning of the admission that this category might be realised in other unimaginable ways? Obviously it can only mean that two such persons, though they have the relation denoted by the category, may also have other relations which are related to this, as specific differences are to the genus to which their species belong. The relation of two such persons is one species, falling under the genus denoted by the category; and Mr. McTaggart only tells us in (2) that there may be infinite other species falling under the same genus. [182] But now let us consider (3). Mr. McTaggart's argument to show that "our selves have characteristics which they could *not* have, *unless* they were" parts of the Absolute, depends upon two premises—(*a*) (which he tries to prove at some length) that the nature of our selves is in a certain respect "paradoxical"; (*b*) that they have a high degree of reality. No paradox, he holds, can be reasonably considered true, unless it can be deduced by a process such as the dialectic. But to admit that our selves have a high degree of reality is to admit that they have a high degree of truth; and hence, he concludes, there is a great probability, until the paradoxical nature of the self is deduced in some other way, that this paradox is the very one which has been deduced by the dialectic. Surely this result should appear surprising! For we have it laid down already in (1) that the very identical paradox, which has been deduced by the dialectic, *is* exhibited in our selves! If the *specific* way in which the self exhibits the paradox, is also itself paradoxical, and if this second paradox is what is meant by "the paradox of the self," it is obvious that the paradox of the self cannot possibly be that which is deduced by the dialectic; and Mr. McTaggart's argument is an attempt to prove a contradiction—that what is *ex hypothesi* a species, is identical with its own genus. If, on the other hand, the "paradox of the self" is the generic paradox, we know already that this has been deduced by the dialectic, and the whole argument is perfectly needless. In fact, the conclusion of the argument, "that the paradox of the self is probably identical with the category," is in flat contradiction with the admission that there may possibly be other unimaginable ways in which the category is realised. If the paradox is even probably identical with the category, it cannot possibly be specifically different from it. Mr. McTaggart's argument cannot possibly prove that any *specific* paradox of the self is the paradox deduced in the dialectic; and since this is impossible, it can only prove over again, this time as a probable conclusion, what [183] was before proved as a certain one—that the self does exhibit the paradox deduced in the dialectic. Mr. McTaggart's conception of the relation of the self to the category seems therefore to be grossly confused. And it is easy to see where the source of the confusion lies. Mr. McTaggart has never precisely conceived what is meant by the category "a whole which is in and for each of its parts." He talks, for instance, of the word "in" being used in different senses, but he does not discriminate these senses from one another. Had he conceived precisely the meaning of the category, it would have been plain on immediate inspection whether the relation meant by it was or was not identical with that of two selves, each conscious of itself and of the other. As it is, he leaves us uncertain, when he tells us that the category does apply to two such selves, whether the relation denoted by the category is actually discernible as uniting those selves, or whether it is only the *words* used in the category which will also apply to a relation, not only specifically, but utterly different, which is discernible as uniting the selves. Similarly, when he talks of the "other unimaginable ways," he does not determine precisely whether all these "ways" have in common some perfectly definite relation, and what that relation is; or whether, perhaps they are completely different forms of relation, which have no real community, are not species of one genus, but are only united by the fact that the same words "in and for" will apply to all of them. It seems, in fact, that when Mr. McTaggart speaks of these other possible ways, he does not really conceive them as species under the one genus of the category, but as having nothing whatever in common with one another. But, if this be so, then his assertion that the category does apply to selves can only mean that the *words* of the category apply to them, their relation has not really anything in common with these other "unimaginable" relations. In that case, plainly his whole argument for the reality of our selves falls to pieces. If, on the other hand, we are to understand that our selves, [184] while really exhibiting the relation meant by the category, also exhibit specific differences, Mr. McTaggart has said nothing even tending to show that these specific differences will be preserved in the Absolute; but, on the other hand, it follows at once that our selves, *so far* as they exhibit the generic relation, are real, since it is assumed throughout that that to which the Absolute Idea does apply, is, so far as it applies, completely real. But, in fact, Mr. McTaggart does not seem to conceive the paradox of the self as thus specifically different from the category. He never anywhere attempts to discriminate what in relations of selves is identical with the relation denoted by the category, and what is not. He only gives us one clearly defined paradox of the self, without attempting to point out in it a generic and a specific element. Finally, he never attempts to discriminate the meaning which he attaches to the category from that which he attaches to the paradox of the self. I conclude, therefore, that the relation between selves, which he defines at some length, is, in fact, the only and veritable relation denoted by the category; and that Mr. McTaggart appears to distinguish them, only owing to the confusion just exhibited. At all events, I have shown that if they are not identical, Mr. McTaggart has not a shadow of ground for his conclusion that our selves are "fundamental differentiation of reality." We thus, at last, get a clear conception of the meaning of "a whole which is both in and for each of its parts." It *means* a whole which has the relations to its parts which Mr. McTaggart describes as belonging to two selves, each conscious of itself and of the other. And it is certain that, if the dialectic is valid, and if, also, the nature of consciousness is such as Mr. McTaggart conceives, the Absolute is exclusively composed of conscious persons. But we have seen already that we have no reason to suppose the dialectic valid; and this conclusion is reinforced by the new fact, just discovered, that Mr. McTaggart himself does not seem to have conceived clearly (he seems even to conceive merely as [185] a form of words) the relation which he is bound to deduce by a stringent logical process. And, on the other hand, we shall now proceed to see that Mr. McTaggart entirely misconceives the nature of consciousness. Even if he could prove strictly that the relation, which he holds to be exemplified in consciousness, fully expressed the nature of reality, we must still maintain that this relation is *not* exemplified in consciousness.

Mr. McTaggart's theory is, that when I know my friend, he is simultaneously both inside and outside my mind: this, he thinks, is the relation in which consciousness always stands to its object. It is owing to this that a universe of conscious selves, each of which knew all about the others, would conform to his "category": such a universe would be a whole which not only contained all its parts, but was itself contained in each of them. This contradiction (for it certainly seems to be one) might of itself be thought sufficient to condemn the theory of knowledge from which it follows; but let us examine a little further into the account which Mr. McTaggart gives of that theory. He at first identifies my friend inside me with my "representation," "reproduction," or "image" of my friend; and since he insists besides on distinguishing between this image and the original (p. 21), it would at first seem that my one friend, when I know him, becomes necessarily two, one inside me, the other outside. But later on it appears Mr. McTaggart prefers to say that it is one and the same friend, who is both inside and outside me. This again seems a flat contradiction; but, waiving that objection, let us consider whether it is a true and necessary account of the relation of consciousness to its object. Consciousness of a thing does not, I presume, mean *nothing but* having that thing both inside and outside my mind. Even though it be true that this relation of the thing to me is involved in my consciousness of it, something else is surely involved too—something quite unique, which we all of us recognise, and which is what we mainly think of when we talk of knowing. I do not know that [186] Mr. McTaggart would dispute this; at all events, it is true. And I think perhaps the falsity of Mr. McTaggart's view can be most convincingly exhibited by showing that when he says that that of which I am conscious is both inside and outside my mind, he is compelled either to define this unique thing which we mainly mean by our consciousness of a thing as meaning in every case both itself and something else (a definition which combines the merit of self contradiction with that of circularity), or else to deny its existence altogether. Which horn of this dilemma Mr. McTaggart is compelled to take he again does not allow us to decide: it depends whether the inside and outside objects, or (to take the second alternative which he gives us) the inside and outside aspects of one and the same object, which he maintains to be necessary to consciousness, are themselves to be regarded, one or both of them, as objects of consciousness; or whether neither is so. His language will support either alternative, and both are equally fatal to his theory. In the first case (1) he analyses my knowledge of my friend into either (*a*) my knowledge of him, as outside me together with his presence inside me, a definition which is obviously both circular and contradictory, as if one were to say "2" *means* "2 + 1;" or (*b*) my knowledge of him, as outside me, together with my knowledge of him, as inside me, to which the same objections apply, as if one were to say "2" *means* "2 + 2." In the second case (2) knowledge *consists* in the mere existence of one and the same thing both inside and outside me, or in the existence of two similar objects one inside and outside, which obliterates what we know and mean by knowledge as entirely as if one were to say that the reflection of an object in a looking-glass were a case of consciousness of an object. And what ground has

Mr. McTaggart for maintaining these absurdities? None but the bare question, which he seems to regard as a knock-down argument: "How can (my friend) be an object of my consciousness unless he is also inside me?" The answer to this question is the [187] simple one, "Quite easily"; it being a fact that we can be conscious *both* of our own states *and* of what is outside us—a fact in which there is no difficulty at all, unless we assume that the relation of consciousness to its object is not merely, what it must in any case be admitted to be, a unique relation, but *must* also be a relation of whole to part. In fact that what I am conscious of *must* be inside my mind is a mere traditional assumption for which there are no reasons, and which, in the sense in which it is intended, *i.e.*, as a definition of consciousness, necessarily leads to the absurdities above detailed. It is commonly supposed, as it was by Berkeley, to be obvious to direct inspection that what I know is always in my mind; whereas the only thing which really is thus obvious, is that my consciousness of the thing is so. The history of philosophy exhibits a uniform inability to distinguish between that of which I am conscious and my consciousness of it—an inability which has found a monument in the word "idea" which regularly stands for both. The doctrine that when I am conscious of a thing there must always be an image of it in my mind owes its plausibility to the neglect of this simple distinction. The existence of this image of the thing is identified with my consciousness of it; whereas it is immediately plain that, even if, when I am conscious of a thing, there is an image of it in my mind, this image must exist *in addition* to my consciousness, and can form no part of its definition, since I must always be supposed to be conscious, in a sense *not* merely equivalent to the existence of an image in me, either of the image itself, or of the thing, or (as Mr. McTaggart seems to prefer) of both.

The first proposition of Mr. McTaggart's Cosmology then—that the universe consists solely of conscious persons—is entirely dependent on these two premises: (1) An incomplete and doubtful chain of reasoning, which *if* complete and evident, would show that the universe was self-contradictory, as being a whole which was also a part of each of its parts; [188] (2) a manifestly false, and also self-contradictory, statement that that of which I am conscious is always both a part and not a part of me. It is plain, then, that he has given us no reason to believe his first proposition; and yet his attempt to establish it must be allowed to have the highest philosophic merit. It has the merit of being an excellent *reductio ad absurdum* of all attempts to construct what Mr. McTaggart would call an "Idealism," *i.e.*, any philosophy which maintains that the universe is wholly "spiritual" and perfectly good. It is qualified to perform this useful service by the fact that, whereas its arguments are quite as good as any that are commonly offered, they and their premises are stated in so exceptionally clear a form that their complete impotence may be easily exposed.

So much for what I have ventured to call the *Cosmological* conclusion of Chapter II. I now turn to the express subject of the chapter—Human Immortality. An essential step in Mr. McTaggart's proof of our Immortality is, as has been said, the above-considered argument that we are "fundamental differentiations of the Absolute." The insufficiency of this accordingly wrecks the argument.

But a second step is essential: granted (what he has thus failed to prove) that we are "fundamental differentiations of the Absolute," Mr. McTaggart goes on to argue that, being such, we must be "eternal." Now what does this mean? Mr. McTaggart distinctly states (p. 8) that he will only prove us to have a "timeless existence." Yet, when he comes to defend his view, that we are immortal, against Mr. Bradley, we find him assuming that the view he is defending is that we shall, in the future, have "another chance"; that "a duration indefinitely prolonged" would be more satisfactory than the space of a single life (p. 44). And similarly, in his argument against Lotze, though he only calls it a *probable* hypothesis that "the whole of reality, in itself timeless, is manifested throughout the whole of time," he seems to consider [189] this probability as only necessary to establish our pre-existence as "a fair inference," not as throwing doubt on the "indefinite prolongation" of our existence in the future. In fact, it seems undeniable that throughout Mr. McTaggart's discussion of the *value* of Immortality, and of the nature of the personal identity possessed by the immortal self, he is assuming that Immortality *means* an indefinite prolongation of our existence in time; although he has distinctly stated that he will mean by it *only* a timeless existence, and though he nowhere expressly argues that a timeless existence involves such indefinite existence *in time.* This confusion as to the nature of the Immortality to be proved, is betrayed in the proof itself. The proof is directed to showing that we can neither change nor perish. But change is said (p. 27) to involve that what changes should *at one time* have a different predicate from that which it has at another; and we may assume that similarly "perishing" involves existing at one time and not at another. If so, then to prove that a thing does not change and perish is to prove *either* that it has the same predicate and itself exists *at all times, or* that it has no predicate, and does not exist at any time: such a proof cannot establish *which* of these two is the true conclusion, and Mr. McTaggart has not therefore established that our existence is "timeless." On the other hand, he seems to assume that both we and the Absolute do exist, and have predicates *at some time*, whence it follows that he has proved our *duration throughout time*, and also (we may add) that our existence is *not* timeless, for though Mr. McTaggart obviously assumes that to exist timelessly and to exist throughout time are at least *compatible*,[1] we must (till further informed) regard [190] it as a contradiction to affirm that one and the same thing both does and does not exist in time; and we can only understand "timeless" existence to mean an existence which is not in time. This contradiction is, indeed, of a piece with his former contention that the object of knowledge is both inside and not inside the knower; and it is explained by the fact that he constantly identifies, without attempting to justify himself, the "parts" or "fundamental differentiations" of the Absolute with the '*manifestation of* those parts in time (*e.g.*, p. 48). To sum up: Even if we admit this self-contradictory identification, Mr. McTaggart's proof that this "manifestation of self" cannot change or perish, only proves that it is *either* timeless *or* existing throughout time; and whereas he says he wished to prove the former, he seems to assume both, first a premiss which could only prove the latter, and then finally that he actually has proved the latter. But when freed from these contradictions and inconsistencies we take it Mr. McTaggart's view is this: (1) Our real self is timeless, *i.e.*, does not exist in time; (2) that manifestation of it which we call our self will certainly(?) have an indefinite prolongation in the future, and *probably* had one in the past. To establish these two conclusions Mr. McTaggart gives us but one argument (pp. 26–34): What are we to say of its validity? That it certainly does not establish the former, since to deny change only proves *either* timelessness *or* duration, but also was not needed to do so: for if we are fundamental differentiations of the Absolute (as we have no reason to think) it seems to follow at once that we do not exist in time since (this we understand to be a premiss) time is unreal. But does it establish the existence of our manifestation throughout time? It does not even attempt to do so, since it is concerned with the impossibility that our *real* selves should change or perish, which, not existing in time, they certainly cannot do. And we can see no argument which would, since there seems no reason why the "manifestation" of an eternal [191] part of the Absolute, since it is temporal, should not be also temporary.

But Mr. McTaggart, as has been said, is not only concerned in this chapter with establishing a probability or certainty that our existence will be prolonged after death, he also discusses the question how much of what we now call "ourselves" may be expected to persist, and the value which may be ascribed to such persistence. With regard to the first point, he argues that since our pre-existence is probable (he gives no reason why it should not be as *certain* as that in the future), and yet we certainly do not remember our past lives, there is no reason to suppose that we shall in our future lives remember this one. What then will constitute our personal identity? Mr. McTaggart maintains that what constitutes it is "identity of substance," from which there also follows an identity of attributes. With regard to this identical substance I shall say more presently. Here I need only remark that it seem to be conceived as identical with the timeless self, *i.e.*, as not existing in time, although, in order to constitute our identity it must obviously be something which exists in and through time. This remark applies to the attributes also, but with regard to these Mr. McTaggart gives us another piece of information, which has a far more important bearing on the nature and value of immortality, namely, that their persistence is compatible with the loss of any or all of the qualities which we actually observe in ourselves or others; we need have identical attributes in the next life, only in the sense in which a man who has been honourable and is become a scoundrel has them at both times in this (p. 38). Apart, therefore, from our substance and these permanent (or timeless) attributes, the bond of identity which connects our present with our future selves is no more than that which connects a man's past virtues with his present vices; and this Mr. McTaggart holds to be a causal relation. "Identity of attributes," he says, "must reveal itself in time as an ordered succession of changes of which each determines [192] the next. So that, admitting that personal identity lay in identity of substance, our way of determining whether two states belonged to the same person would be to endeavour to trace a causal relation between them" (p. 40). It is, therefore, a succession of states, causally connected with those which we call ours, in this life, that will constitute our future lives; and only in proportion as the future existence of a series so connected with our present selves seems satisfactory, shall we have reason to prize the hope of immortality which Mr. McTaggart offers to us. Now in trying to make it seem satisfactory we think that Mr. McTaggart goes beyond his data in three respects:—(1) He admits that our states are causally connected, not only with one another, but also, both as causes and effects, with our "circumstances," and the states of other people; and he does not explain in what way the causal connection between our states, which shows them to be ours, differs from that which may subsist between them and those of other people. Now I do not wish to deny that there is some such special causal connection between the states of each of us—a connection which may serve to define the life of each as a unique series; but it seems to me that, so long as we do not hold with Leibniz that each series is wholly independent of the rest, we cannot deny that in the case of two states of the same man, separated, say, by an interval of 40 years, the earlier of the two may have had far less influence upon the nature of the second than the cumulative effect of external causes. If this be so, the influence of our past upon our present character may, in the course of time, become infinitesimal, even if it does not vanish altogether; it will no doubt have had its effect upon the universe, but the main part, if not the whole of that effect, may now consist in the states of others, and conversely our present state may be, mainly due to the past states of others. That this *may* be so, at all events, Mr. McTaggart gives us no reason for denying: nor can it be denied, if we both distinguish (as he does) our own state at any given moment, as a different effect and cause [193] from the states of others at that moment, and allow that our states and those of others have in the past and will in the future interact. Moreover, it certainly seems that such things do happen, *e.g.*, to take his own instance (p. 54), "when a personal relation has existed for many years, many of the events which formed its temporal content . . . are completely forgotten. But we do not regard them as lost, for we recognise that each of them has done its part in moulding the relationship which exists at present. . . . As factors of disposition, they are all permanently real." Certainly we may admit, that our present relation to a person in this life could not have been *altogether* what it is, unless our past relations had been what they were: but can it be denied that our present relation may *in the main* be due to quite other circumstances, *e.g.*, to long familiarity with someone of a very different character? Nothing seems more certain, *empirically*, than that the effect upon us of a personal relationship, in the past, may in time become not only different from, but very much smaller in degree than, what it once was: and it must be remembered that we are here speaking of attributes that are *empirically* observable and subject to change, not of those others which Mr. McTaggart tells us are absolutely permanent and always the same. In short, even though "each event" has done "its part" in moulding our present relationships, "its part" in moulding that present may be very much smaller than was its part in moulding a part nearer in time to the original event. We think, therefore, that Mr. McTaggart misleads us seriously when he says, on the ground of this causal relation, "It is certain that whatever modifications in (the self's) nature took place in one life would be reproduced in the next" (p. 50). For there may, in spite of such causal relation, remain in us, after a time, scarcely any attribute that can be regarded as an effect of relationships which, when they existed, affected, in the most important manner, almost the whole of our mental life. But, further, (2) the assurance last [194] quoted actually denies the fact that even if a thing's effects persist, it need not itself be reproduced. Mr. McTaggart seems here to have forgotten completely that an effect does not always resemble its cause, either in quality or in value; so that, even if our state in a far future were far more largely determined by our present relationships than we have any reason to expect, it would not follow that it had any similarity to, or retained the value of, those relationships. Mr. McTaggart himself later on (p. 53) recognises that the reproduction of a cause does not follow from the persistence of its effects, and in order to establish the probability of the former he now appeals to a second principle, the assumption of which is the third point in which he appears to go beyond his data. (3) This principle is that there must be "development" in time—development "towards an end according to final causality" (p. 50). "All change in time," he says, "for the individual as well as for the universe, must be taken as ultimately determined by the end of developing as a series the full content of the timeless reality." Now, by such development it is plain that on p. 54, where the principle is appealed to, Mr. McTaggart understands the addition *in the future* of new valuable attributes to the old ones which persist. "Development," then, means "progress," and we are rather surprised to find here assumed as if certain, what on p. 44 was only called (without reason given) "the more probable conclusion"—namely, that "progress is as real as the imperfection for the removal of which it is needed." Mr. McTaggart then makes two distinct assumptions, for neither of which do we find that he has given or can give any reasons: (*a*) He seems to assume as a certainty "that every addition to the series of temporal events must make that series a more complete manifestation of the timeless reality." Now we understand that the timeless reality itself is absolutely perfect, and therefore that no manifestation whatever can constitute any addition to the perfection of the universe; and this being so, it is plain that [195] a more complete manifestation (though, as Mr. McTaggart might say, better *as* a manifestation) is not one whit better absolutely than any other. Yet we can only understand that "*must*" make and "end according to final causality" as meaning that a complete manifestation of the timeless reality is demanded by the *perfection* of the universe—*i.e.*, we *must* assume that every addition to the series of temporal events makes it a more complete manifestation, solely because a more complete manifestation will make the universe more perfect than a less complete one. It is, in fact, impossible for any philosophy which, like Mr. McTaggart's, distinguishes between a perfect timeless Reality and its manifestations or Appearance in time, consistently to ascribe any value whatever to the existence of anything in time; and that for two cogent reasons: (1) that it must maintain that nothing does really exist in time, and (2) that it cannot hold that the existence of anything in time can make any difference whatever to the perfection of the universe. Even if it allowed that things really existed in time, it could not allow any real value to such existence; and as it is, its whole Ethics must consist in ascribing a value, which they cannot have, to things which do not exist. Thus, in considering his Immortality, Mr. McTaggart plainly judges that it is better that he should exist at certain future moments than that he should not. But if, as he also maintains, that which exists timelessly is, in itself, absolutely perfect, then all possible good is realised by the timeless existence of the Absolute, and that one thing rather than another should also exist in time cannot be any good whatever. Mr. McTaggart's Ethics, then, necessarily contradict his Cosmology. But it may be held that his Cosmology is here in fault; that we may really be immortal, and that the Universe will be more or less perfect according as we are so or are not. And hence it is worth while to consider Mr. McTaggart's conception of the value of an Immortality, which will be the same in nature, whether it be held to be real or unreal. [196] (*b*) Even, then, supposing that all the parts of the temporal series contributed to make it a more complete representation of reality, there can be no reason to suppose, as Mr. McTaggart does, that the series would be a progress—*i.e.*, a series of which the future members were better than the past. Yet this, as we have seen, Mr. McTaggart at one time assumes for certain, and at another calls "more probable." But many alternatives are possible: Even if it remained at the same "dead level" of value throughout time, or underwent fluctuations regular or irregular, the whole of it might yet be necessary to manifest reality as completely as possible; supposing there was reason to think it exhibits a regularly increasing or decreasing series of value, it is quite as likely that this series increases in the direction of the past as in that of the future. Why, then, is it "more probable" that it should increase in the future? Even if it does, Mr. McTaggart admits that the early stages, which were inferior in value and manifested reality less completely, were necessary to the greatest possible perfection of the whole. If so, then, supposing the case reversed, and that the manifestation of reality is doomed in the future to become more and more incomplete, yet all these more incomplete stages, though inferior in themselves, might by a parity of reasoning serve the purpose of making the manifestation contained in the *whole* series more complete. In short, Mr. McTaggart's optimistic view that every event in time contributes to the perfection of the whole temporal series (a view which, as we saw, flatly contradicts his premises) is further quite compatible with a thoroughly pessimistic view of our whole future: if it was compatible with the greatest possible perfection of the whole that our past characters should have been worse than our present and future, it is equally compatible with that perfection that our future characters should be worse than our present and past. It is quite as likely that all the perfections which Mr. McTaggart supposes we shall have as we approach the end of our existence in time, were really [197] possessed by us when we first began it, and have gradually been lost in successive lives ever since, and will continue to be so. Nor can any empirical argument serve to render this less probable. So far as such arguments tend to show anything with regard to the whole temporal series, they make it probable that this series exhibits mere alternation of periods of more with periods of less value—*e.g.* an alternation of the existence with the non-existence of human life, and if Mr. McTaggart maintains that, nevertheless, there is a continual progress towards the future, a continual decrease in value towards the future is at least equally compatible with the facts.

To sum up, then: It does not seem that a series of future lives merely bound to one another and to our present lives by causal relations of the same kind, as those which bind the various periods of those present lives themselves, offers by any means so desirable a prospect as Mr. McTaggart tries to persuade us that it does. When he says (p. 54): "We know that nothing can be lost," the most that he is entitled to mean is that there will always be effects, of some kind somewhere, causally connected with that which happens to us now. But this is by no means all that he does mean, nor is it what, to anybody else, will make that assurance sound so comfortable. He does, as we have tried to show, mean also (*a*) that the effect of our past *within each one of us* will always be very great; (*b*) that this effect will have considerable similarity, not only in value, but also in quality, to its cause; and the arguments which he gives for these two conclusions cannot, as we have seen, justify them. The most that he is entitled to assume is that the middle of our next life will have to the end of this one as close a causal relation as the end of this one has to its middle. But it certainly seems that the most valuable states and relations of middle life may have ceased to have any but the slightest effect upon our condition in old age: there may certainly be a great difference between the two, and the change [198] may be greatly for the worse. This being so, it is as likely as not that, after two or three lives, the effect of our present lives upon *us* would have become quite negligible, and that our character and value would differ as much from what they now are, as those of any two living men differ from one another. Under these circumstances Immortality seems to promise us but little advantage. Only one of the arguments, which Mr. McTaggart advances in its favour, seems to be sound in principle. This is that the indefinite prolongation of our existence would increase the chances of the consummation or renewal of personal relations, with which misfortune has interfered in this life (p. 44); but I am afraid that even the chance thus obtained would turn out to be so very small as to be scarcely worth considering; and there must, in any case, be set against it increased chances of misfortune for those who have been fortunate in this life.

So far we have been considering the value of such future lives as Mr. McTaggart is, consistently with his premises, entitled to promise us. And it is well to remember two points:—(1) That his arguments to prove that we should have even such future lives as these, entirely broke down: we have no reason to believe that we are immortal even in his sense; and (2) that we have only been considering the "*actual*" character of those lives, neglecting, on the one hand, the substance and unchangeable attributes, with regard to which there seemed such doubt, whether they did *not* exist in time at all, or existed permanently through time, and, on the other, those "*potential*" characters, by which we understand Mr. McTaggart to mean any past or future character of one and the same person, which, at the time in question, he does *not* actually possess. Mr. McTaggart himself, as we have seen, rests his pleas for the value of immortality upon the *actual* characters which he thinks he can prove we shall possess; and there can be no doubt that our desire for immortality largely depends upon them; nobody can set much store [199] upon the hope of a future perfection, such as according to Mr. McTaggart he possesses already—a perfection which is and will be utterly imperceptible both to himself and to others; nor upon a future life in which, what he has lost in this, will still be just as truly lost and past, as it is now, even though he may believe that it is now *potentially* present and will be then.

So far, then, we have seen Mr. McTaggart maintaining (without good reason) that there will persist something which may fairly be called *we*; and ascribing to this something a character much more valuable than his premises will justify. But he also raises another question, important enough to deserve some notice. Let us grant (what I cannot see my way to deny) that a certain kind of causal relation between a series of mental states is sufficient to justify us in saying that they belong to the *same person*. There still remains the question: Is a series of states having this causal relation *all* that we mean by ourselves? Is the continuance of such a series what we desire when we desire that ourselves should persist after death? I think Mr. McTaggart has not given sufficient consideration to these questions. His definition of personal identity is perhaps adequate to one sense in which the word is used: "personal identity" may be sometimes used in philosophy, and rightly used, to mean no more than this; and it certainly cannot be rightly predicated of anything which does *not* possess the properties by which Mr. McTaggart defines it. But it is quite another question whether, when we desire the continued existence of our own or other selves, we are not desiring the existence of something quite different, and I think that Mr. McTaggart's argument is apt to convey the delusive impression that this is not another question: his definition of "personal identity" is, he says, *the* right one, and it would seem to follow that, if we desire the continuance of our personality at all, we must be desiring that which he defines.

[200] Mr. McTaggart has, no doubt, given himself the right to reply that what we mean by ourselves is not only such a causal series of states, but the whole formed by such a series together with the identical substance of which they are attributes. But he has himself admitted in this chapter that it is not the substance but the attributes which give to such a whole the chief part of what we mean by "personal identity." "All substances," he says (p. 37), "if abstraction were made of their attributes, are absolutely indistinguishable, and the distinction between persons would be non-

existent." And later (p. 39) we find:—"Nor does personal identity seem to have much meaning, if it loses its connection with the special and unique interest which we feel in our own future as distinguished from that of any one else?" It is plain, then, from these two passages, that according to Mr. McTaggart (1) when we speak of "the same person," the phrase has not "much meaning," unless it refers to that which distinguishes the person in question from all other persons; (2) that what does distinguish each of us from any one else is not our substance. To this we may add that what gives "special and unique interest" to our own future, cannot be the permanent and unchangeable attributes, with which Mr. McTaggart endows us, since these are *ex hypothesi* unknown to us. It follows that what thus interests us, and is therefore the only thing which gives "much meaning" to personal identity, must lie somewhere in the causally connected series of changing states. And our question is:—Does that which thus interests us in this series of states, and which alone gives "much meaning" to personal identity, consist in the mere fact that they are causally connected with our present state? If it does not, then that by which Mr. McTaggart defines personal identity is *not* that which, by his own admission, will alone give "much meaning" to personal identity.

Now I cannot but think that what gives to our own future a special and unique interest for us, is not this mere fact that it [201] will have a special and unique causal relation to our present. And, at the same time, I agree with Mr. McTaggart that that which does give to our own future this special interest *is* that which constitutes our main reason for calling it *ours*: when we think of a future person as identical with ourselves, the chief part of what we mean by this is that he has that relation to our present selves, which makes him uniquely interesting to us. What is it then in our own past and future, which at the same time makes us call it ours, and gives us an unique interest in it? What is it which we really desire when we desire the continuance of our personal identity?

This is a very difficult question, and one in answering which we should be glad to have had more help than Mr. McTaggart gives us. His treatment of the subject seems to be almost entirely governed by the desire to prove that this valuable element which constitutes our "selves" is *not* memory, whatever else it may be. His argument that we shall live again must, he sees, prove equally that we have lived before; and since we certainly do not now remember our former lives, he recognises, as we have seen, an improbability that we shall in the future remember this one. This being so, he must either admit that what he promises to us is of little value, or else he must maintain that "memory," which he cannot promise us, is *not* the valuable element in personal identity. This latter, therefore, he tries to prove; but, having refuted the claims of memory, he seems to assume at once that there can be no other candidates, except his "causal relation," for the honour of being what we value in "personal identity," and what we mean by it, when we give it "much meaning." I think he both grossly underrates the value that is and ought to be set on memory, and also fails to see what other elements there are for which we justly prize *ourselves*.

"Suppose a man," says Mr. McTaggart (p. 40), "could be assured that in a short time he would lose for ever all memory of the past. Would he consider this to be annihilation, and take [202] no more interest in the person of similar character who would occupy his old body than he would in a stranger? Or, would a man approaching the gate of hell lose all selfish regret for his position if he was assured that memory, as well as hope, must be left behind on his entrance? It is not, I think, found that believers in transmigration are indifferent to their fate after their next death. And yet they believe, in the majority of cases, that the next death will, for the time at least, break the chain of memory as completely as the last did?" Let us grant that all this is true. Does it prove either that the possession of memory is not essential to any personal identity, which is to have "much meaning" for us, or that a causal relation to ourselves is the only thing which is essential to this? Surely not; and that mainly owing to the very elementary psychological fact, which we might think Mr. McTaggart had never noticed, namely, that a man may be fully convinced, in any ordinary sense of conviction—may even be ready to die for the truth of his opinion—that a certain predicate does *not* attach to a certain subject, and yet whenever he *imagines* that subject, as he must do when he is impressed by its desirability, may quite unconsciously include in it the very predicate, of which both then and at all other times he is ready to asseverate the absence. This certainly *may* be the case with the believer in transmigration; and if it even *may* be, what Mr. McTaggart says, affords no jot of support for his conclusion. But I am inclined to believe that it not only may be, but is the case; and in the hope both of making this opinion plausible, and of throwing some light on what we really mean by our "selves," I will dwell a little upon the psychological analysis of the supposed cases.

A man says, "It is *me* that the devil will be torturing," and he at once feels for the sufferer a pang of pity, which would not be excited in him by the idea of a very much better man suffering the same torture. Such an interest certainly is normally excited, whenever the subject under discussion is conceived as "me" or "mine." But, this being the case, [203] that interest will not cease to be excited, merely because I have arrived at a reasoned conviction, that "me" *can* only include something in which I take no interest. Hume was not prevented from having the same selfish feelings as Mr. McTaggart by the fact that he believed his self to be quite a different kind of thing from that which Mr. McTaggart believes his to be. Let us apply this doctrine to the believer in transmigration. Mr. McTaggart grants us that he conceives the future soul as "*his*." That being so its fate will excite the same emotions which the fate of anything conceived as "his" normally excites; and even if he has made a wrong philosophical analysis of what that "his" includes—though he has, for instance, excluded memory from it—this opinion, however strongly held, will not prevent him from being influenced by elements which really enter into what he means by "himself," and which are far more closely associated in his mind with the word "me" than any philosophical definition can be. A materialist's opinion that his body is all that he cares about offers not the slightest evidence that his soul may not be the almost exclusive object of his attention: what it is good evidence of is that his powers of analysis are defective. And since the meaning of "self" is notoriously one of the most difficult problems of analysis—so much so that the ablest intellects have always differed as to its meaning—there can surely be no reason to think that the common herd, even of believers in transmigration, have succeeded in discovering what they mean by it—in knowing what it is in the idea of themselves which really influences feelings. If so, when a Buddhist thinks "The soul in that animal will be myself, but it will not remember its present state," can there be any reason to suppose that when he imagines it as *himself*, he does not imagine it as remembering his present state? In other words, that the thought which is expressed by the first half of his sentence, may flatly contradict that which is expressed by the second, without causing him the slightest uneasiness?

[204] What, then, do we really think of when we think of our future selves, or when we try to put the case, "Supposing I had been you?" Our feelings certainly may be influenced by the thought of our *body* or of our *character*. The importance of both these considerations is implied by Mr. McTaggart when he says, in the passage just quoted, "Would he take no more interest in the person *of similar character* who would occupy his *old body* than he would in any stranger?" and yet, as we have seen, he takes no account of the *body*, in his description of what gives "meaning" to personal identity, while he is mistaken in supposing that similarity of character follows from that description. But, after all,

neither the nature of our body nor that of our character is what chiefly interests us in ourselves. This may be plainly seen by considering a case, which is certainly imaginable, though Mr. McTaggart denies it to be possible (p. 51), that of an exact double of ourselves, exactly similar to us both in body and in character. Such a double, Mr. McTaggart here implies, would, if it were possible, be the *same* person with ourselves; for, says he, identical attributes imply identical substance; but it is obviously self-contradictory to suppose it the same, and hence this conclusion, if it does follow from Mr. McTaggart's theory of personal identity, can only serve to refute that theory. The imaginary case of a double does, in fact, absolutely refute the theory that what interests us in our past and future, and makes us call them ours, is *identity* of attributes; but I think that Mr. McTaggart is in this passage unjust to his own theory, since he appears to confuse identity of attributes with their continuity, although he has elsewhere explained that continuity means causal connection, which is quite a different thing. A double of ourselves, existing simultaneously with ourselves, could obviously not have to us that causal connection, which, we agreed, is a necessary condition of personal identity; and hence the absence of this connection might conceivably be what we should predicate of it when we called it a different [205] person. It *might* be so, but it certainly would not be so: the consideration of this case does, in fact, refute the theory that either identity or continuity of attributes, or both together, is what we *mean* by personal identity.

We can, in fact, imagine a future series of mental states, which should be both causally continuous and identical in character with ours, and which yet should not be what we mean by calling them ours: the hypothesis of a new self like us, coming into being at some point of time, instead of our present self continuing , has, in fact, a *meaning* for us, as Mr. McTaggart shows by arguing that it is actually impossible. It is, I admit, actually impossible: such a series of states would, in fact, be *also* what we mean by ourselves; it would not be a new self: but that this statement should be significant, that we should understand the proposition that a series of states, both causally continuous and identical in character with our present self, would, in fact, be not a new self but our own self, shows conclusively that what we mean by personal identity is neither causal continuity nor identity of character, nor both together. What is it, then, that we do mean? I can quite well imagine that a person exactly similar to me, both in body and character, should now be sitting in that chair opposite to me; and it is certainly not the mere fact that he is sitting in that chair and I in this, which causes the profound difference which I feel between my interest in his fate and in my own. If I have certain qualities which I admire, and which others are without, I may care slightly more for him than for those people, because he possesses those qualities, and I may think that they give him a better claim to immortality. Only in so far as I give him this preference can it be supposed that the *character* of my body and my mind is what interests me in myself; and, in fact, the preference which I allow him on this score is extremely small compared with that which I give to myself over the same people. To confess the truth, I feel a positive repugnance to him; and, in any case, my desire for his immortality is [206] immeasurably weaker than my desire for my own. It would be just the same to my friends in all obvious respects if I were annihilated at once and he continued to exist; and it would certainly have the same effect upon the world at large; and yet I cannot contemplate this event with the smallest satisfaction. Surely, then, what I chiefly *mean* by myself, what is the object of my self-love, must be that which distinguishes me from him.

It is, in fact, absurd to suppose that that which, when it exists simultaneously with us, entirely lacks the special and unique interest for us, which gives meaning to "self," would, by the mere fact of a special causal relation to us, acquire that interest. We do not value our past and future merely because they are like us and causally connected with us. What gives meaning to "self" for us is that which distinguishes our *present* self from any conceivable simultaneous existent, however like us it might be; and we value the states causally connected with our present self, not because they are so connected, but because they are states of that which thus distinguishes our present self: it is this which we mean when we call them *our* past and future. The permanent self must, in any case, be defined as the causal series connected with *our present self*: our self can only be defined by reference to that which makes us ourselves *now*. This, then, which distinguishes us from any other thing or person *at the present moment* is certainly what constitutes the chief element in the meaning of self; and this being so, it seems extremely unlikely that, when we come to think of ourselves as continued in the past or future, when, in fact, we consider personal identity through time, we should mean by that continued self something merely related causally to our present self. Since "self" means to us mainly our *present* self, it is almost unavoidable that, when we think of our self at another position in time, we should mean our present self at that position; and this seems to me to be actually the case.

[207] What, then, is it which gives this special and unique interest to our present self? What *is* the present self whose continued existence we desire? In order to answer these questions, we must, I think, take two distinct points into account. (1) When we consider our present selves, or are impressed by their value, we are, of course, self-conscious. But what we have to note is that this consciousness of ourselves is an experience completely different in kind from our consciousness of any other person. We never know any one else's consciousness in the same way in which we know our own, namely, by direct perception. That is to say, the object of our consciousness, when we are conscious of our self, is

not the same in kind as when we think of any other self; and this difference in kind is equally great, in spite of complete identity in character, emotions, or other objects of consciousness. But (2) we know that every other person is conscious of an exactly similar object, and each of only one such object—himself. And to know this is to know that our self is, in fact, identical in kind with every other self. The self which we perceive is the same in kind with the self which another perceives, though it is different in kind from any other self which we or another person think of. That is to say, it does, in fact, differ *numerically only*[2] from any other self, although its perception of itself also differs in kind from its thought of any other self.

Putting these two points together, we get the result that what we value in ourselves is (1) of the kind of that which is presented to us in self-consciousness, and (2) differs numerically only from many other beings of the same kind. When, therefore, we desire that ourselves should persist in preference to others, we are desiring that one single instance of a certain kind, differing in no respect from other instances, except that it is one and they are others, should persist in preference to [208] others: *i.e.*, we do set a value on our mere numerical difference from others. But, on the other hand, we do not strongly desire that this numerically singular self, merely as it is conceived or thought of, should persist, but as it is actually perceived; and it is this second point which seems to me to show the importance of memory in our conception of personal identity. We must, of course, admit that this unique thing, having the qualities perceived in it, may continue to exist, even at times when those qualities are not perceived in it. It may, too, perceive itself at such future times. But the thought of either possibility leaves the imagination cold: we are only conceiving it when we thus think of it. And this defect is remedied by memory and by memory only. The only sense in which we use personal identity with "much meaning"—the only sense in which we much desire it—is that in which what is meant by the past or future self has the same relation to the present self, as the present self has to itself. And this relation is given by memory. When we remember our past states we have to them the same unique relation which we have to the present object-self, and when we think of our future self as remembering our present, it is again not mere thinking, since we are relating it as subject to the present object-self which is actually perceived. Of course, we do speak of retaining our personal identity, without meaning that the future self will have memory of our present self at every moment; but we feel hesitation, even in so speaking of it, unless we think of it as *capable* of so remembering, as it is in this present life. And by this *capability* we do not mean a mere potentiality: we mean a very real relation, which does exist between the various periods of our present life, and which would not exist between that and such a future life as Mr. McTaggart promises us. Even when we are remembering no past state, our present state is one which will probably be remembered, and remembered along with some other state which it does not now remember. And when we think of a future state which [209] does not remember our present, it will yet probably be one which remembers some other, which did remember our present, or which remembered what our present now remembers. Even if this be not the case, the future state will at least be one which remembers some other, which in its turn remembers some other, which in its turn remembers or is remembered by the present. Such relations of memory may, of course, have any number of steps. But it seems to me that, however many the steps, they are very important constituents of our conception of personal identity. For it must be insisted that each step involves a relation, which, unlike the causal relation, is only possible between two states of one person; and that by a series of such steps every state in our present life is probably related to our present self in a way in which no state of any other person ever can be so related.

To conclude, I will sum up the most important points in which this theory of what gives "meaning" to personal identity, appears to me an improvement on Mr. McTaggart's. (1) Mr. McTaggart appears to attribute far too much importance to a causal connection between our states or characters in the sense in which these, or a combination of them, may be different in kind from those of other persons, or from one another. In his own language, he lays in this chapter too much stress upon the connection of our "attributes" as distinguished from our substance. But, in fact, it seems plain that our present attributes are specially valued by us chiefly because they are *ours*; and those that are causally connected with them, not because of that connection, but partly because of the indirect connection which they thus obtain with our present self, and still more because they are related to a past and future self, which is directly, and apart from them, identical with ours. Thus the causal connection, on which Mr. McTaggart insists so much, is only important as giving a partial explanation of how some of our attributes come to be thought *ours*: it [210] does not at all explain what we mean by calling them ours. The relation of the attributes and the substance in respect of value is that, though the attributes may have some value in themselves, and the substance perhaps none at all, yet the two together have an immensely greater value than the attributes by themselves could have; and the attributes can only have this value, not as being causally connected with an attribute which has it, but only as being related to the substantial self, in the same way in which that attribute is related to it. (2) But Mr. McTaggart does also insist on the necessity of identity of substance for personal identity; and so far he may be thought to agree with the view I have proposed. In fact, however, his view of the substance of the self suffers from a defect which is due to the same cause as his emphasis of the attributes. Mr. McTaggart probably emphasises the part played by the attributes in the notion of self, because he thinks that two things, if they differ at all, must differ in kind: that this is the only kind of difference is indeed an almost universal assumption of philosophic tradition. He must, he thinks, explain the uniqueness of each self, by its having sole attribute which no other self has, since, as a self—*i.e.*, in respect of its substance—it is identical in kind with every other. Accordingly, in the quotation given above, he states that "all substances are absolutely indistinguishable." This constitutes a very important difference between his view and that which I now advocate. I have been compelled to look for the unique interest which we take in ourselves, not in our attributes, but in the fact that they are *ours*. But this (except by a vicious circle) can only mean: in the fact that they belong to our substance. Then, recognising, with Mr. McTaggart, that "all substances are absolutely indistinguishable" *in kind*, it follows that we are interested in ourselves as distinguished from others, solely because we are capable of taking an interest in something which differs merely numerically from others, and on account of its numerical singularity. With regard to [211] the justness of this valuation, we must, of course, allow that we are not really more valuable than others; but we need not, therefore, deny that the loss of ourself would be a loss, which the existence of none other could replace. Not to deny this recognises that mere numerical difference can give a value to a thing; and this principle, it seems to me, is implied in our preferential valuation of ourselves. Finally, (3) Mr. McTaggart does not give sufficient consideration to what is meant by the persistence of an identical substance throughout time. It has been already pointed out that he does not clearly distinguish whether the substance, which is ourself, exists timelessly or throughout time. But waiving this point, and assuming, what he certainly implies, that the identical self may *persist*, it must be insisted (1) that this persistence cannot be regarded as a mere causal connection between the existence of the self at one time and its existence at others, and (2) that the mere existence of the identical self at all times does not seem to be all that we mean by personal identity, nor what we mainly set a value on. It seems to me that, if we are to regard a past and future self as really identical with ourselves, we must regard it not merely as an identical substance with our present selves, nor as having an unique causal relation to them, but as bound to them by a relation of self-consciousness—the perceptual relation which we have to our present selves. That such a relation does exist in our present life I have tried to point out; and also that Mr. McTaggart's attempt to convince us that we do not set much store by it does not prove his point. Personally I may say that the future life he promises me—a life in which I should have no memory at all of this life—is to my feeling barely distinguishable from the future existence of another person.

So much, then, for the first of Mr. McTaggart's cosmological chapters. I have divided my criticism of it into two parts, and will now briefly sum up what I have tried to prove.

[212] I. Mr. McTaggart tries to prove that Reality consists exclusively of minds, similar to and including our own. This proof constitutes what I have called the properly Cosmological part of the chapter; and its validity is essential to the importance of the other two cosmological chapters, which only try to decide upon the nature of and relations between these minds, which alone are real. Obviously they will not be cosmology, unless it is certain that such minds do constitute the whole of reality.

But so far from this being certain, I have urged that Mr. McTaggart has not given us the smallest reason for thinking it probable. For the proof depends partly upon an exceedingly long chain of argument (supposed by Mr. McTaggart to be contained in Hegel's *Logic*), of the complete validity of which nobody ever has or ever will be rationally, or otherwise, convinced. And, if this were not sufficient to condemn the conclusion as the idlest supposition, there is further necessary to the demonstration a false and self-contradictory theory of the nature of consciousness, and its relation to its object.

II. Deals with Immortality. So far as this bears its ordinary meaning of existence throughout time, I think Mr. McTaggart should have clearly separated his discussion of it from Cosmology proper: since he holds that nothing which exists in time is real, and hence the question whether we exist throughout time is merely a question of phenomenology—a question of what, though certainly false, "appears" (to whom?) to be true. To those, indeed, who hold that what exists in time is real, this discussion may seem more important than and quite as cosmological as the other.

On this head I have urged the following points:—

(1) Mr. McTaggart, though he states the contrary, certainly implies that he has proved not merely our "timeless" or "eternal" existence, but our duration throughout time.

[213] (2) He does not see that the two are incompatible; and since his arguments prove only (if they prove anything) that *either* the one *or* the other is true, he certainly has not given us the smallest reason for supposing that we shall endure throughout time.

(3) He ascribes to our duration through time several valuable qualities which his premises (especially that which defines the relation between the successive states of the *same* person) utterly fail to justify.

(4) He is mistaken in supposing that that which he defines as constituting, or as a sign of, personal identity, is what we really mean by that word or desire under that name. On the contrary, he omits from his description of the next life, much of what makes our continuance in this life really valuable, and almost everything that makes us desire it.

We are left then with the conviction that we have no reason to think ourselves immortal even in Mr. McTaggart's sense; and that, even if we were, such immortality would, in all important points, be indistinguishable from the future existence of other persons, and these, for all that Mr. McTaggart can tell us, continually worse and worse.

The two remaining cosmological chapters must now be dismissed very briefly.

The first of these (Chapter III) tries to show that the Reality, which the last chapter has concluded to be composed of a number of persons, is not itself also one person; from which it follows that, since the word God properly denotes a person, the Absolute, if Mr. McTaggart is right about its nature, is not God, and also (since the word also denotes a supreme being) that "there is no God." This latter conclusion depends, of course, upon the correctness of that arrived at in Chapter II; and we cannot, therefore, allow to it the smallest validity. The chapter can have no direct bearing on the view we are to take of the nature of reality as a whole or of supersensible reality. The most philosophically interesting question [214] which is relevant to Mr. McTaggart's argument is the question whether, and in what sense, one person can be part of another person. But even with this question Mr. McTaggart does not deal directly, confining himself to criticising some confused arguments of Lotze, which are intended to show that it is the case.

The importance of the conclusions of Chapter IX also depends mainly upon the validity of Chapter II. If, as I have tried to show, there is no reason to think that Reality is composed exclusively of conscious spirits, Mr. McTaggart's view as to how these spirits are related to one another ceases to have any profound interest. The chief interest of the chapter lies in its ethical conclusion, that the love of persons for one another is not only the greatest, but the sole, Good. But this conclusion Mr. McTaggart does not attempt to prove directly. He assumes, as a result of the Dialectic, that the Universe is perfect, and then tries to prove, by a combination of the results of Chapter II with the Dialectic, that the Universe consists of loving persons. That such a Universe would be perfect, therefore, only follows as a result from one argument, which is not given to us, in combination with a further development of others which we have seen every reason to distrust.

This further development, which consists chiefly in a discussion of the nature of Knowledge and Volition, and of the questions (1) whether they can be real; (2) whether they do not "postulate an ideal which they can never reach as long as they remain" themselves; (3) whether this ideal is Love is of considerable interest in itself, but I have not space to discuss it here.

NOTES

1. They are in fact compatible in a sense; but the existence in time cannot be the same thing as the existence out of time, and since, in speaking of one and the same *object*, we usually *include* its existence in its notion, it is a contradiction to affirm that an object existing in time also exists timelessly. The same defence applies to my statement made on p. 186, that "one and the same person is both inside and outside me" is self-contradictory.

2. For some explanation of the meaning of this term, *see* my paper on "Identity," *Proceedings of Arist. Soc.*, 1900–01.

8

Experience and Empiricism

Almost all philosophers now-a-days are agreed in speaking respectfully of "Experience." Before Kant's time philosophers were divided into Empiricists, on the one hand, and, on the other, those who held that so many and such important conclusions could be derived from "innate truths" alone, that they despised the aid of "Experience." Now-a-days "innate truths" are wholly out of fashion; and though "pure thought" may still be thought to do a great deal, its function is generally limited to the "interpretation of experience." This change is due to Kant, and its full significance is, I think, rarely recognised. The statement that Kant made "experience" the *sole premiss* of all our knowledge will probably sound strange to many; and it may seem even stranger to hear that those who reject his conclusion that our knowledge is *limited* to "possible experience," do not for the most part differ from him in making experience their sole premiss. Yet I think it is easy to see that Kant did do this. Kant tries to defend the truth of "synthetic *a priori* propositions" by showing that they are "conditions for the possibility of experience." This he can only do by

Originally published in *Proceedings of the Aristotelian Society* n.s. 3 (1902–1903): 80–95.

showing that they are implied in actual experience. But to show that A is implied by B will not prove that A is true, unless it is assumed that B is true. That Geometry has a claim to validity, which Spinoza's "geometrically demonstrated" Ethics has not got, rests for Kant on the fact that the former is and the latter is not implied in "experience." Spinoza's system may quite well contain nothing but "conditions for the possibility" of something other than actual experience; but the difference in validity between it and geometry would still remain for Kant. It is, therefore, only [81] the fact that actual experience is true which gives Kant a reason for asserting the validity of "transcendental" and denying that of "transcendent" knowledge. Experience is true, and geometry is implied in it; therefore, geometry is true. Such is Kant's reasoning. To have rested the claim of geometry on its bare self-evidence would not have satisfied him; for the "transcendent" metaphysics, which he declares to be "unscientific," might make exactly the same claim. He thinks he has *proved* the validity of geometry, and *disproved* the possibility of transcendent metaphysics; and for this proof "Experience" is his *sole premiss.*[1]

Now subsequent non-empirical philosophers differ from Kant, for the most part, only in maintaining that more is implied in "experience" than he could find to be so. They do not claim, any more than he did, to have other and independent premisses for their conclusions, such as the pre-Kantian dogmatists assumed. But this fact suggests two questions, which the following paper attempts to answer:—I. How much do philosophers assume when they assume "Experience" as their sole premiss? II. In what essential respect do Kant and non-empirical post-Kantians differ from such philosophers as Hume and Mill, who are deservedly called "empirical?"

In answer to the first question, I shall endeavour to show that, in assuming "Experience" as a premiss, philosophers assume the truth of a vast number of propositions, which, as a matter of fact, they subsequently conclude to be false.

In answer to the second, I shall endeavour to show that empiricists are distinguished, not by any theory of the *source* of knowledge, but by the fact that they constantly imply that all known truths are of *the same kind as* experiences, although, in fact, they assume the knowledge of truths which are not of this kind.

[82] I.—*Experience,* in its common philosophical significance, seems to denote a sum of actual experiences. Thus "my experience" or "your experience" means the sum of my or your experiences; and "experience" without such qualification commonly stands for the sum of human experiences. "Experience" does, however, also denote that common character, in virtue of which actual experiencs are classed together; and it is obvious that only this common character is susceptible of definition, since the number and variety of actual experiences is too great to be exhausted. "Experience," then, denotes a kind of cognition; and, like "cognition" and "knowledge" themselves, the word stands for a double fact: (*a*) a mental state, and (*b*) that of which this mental state is cognizant. Thus "an experience," like "an observation," may stand either for the observing of something or for that which is observed.

The kind of mental state denoted by cognition or consciousness is itself of too simple a nature to admit of definition: it is something which can be easily recognised as one and the same, existing in all instances of cognition, and differing from the various objects of which it is the cognition. It will not be disputed, however, that cognitions are *also* distinguished from all other kinds of mental existents, if any such there be, by the fact that they always do stand in a unique kind of relation to something else—something, namely, of which they are cognitions; and the kinds of cognitions are commonly distinguished by the kinds of object of which they are cognitions. That they also differ in themselves would appear to be proved by the fact that one cognition may be the cause of another cognition, although the object of the first is the cause of something entirely different from the object of the second—*e.g.*, in the case of association by similarity. But that there is nevertheless no objection to distinguishing the kinds of cognition by the kinds of their objects would appear to be proved by the fact that in all cases where we know the effects [83] of a cognition they seem to be connected by a uniform law with the nature of the object of that cognition. It would seem, then, that though cognitions are distinguished from one another by intrinsic differences, these differences always correspond to some difference in the nature of their object. In dividing them, then, according to the nature of the objects, we shall be dividing them truly; and no other course seems open to us, since no one has yet succeeded in pointing out wherein the intrinsic difference of one cognition from another lies.

(1) The first great division between objects of consciousness is between those which are true and those which are false; and "experience" is generally and properly confined to the class of cognitions of what is true: a "false experience" would be commonly allowed to be a contradiction in terms. The word "cognition" itself is sometimes confined, as its etymology suggests to awareness or consciousness of what is *true* in which case it is equivalent to "knowledge." But a "false cognition" would not be so generally recognised as a contradiction in terms, as "a false experience" or "false knowledge"; and since the word is grammatically more convenient than "awareness" or "consciousness," I have used it above, and shall use it below, as equivalent to these terms. "An experience," then, is a true cognition; and it must be noted that there is no evidence that a true cognition has any intrinsic difference from a false one, since none of the properties of objects with which the psychological laws of sequence appear to be connected is universally a mark of truth. Thus a true cognition may as readily cause a false one by the laws of association, or a false cognition a true one, as either may produce one of its own kind in this respect. Any cognition of which the object is "that a thing is true" does indeed differ intrinsically from any cognition

of which the object is "that a thing is false;" but the cognitions of the things themselves do not so differ. In truth, then, we have a mark of all the [84] *objects* of experience to which, so far as is known, no intrinsic property in the states of mind cognizant of them corresponds, although every true proposition differs from any false one.

But (2) not all cognitions are true experiences. The objects of experience all fall within the class of true propositions about existing things; and existence is a mark to which we have reason to suppose that something in the state of mind corresponds—*i.e.*, states of mind cognizant of existential truths differ intrinsically from those which are cognizant of any other class of truths, although they do not differ intrinsically from those which are cognizant of false existential propositions.

But (3) the very same existential truths which we experience may at another time be known to us by memory, or at the very time when we experience them another mind may have attained to a knowledge of them by inference or mere imagination. What is it which distinguishes our experience of them from that knowing of them to which we give these names? The distinction for which we are to look is that which, in Hume's language, divides "impressions" from "ideas." He held that this distinction consisted merely in the superior "liveliness" of the impressions; and it seems to be true that, at most times when we are experiencing, some part of what we experience is cognized with a "liveliness" superior to that, which belongs to most of our memories or imaginations; so that by far the greater number of our "lively" cognitions are experiences. But (*a*) it must be remembered that at each moment of normal experience we have experience of a vast variety of objects: and it would seem certain that, whatever this "liveliness" may be, only a comparatively small number out of this variety—namely, those which are near the centre of attention, are cognized with more liveliness than most imaginations; yet all are certainly experienced. And (*b*) there seems no reason to doubt that some true imaginations may, like hallucinations, possess as high a degree of liveliness as any experience. There does not, therefore, seem to be any intrinsic [85] property either in an experience or in its object which will serve to distinguish it from all imaginations. We are driven to the conclusion that an experience is in itself quite indistinguishable from a true imagination, memory, or inference, and, if it is to be precisely distinguished from these, can only be so by the circumstances under which it occurs. But language certainly demands such a distinction; it would be generally felt that the term "experience" should denote something which cannot, even in a single case, be identical with that which is denoted by mere imagination: and hence we must say that exactly the same cognition, when occurring under certain circumstances, is properly called an experience, and, when occurring under different circumstances, a mere imagination.

When once it is thus recognised that an experience is to be defined not merely by any intrinsic properties of itself or its object, but also by its circumstances, it becomes easy to distinguish it from *memory* and *inference*. The only difference which seems to differentiate these from it in all cases is one of this extrinsic kind —namely, (*a*) in the case of memory, that it has among its causes a previous cognition of the same object, whereas any object can be *experienced* only once; and (*b*) in the case of inference, that it has among its causes a mental process of a peculiar kind, which is never among the causes of an experience. Moreover, this method of defining experience has been very frequently adopted; an experience has been generally held to be distinguished from other cognitions by its origin or accompaniments.

There still, however, remains the case of certain true imaginations. What kind of circumstances will always distinguish these from experiences?

1. It has been proposed to define experience as "immediate"

knowledge. This is a negative definition, referring to the absence of mental causes. But there are certainly some imaginations of which we do not know the mental causes. We [86] cannot, therefore, assign any definite class of mental causes which is invariably found among the causes of an imagination and invariably wanting among the causes of an experience; and to say, what is probably true—namely, that imaginations always have some kind of mental cause, which experiences are without, is merely to say that they *can* be defined by their mental causes: it does not itself constitute that definition. It may, perhaps, be said that among the causes of every imagination is some previous experience; but, even if this be true, it requires an independent definition of experience before it can itself be taken as a definition of imagination. Nor, finally, are we entitled to assert that experiences have no mental causes, because we know of none. Accordingly in any sense in which we are entitled to assert that experiences are immediate, except that which makes immediacy deny causation by previous experiences, we have an equal right to call some imaginations immediate.

2. It is, perhaps, true that all experiences are accompanied by cognitions of objects closely related to their own—that their objects are always members of a simultaneously cognized continuum. But it is certain that some imaginations, if only their objects be true, may be thus related to both experiences and imaginations occurring simultaneously.

3. It would seem, then, that the only method of distinguishing an experience from an imagination is by means of antecedents or accompaniments other than mental. Let us take the case in which the same object is simultaneously experienced by one man and imagined by another. The total antecedents and accompaniments of both cognitions are the same. If, then, they are distinguished by their antecedents, this must mean, not that they have different antecedents, but that the one has to some of their common antecedents a relation which the other has not got. Nor can this rela-

tion be identified with invariable antecedence, since in this case the imagination and the experience have the relation in [87] question to different antecedents, and consequently neither set of antecedents can be said to precede invariably the cognition which is in one case an experience and in the other an imagination. We must, then, understand the statement that an identical imagination and experience are distinguished by the circumstances under which they occur, as meaning that the one has the same relation to some of its circumstances which the other has to others, and that this is a relation which neither has to all; and this relation would seem to be sufficiently defined by the fact that from the circumstances in question you could infer the future existence of the cognition, although from the existence of the cognition you could not infer which set of circumstances had preceded it. If we call this relation "causal," then we may say that an experience is always distinguished from a true imagination by the nature of its physical causes; and there does, in fact, seem to be a class of causes, capable of exact definition, some member of which class is always among the causes of an experience, but never among those of an imagination. Each different experience has, indeed, a different cause; but the class to which all such causes must belong may be defined in the following way:—

Every event, and consequently every experience, has this causal relation to some set of circumstances at every preceding moment, the set becoming larger and larger as you recede in time from the event in question. Among these sets (which may each be called *one* of the causes of any given experience in a different sense from which each member of any one of them may be called *one* of its causes) there will always be one of which the thing or event, the existence of which is the object of the experience, is a member. Among the causes of an imagination, on the other hand, the thing or event, whose existence is its object, will never be thus included. It follows from this that among the *accompaniments* of an experience there will always also be some having to it the special relation that its existence could be inferred from theirs, and that these accompaniments [88] will be different for an experience from what they would be for an imagination; but *this* difference is not capable of a definition which shall be at the same time general and exact, since the condition which renders such a definition possible in the case of antecedents—namely, the identity between part of the object of an experience and part of one of its causes, does not hold for its accompaniments. It must be noticed that in cases where the object of the experience is the existence of something mental—*i.e.*, in the case of what have been called "experiences of the inner sense," the causes by which it is characterised as an experience will thus *ex hypothesi* include something mental. But it may be useful to observe that in this one case an alternative definition is abstractly possible, if, as seems probable, every kind of mental occurrence both invariably accompanies and is invariably accompanied by one peculiar kind of physical event—namely, that any cognition of a mental occurrence, among the causes of which is included the physical event having such relation to that occurrence, is an experience.

(4) Having thus defined the difference between experience and all other ways of cognizing the same objects, it remains to say something more with regard to the kinds of object which can be properly said to be experienced. It has been laid down above that all such objects must be true, and must be existential propositions. (i) From the first of these conditions it follows that every object of experience must be complex. That this is so is implied by all philosophers who hold, as all do, that inferences can be drawn from the subject-matter of experience; but it may be thought to conflict with the very common theory that *sensations* or *sense-impressions* are experiences. "Sensations" are frequently spoken of as if they or their objects might be simple; they are regarded as being or supplying the elements of knowledge. This difficulty,

however, seems to be merely due to the fact that "sensation" is commonly used to denote two quite different forms of cognition, which are not in [89] general clearly distinguished from one another. The proper and usual meaning of "sensation" is that in which it denotes a cognition of *the existence of* a simple quality; a sense in which "sensations" are experiences. But it is commonly thought that this is identical with the cognition of a simple quality, a form of cognition, which is undoubtedly possible, but which is by no means so important.

(ii) It may seem strange to some that the object of an experience should be called a proposition. But such object may undoubtedly be "the existence of such and such a thing," and it seems impossible to distinguish the cognition of this from the cognition "that such and such a thing exists." The object of experience, moreover, is undoubtedly true, and allows valid inferences to be drawn from it, both of which properties seem to be characteristic of propositions.

(iii) What types of proposition can be properly included under the description "propositions about existing things," and hence, as objects of experience, is a more difficult question. In ordinary life we do undoubtedly include, among the objects which we say we experience, successions and coexistences; and the usage of philosophers seems to be generally in agreement with this use of the term. We might thus be said, for instance, to experience the motion of a coloured point. Now, it would seem that this proposition would be properly interpreted in the form: "Such and such existing things, having this and that spatial position at this and that time, are divided from one another by such and such a spatial distance and such and such a temporal distance." But this is not strictly an existential proposition, nor can its meaning ever be exhausted by any number of such; it does not assert the existence of anything: it asserts that two or more existing things have certain relations. At most it is capable of analysis into "the position in space, occupied now by this, has such and such a spatial distance from the position occupied then by that," and "the position in time occupied by this here has such and such a temporal [90] distance from the position occupied by that there." But to allow that such propositions may be objects of experience involves a twofold modification of our definition. (*a*) We must extend the definition of "existential proposition" to include the assertion of a relation between existents of which the existence may be the object of experience. It is by such an inclusion of relations between existents that *perception* is distinguished from "sensation"; and perceptions are generally held to be experiences. (*b*) We must also allow that the existence of a position in space or time may be an object of experience. Yet it would be paradoxical to assert that positions in space or time could be among the causes of anything. We must, therefore, extend the definition of experience by adding that the existence of a thing which is not itself among the causes of an experience, yet if it be included in the proposition from which the effect may be inferred, may be an object of experience. This extension of our definition will certainly allow the existence of positions in space and time to be included among objects of experience. For every causal inference is from the fact that a thing exists *at a particular time and place* to the fact that something else will exist at a particular time and place. Though, therefore, we do in ordinary language restrict the term cause to the thing which so exists, yet the necessary connection involved in the term does not hold between its existence and that of its effect, but between their existence at their respective positions in time and space. The same extension of our definition will, however, also allow us to include among experiences cognitions that such and such a quality exists, apart from any specification of time and place. We have it, then, that an empirical proposition must either (*a*) assert truly the existence of one or more members of one of the following classes of entity—classes none of which is identical with any other or with the sum of any others: namely, (α) this here now, (β) this now, (γ) this here, (δ) this, (ε) this place now, (ζ) this place, (η) this time; or else (*b*) [91] must assert a relation between some members, not of these classes, but of the new classes formed in each case by all the existing members of each of them; or, finally, (*c*) must assert something collectively of some members of the classes last defined. Classes (*b*) and (*c*) may perhaps be more clearly defined in the following way—namely, that those only among relational and collective propositions can be objects of experience, or empirical, in which the terms related or grouped presuppose propositions of class (*a*).

(5) In the above manner (3) must an experience be defined if it is to be distinguished from every case of true imagination. It is to be noted, however, that the use of the word is commonly extended to include cases of imagination which resemble experiences in a respect which can only be defined by means of the above definition. For instance, when we see that a table is wooden, this would commonly be called a case of experience, although some part of the properties which we mean by "wooden" are certainly not among the objects of any cognition caused by the action of the table upon our eyes. In such a case our knowledge of the existence of these properties which have a certain spatial relation to those which *are* among the objects of sight, and are experienced, must be allowed to be a mere imagination, since it has not its objects among its causes; but we call it an experience, because its object is simultaneous with the object of an experience which is simultaneous with it. When, therefore, an imagination resembles a simultaneous experience by having the same temporal relation to its object, we commonly rank it as an experience of class (*a*); and cognitions, into which it enters in the same way as true experiences of class (*a*) enter into cognitions of classes (*b*) and (*c*) may also be called experiences.

II.—Having thus given a precise meaning to "experience," we

may now inquire in what sense, if any, *empiricism* can be defined as implying that "experience is the origin of all our knowledge."

[92] It is plain, in the first place, it cannot mean that experience is its own origin; and, therefore, that by "all our knowledge" we must understand all that is not itself experience.

But with regard to that part of our knowledge which is not itself experience: (i) it is certain that not every empiricist need deny, or imply the denial of, the fact that the brain co-operates with experience in determining what inferences, imaginations, and memories we shall have, just as it co-operates with the object in determining what experiences we shall have. It is not, then, essential to empiricism to hold that experience is the sole *cause* of all knowledge other than itself. And (ii) if our definition merely means that experience is *one* among the causes of all such knowledge, then this is not denied, but constantly implied, by many philosophers who are not empiricists: *e.g.*, when it is allowed that experience is necessary as an *occasion* for the knowledge of a necessary truth.

It remains, then, to inquire in what sense, if any, this definition will hold, supposing that by "origin" be meant "premise," and by "experience" and "knowledge" not our mental states, but the truths of which they are cognizant. Understood in this sense, the definition must mean that experience is the *sole premiss* of any truths we know which are not themselves experienced. But this doctrine, as was said above, fails to distinguish empiricists from Kant and from post-Kantian non-empirical philosophers; since they too imply that we have no title to asset the truth of any proposition which is not implied in experience.

It appears, then, that no implication with regard to the position of experiences as causes or as premises of all our knowledge will suffice to define empiricism. Yet empiricism does undoubtedly imply the assignation of some kind of pre-eminence to experience in respect of truth. There seems to remain but one way in which this can be done—namely, by implying that all the truths we know are of the same *kind* as [93] the objects of experience. From this principle it would follow that, in a sense, actual experience was the sole *test* of all our knowledge; since it would be true that we could know nothing but what *could* be experienced, and that consequently any piece of knowledge might be disproved by a possible observation or experiment. On the contrary, it is characteristic of non-empirical philosophers to hold that we have some pieces of knowledge which no possible experience could disprove, although almost all suffice to prove them. It would remain true, no doubt, that the empiricist must imply that we have pieces of knowledge which never are tested by actual experience, and which cannot (humanly speaking) be so—*e.g.*, that the moon is spherical. But this very fact helps to explain why the doctrine that "experience is the origin of all our knowledge" has been commonly supposed to define empiricism. For that doctrine by its very terms admits that we do know more than we actually experience, and yet, at the same time, exhibits a wish to maintain that experience is more certain, more truly knowledge, than anything else we know. This inconsistency may very naturally be suggested by the fact that what is of the same kind as an object of experience is just what *can* (in one sense) be experienced, although, as a matter of fact, it never can (in another sense) be experienced.

There seems, then, sufficient reason for taking this implication "That we can know nothing but what could be experienced, *i.e.*, what is of the same kind as what we do experience," to define empiricism; and this, if our definition of experience has been correct, is exactly equivalent to the definition—that empiricism is distinguished by the frequent implication that all known truths are truths about what exists at one or more moments of time. And the correctness of the definition is further confirmed by the fact that the most general and obvious characteristics of empirical systems seem naturally to follow from this presupposition. Thus

(1) empiricists are [94] always characterised by their treatment of so-called necessary truths, of which an extreme instance are the truths of arithmetic. These truths are not existential truths, and hence we find that empiricists tend either (*a*) to admit their truth, but to interpret them as analytic or insignificant; or (*b*) to interpret them as universal, and deny that we can know them. By the former device they are enabled to hold that such truths are mere parts of what we experience, not something different, which can indeed be inferred from experience, but cannot be disproved by it. On the other hand, the device of interpreting all such truths as universal is due to an attempt to assimilate them to existential truths of the form "all these things have this character," and thus to make them *possible* objects of knowledge. And the denial that we can know them is due to the fact that these are a limiting case in which it is impossible not to recognise the incompatibility of possible knowledge in the one sense with that in the other. It seems obviously absurd to maintain that we can observe every instance of a given class; whereas it is not obvious that the same absurdity, if it be an absurdity, is involved in maintaining that we can observe *some* instances, which we do not observe. The empiricist fails to see the difference between the assertions "all these things have this character" and "so many things *of this class* have this character." When he says, "all things of this class, *within the limits of observation*, are of this character," he can still think that he is making an empirical proposition, a proposition in extension, because he seems to himself to be making an assertion not about a whole class, but about a part of a class. His assertion, then, that we can know only *general* and *probable*, not *universal* and *necessary* propositions, seems to be due to the fact that he applies to all truths the test of conformity to the type of objects of experience, and admits as certainly true those only which seem to him, because he confuses this test with the test of actual experience, to have such conformity. (2) A second characteristic of empiricists,

which [95] seems also to follow naturally from this presupposition, is the tendency to regard all inference as either analytic or causal. The view that it is analytic harmonises with their presupposition in the same way as the view that necessary truths are analytic, and the characteristic of causal inference is that it is inference from the existence of one thing to the existence of another.

NOTE

1. The proposition "geometry is implied in experience" is not a premiss of the conclusion "geometry is true," in the piece of reasoning given above. (*See* Lewis Carroll, in *Mind*, N.S. 14, p. 278.)

9

Mr. McTaggart's Ethics

The subject of this article is the general ethical principles maintained by Mr. McTaggart in his recent book, entitled "Studies in Hegelian Cosmology."[1] Four chapters of this book are devoted to ethical subjects; and all of them certainly contain valuable contributions to the subjects with which they deal. Three of them, however, those on Punishment, on Sin, and on The Conception of Society as an organism, I shall not have space to discuss. The chapter on "The Supreme Good and the Moral Criterion" gives us Mr. McTaggart's fundamental principles; and this chapter by itself supplies matter enough to deserve very full consideration.

Of the five metaphysical chapters, which constitute the greater part of the book, it is only necessary here to say that their chief content is a very elaborate and original argument in favor of the unusually definite conclusion that the Universe consists exclusively of a number of finite persons, including ourselves, which exist timelessly and whose consciousness is solely occupied with love for one another. This conclusion it was necessary to state because Mr. McTaggart's two fundamental ethical principles are

Originally published in *International Journal of Ethics* 13 (April 1903): 341–370.

contained in the assertions: (1) That this state of things, which Mr. McTaggart holds to be the *sole reality*, is also the Supreme Good; and (2) that the best means of deciding what course of action it is right for us to pursue is, in the majority of cases, to consider which course will bring about the greatest balance of pleasure over pain "immediately, or in the comparatively near future which we can predict with reasonable certainty" (p. 99).

Now it should be noted, to start with, that these two propositions are so related that if the one is true the other must be false. This follows from Mr. McTaggart's metaphysical conclusion that the sole reality is timeless. For to say that one course of action is better than another is to imply that it either [342] is itself or causes to exist, some real good, which, but for its existence, would not have existed. But assuredly our actions neither are themselves, nor can produce anything except the existence of something or other in time. Accordingly, if what exists timelessly is the sole reality, neither our actions nor what they produce can be real; and the unreal existence of one thing rather than another, even if it have any meaning, can certainly not have any value. This contradiction is, perhaps, concealed from Mr. McTaggart by the fact that, following ordinary usage, he speaks of the thing which is real or exists, and not of its existence or reality as the good to be attained, while he certainly conceives it possible that one and the same thing may exist both timelessly and in time. But it is, I think, plain that what we judge to be good is always that a thing of a certain sort should be real or exist; and it is certainly only the existence of certain things in time, not these things as they are apart from any existence or in their timeless existence, that our actions either are or affect. The point may, perhaps, be brought out most clearly by reference to the other form in which Mr. McTaggart expresses the doctrine that what exists timelessly also exists in time—namely that it "manifests" itself in time. For it is certainly only the manifestations, as such, that our actions can affect; and I contend that no manifestation can be better than another or good at all, since none, as distinguished from the reality of which it is the manifestation, has any reality whatever. And even if the principle that, in order to be good, a thing must be real, be not sufficiently evident, the contradiction will still follow from the fact that Mr. McTaggart uses Supreme Good in the sense of sole or complete Good. For if the timeless reality is in itself the sole Good, it follows that the fact of its also having one manifestation rather than another, or any manifestation at all (even if these suppositions do not contradict themselves) cannot be *any* good.

This contradiction, however, is only between Mr. McTaggart's Metaphysics and his Ethics; and it may be that it is his Metaphysics which are wrong. It is only the metaphysical assertion that the sole Good exists timelessly which leaves no [343] possibility that the existence of anything in time could be any good whatever. Mr. McTaggart's *ethical* assertion about the Supreme Good, namely that it would consist in the existence of that, which he actually holds to be the sole existent, may still be true, whether it does exist or not; and it is at least consistent with his second ethical principle about the nature of the moral criterion.

We have, then, to consider the ethical assertion that the existence of a number of persons, loving one another perfectly, would be perfectly good, and that nothing else can be any good whatever. And it may be noted again at once, that, if this be true, no action can be either right or wrong except as it tends to produce or to prevent the existence of such a state of things. Nothing that happens, until this state of things is completely realized, can be any good whatever in itself; it can only have value as a *means* to such complete realization. As such a means, indeed, it may have value; and therefore, Mr. McTaggart's second ethical principle is consistent with this his first. But Mr. McTaggart's view of what actually makes our actions right is not consistent with it. For he holds that we cannot tell whether any course of action, rather than another, will tend "to advance or retard the eventual complete realization of the complete good" (pp. 98–99); whereas we can tell that one course of action is better than another; and it is so, if it "will bring about," in that near future defined above, "the state which conforms as closely as possible to that perfection" (p. 99). Mr. McTaggart does, then, hold that the immediate realization of something more or less like what he asserts to be the sole Good is in itself a good; and, if this be true, it follows that what he asserts to be the sole Good, is *not* the sole Good.

Accordingly the fundamental principle of Mr. McTaggart's *practical* ethics, namely that one action is better than another, if it will bring about, in a near future, the state which conforms as closely as possible to perfection, compels us to deny both (1) his two metaphysical doctrines (*a*) that only the Absolute is real, (*b*) that only the Absolute is good; and (2) his ethical doctrine that only the eventual realization of the [344] Absolute would be good. We still, however, have left the ethical assertion that the state of things described would be *perfectly good*, in some sense which does not deny that other things are good too, but, on the contrary, implies the corollary that they are more or less good according as they more or less resemble it.

In this assertion we have the fundamental principle of Mr. McTaggart's Ethics—his doctrine of the Supreme Good; and it is not an assertion which we can be expected to accept without argument. Nor does Mr. McTaggart ask us so to accept it. He professes to give reasons for it. But whereas the assertion itself is only doubtful, the reasons he gives for it betray the utmost confusion on the most essential points of ethical reasoning.

It is, in the first place, remarkable that Mr. McTaggart should suppose such a proposition capable of being proved in three sentences. But, when we examine the supposed proof, we find still further reason for astonishment. It runs as follows:

"In the reality so defined, every conscious being—and there are no other beings—will express all his individuality in one end which will truly and adequately express it. The fulfillment of such an end as this would give satisfaction, not partial and temporary, but complete and eternal. And since each individual finds the whole universe in harmony with his end, it will necessarily follow that the end is fulfilled" (p. 96).

Mr. McTaggart argues, then, that the Absolute must be perfectly good, *because* it would give complete satisfaction to every being in it. That is to say he assumes as his fundamental principle that whatever universe would give complete satisfaction to all the beings in it (no matter what they were satisfied with) would be perfectly good. This principle certainly seems far from self-evident; and moreover it directly contradicts what is implied in the principle, which it is offered to prove, namely, that the Absolute is *better* than any other conceivable Universe. We are, then, naturally prompted to ask what considerations can have induced Mr. McTaggart to be satisfied [345] with so extraordinary a piece of reasoning; and indications are not wanting.

(1) The natural meaning of the argument would be that complete satisfaction itself was the sole good; since, when we say that a thing is good *because* it has a certain property, we commonly mean merely that since it contains this property it contains something that has intrinsic value. It is, of course, possible that all things which contain a certain property are themselves good as wholes; but, if this be meant, it is a mistake to say that they are good *solely because* they possess this property. It will be true to say that they would not be good, *unless* they possessed it; but for the same reason it will also be true to say that they would not be good unless they also possessed their other constituents: since in both cases the judgment rests on the fact that it is the thing as a whole which is good, and that it would not be the whole it is unless it had all the parts it has. Now it is plain that Mr. McTaggart means us to understand that his Absolute *as a whole* is good: he immediately goes on to say: "The supreme good is not pleasure as such but this particular pleasant state" (p. 96): and later we find

him using language which implies that it is good *not only* because it contains complete satisfaction but *also* because the ideals which it satisfies are perfect (p. 119). This being the case it is at least misleading to argue here that it is good because it contains complete satisfaction; though such an expression might be excused if it were a self-evident truth that all universes which contained complete satisfaction were equally good, and that all good universes had this and no other property in common. But it becomes inexcusable, if we assume that Mr. McTaggart intends us to understand that the Absolute is *better* than any other conceivable Universe: if, of two wholes which contain a common element, one is better than the other, it is obviously absurd to maintain that the former owes *all its* goodness to the fact that it possesses the element which is also possessed by the latter. We are therefore, I think, justified in assuming that Mr. McTaggart was influenced by the idea that complete satisfaction is itself the sole good: the more so, as he expressly states elsewhere that "It is *only* in respect [346] of the element of feeling in it that any state can be deemed to have intrinsic value" (p. 261). Mr. McTaggart is plainly unaware that this is inconsistent with the doctrine that the Absolute is better than any other conceivable universe, which might contain the same element of feeling, *because* the ideals realized in it are also perfect.

(2) But there is reason to think that Mr. McTaggart is also influenced by another fundamental confusion with regard to the principles of ethical reasoning. It is possible that when he says the Absolute is perfectly good, because it would give complete satisfaction, he means us to complete the argument by adding "and because nothing else could." The use of language is such that it does seem very plausible to argue: Since complete satisfaction is necessary to perfection, the only thing which could give it must be better than anything which would not. And Mr. McTaggart actually does suggest this reason for a principle, which he strongly

emphasizes in Chap. IX, and which, taken strictly, is inconsistent with the argument we are now considering. In Chap. IX we are told that it is not the satisfaction of all desires, but only of those which are "fundamental demands and aspirations of our nature" (pp. 259, 266), that is necessary to the perfection of the universe. Now it is obvious that here again Mr. McTaggart is contradicting his principle that all universes which give complete satisfaction to all the beings in them would be perfectly and equally good, and asserting that a universe which completely satisfied some kind of desires would be better than one which satisfied others. But instead of asserting that the satisfaction of some desires is better than that of others, *because* the former are directed to more perfect ideals, he seems to suggest that it is better *because* they are more fundamental. Nor does he anywhere try to prove (what would be extremely difficult) that all desires for what is good are in fact fundamental (whatever that may mean) and that all fundamental desires are in fact desires for what is good. But he does suggest that the reason why fundamental desires are to be preferred is *because* "their realization is essential to permanent harmony" (p. 266); or, in other words, because we *could* not be completely and permanently [347] satisfied with the objects of any others (p. 259). It would seem, then, that Mr. McTaggart is influenced by the plausible argument that the only thing which *could* give complete satisfaction, is therefore better than anything else. And yet this argument is merely an instance of the very fallacy against which he rightly protests elsewhere (pp. 96, 266) in the most emphatic manner—a direct inference from "is" to "ought"! Because the nature of the Universe is such that only certain kinds of things *could* give complete satisfaction, we are "therefore" entitled to say that it is better than others in which a different natural law would allow us to be completely satisfied with other kinds of things! We might just as well say that because in this world certain evils are the only means of obtaining certain goods, *therefore* this world is better than any other in which the same goods might be obtained without the aid of any evils! It is, of course, better *as a means* that we should undergo the greatest evils, if the constitution of the Universe is so bad that by that means we can obtain greater goods than by any other: but it can be better *as a means* only. And similarly the empirical truth (and it can be no more) that only certain desires *can* be permanently satisfied may be a reason for regarding the satisfaction of those desires as the best thing that we can get; but it can be no reason for regarding a Universe in which only those desires are permanently satisfied as *therefore* supremely good.

(3) But finally we have to think that Mr. McTaggart is also influenced by a third error. His words might be interpreted as meaning not that, since the Absolute would give complete satisfaction, it is therefore *also* supremely good; but that to call it supremely good is simply another way of saying that it gives complete satisfaction. And, in fact, one of the many errors on which his whole argument in Chap. IX is based seems to be the vicious traditional assumption that the distinction between what is and what ought to be is identical with that between what is known and what is willed—that "the difference of meaning between the predicates 'true' and 'good' " is the same as that between the predicates "known" and "willed" (p. 268). Thus on pp. 266–7 we [348] find treated as if they were identical in meaning the two statements: "If no amount of 'ought' can produce the slightest 'is,' it is no less true that no amount of 'is' can produce the slightest 'ought,' " and "While our desires must serve in the kingdom of the true, they rule in the kingdom of the good." It is difficult to imagine that, when he wrote this passage, Mr. McTaggart was very clearly aware of any difference between the propositions "This is good" and "This is desired"; since, if there be such a difference, it seems only too obvious that what we desire may just as easily be bad as it may be unreal.

Mr. McTaggart's treatment of the fundamental question of

Ethics, the question, What is best in itself? can hardly, then, be censured too severely. He seems not to have realized that it is a difficult question at all. His answers to it are both ambiguous and mutually inconsistent; and the reasons which he gives for them both mutually inconsistent and fallacious.

But his argument in favor of the doctrine that a calculation of pleasures and pains will generally give us a correct criterion of what we ought to do, deserves considerably more respect. It is here rather the truth of Mr. McTaggart's premises than the cogency of his reasoning, which may be called in question.

One part of the argument (pp. 108–118) is devoted to pointing out, what is certainly true, that quantities of pleasure *can* be compared with success. It is possible, Mr. McTaggart argues, to know that the amount of pleasure which we get from one thing is greater than that which we get from another and not only this, but *also* that the amount got from one thing is *so much* greater than that got from another that, even if we were to get the latter twice, we should not have had so much pleasure as if we got the former only once. All this is unquestionably true, whatever may be the difficulties of deciding precisely what is meant by saying that one pleasure is more than twice as great as another or greater than the sum of five others; and Mr. McTaggart justly points out that exactly the same difficulties must be incurred by any system of Ethics, since any such system must hold that we know the *value* of one thing or of one set of things to be greater than the sum of the values of another set.

[349] So much, then, must be granted; but this is only a preliminary. Mr. McTaggart's main thesis in this chapter is what he expresses in the proportion: That the calculation of pleasures and pains is both, in general, a *correct* criterion of how we ought to act, and also *the only available* criterion (p. 127). The question whether this thesis is true is certainly of the utmost importance; and this question I now propose to consider at length.

In the first place, great care is needed to distinguish exactly what it is that Mr. McTaggart means to maintain. For he does *not* hold, as his words might imply, that wherever one course of action will produce a greater balance of pleasure than any other, the results of that course will be the best. He admits (1) that, even where we ought to choose the course that will give the greatest pleasure, the total results of that course *may* be worse (p. 124, "third case"); (2) that in some cases it is impossible to decide whether we ought to choose the course that will give the greatest pleasure, or not (p. 124, "fourth case"). Accordingly his thesis may be most accurately expressed in the following propositions: (1) that it is *never* plain we ought to choose a course which will give the less pleasure, (2) that in all cases where one course will give greater pleasure, if we can decide at all which course is right, that one is right, (3) that we often can decide that one course both will give greater pleasure and is right.

Now, it should be noted that, if this be all, to say that pleasure is "the only available criterion" is quite inaccurate. Mr. McTaggart wholly neglects to consider a case, which he plainly admits to be possible. For suppose, that one course will plainly cause less of goods other than pleasure (as in the "fourth case," p. 124), and that instead of this also giving less pleasure (as Mr. McTaggart there supposes) the amounts of pleasure produced by both courses are as far as we can judge, equal. In such a case it would plainly be our duty to choose the course which produced most of other goods. Here, therefore, we have a case, where a criterion other than pleasure, would, by Mr. McTaggart's own admission, be available. And Mr. McTaggart has not tried to show that such cases do not [350] occur, or are even rare: he has apparently simply failed to think of them. That one of the conditions for their occurrence, namely, the apparent equality of the pleasure produced by two courses, is by no means rare, I shall presently maintain.[2]

Mr. McTaggart has, then, certainly failed to show that pleasure is the only available criterion of moral action. He has failed to notice a class of cases in which, provided they occur, another criterion would, on his own doctrine, be available. But these cases are only those in which, because the amount of pleasure that would be produced by alternative courses appears to be equal, there is no balance of pleasure to serve as criterion between them at all. How are we to understand the important proposition which still remains, namely that where one course does promise more pleasure than another, this fact is, *in general* a *correct* criterion of its rightness?

It should be noted precisely what is meant by that limitation "*in general.*" It is inserted in order to allow for those cases, mentioned above as admitted by Mr. McTaggart to occur, where the course which promises the greater pleasure also promises a decided loss in other goods. "In this case," Mr. McTaggart says (p. 124), "there seems no reasonable solution." A balance of pleasure is, accordingly, in this case *not* a correct criterion, in Mr. McTaggart's sense. The course which brings it *may* be the one which also brings the greatest total of good, but we cannot tell whether it is or not. But Mr. McTaggart holds such cases to constitute only a small part of those which we actually have to decide. He alludes to them as showing "the *occasional* failure of the only available criterion" (p. 127). They do, therefore, on his principles, prevent him from holding that pleasure is *always* a correct criterion, but they leave him entitled to hold that it is so *in general.*

So much by way of making quite plain what Mr. McTaggart's thesis is. His most general proposition is the first of the three given above: That in no case is the course, which would produce less pleasure, plainly the right one. The next in [351] generality is the second of those three: That, in most cases, the course which would give more pleasure, is plainly the right one. These two propositions involve the chief points of principle, which I propose to dispute: and I propose to deal with them first. Discussion of the third, namely: That we can often tell which course would give more pleasure, in cases where that one is right, may be conveniently postponed till the main questions of principle have been dealt with.

And, first of all, I propose to consider the proposition: That, in most cases, the course which would give the more pleasure, is plainly the right one; because, although it does, equally with the first, involve one of what I shall call Mr. McTaggart's two main premises, namely that pleasure is good in proportion to its amount, it is mainly to be rejected owing to an objection, which will hold whether those main premises are true or false. This objection is as follows:

The "most cases," in which the course which gives a balance of pleasure is the right course, are divided by Mr. McTaggart into three classes, which may perhaps be as briefly and clearly described in his own words as in any others.

> "In the first [case]" he says, "the action to which the hedonic criterion would guide us, involves in our judgment a greater development of ideals. In this case it is clear that we should take this course, since both elements of the good are increased.
>
> "In the second case, our action, whichever way we act, will, as far as we can see, make no difference to the development of ideals. Here, too, we can safely abide by the hedonic criterion, since that measures the only element of the good which our decision can be seen to affect.
>
> "In the third case, our action may make a considerable difference to the development of our ideals, but we are unable to tell whether the difference will be for good or for evil. Once more we shall do well to follow the hedonic criterion. For then, at any rate, we shall gain in respect of one element of the good. We *may* indeed lose much more in respect of development. But then we *may* gain in respect of that element also. Since the effect on development is unknown, the only rational course, if we must act, is to be guided by the effect on happiness, which is known." (p. 124)

Now, in the first of these three cases it is plain that the course which promises the greatest pleasure is the right one to adopt, *provided only* that by "our judgment" to the effect that it also involves the greatest amount of other goods, be meant a judgment, to assure the correctness of which all reasonable [352] precautions have been taken. A proviso of this sort we have to understand throughout. Here it need only be said, that, if it is clear that a certain course will bring a gain on the whole in all other respects as well as in pleasure, Mr. McTaggart is, if pleasure be a good, justified in holding that course to be the right one. It is, however, important to notice that this assurance, that we shall gain on the whole in all other respects, is precisely what Mr. McTaggart has previously maintained to be "impossible in most cases, if not in all" (p. 101). According to Mr. McTaggart, then, this first class of cases, in which pleasure is, on Mr. McTaggart's principles, a correct criterion, will be very rare.

But the second and third class of cases present more difficulties. In the first place, how do these two cases differ from one another? In the first it is only "*as far as we can see*" that our action will make no difference: here, therefore, it is not denied that our action "may make a considerable difference," as is the case in the second. It is impossible to discover exactly what distinction Mr. McTaggart meant to make: but three alternatives are possible. (1) He may have meant the first case to be that in which we doubt whether our action will make any difference at all; and the second to be that in which, *knowing* that it will make a difference, we doubt whether the difference is for good or for evil. Assuming him to have meant this, how does it affect his argument? We cannot refuse to admit that where the effects of two courses differ *in no respect*, as far as we can see, except in amount of pleasure, Mr. McTaggart is, if pleasure be a good, right that what gives more pleasure should be preferred. The first of these two cases, then, if this be meant by it, seems to be in Mr. McTaggart's favor. *But*—the case never occurs; for our actions always do make *some* obvious difference, other than gain or loss in pleasure: and the question whether this difference is or is not a "development in ideals," is, under another name, merely the question whether it is for good or evil—the question, which is to be dealt with under the other case. (2) Mr. McTaggart may have meant the first case to be that in which we *can* see that our action will make no difference for good or evil, and the second [353] to be that in which we *cannot* see whether it makes such a difference or not. If this be so, we may again admit that Mr. McTaggart's conclusion as to the right course to pursue in the first case, is theoretically correct. But it is also again quite evident that such cases can never occur. We can never judge with security that the total values of two alternative sets of goods are absolutely equal; for such a judgment would require an immensely greater accuracy than those which Mr. McTaggart himself maintains to be very rare—namely that one such total is greater or less than another. But (3) it is possible that Mr. McTaggart may mean by his first class cases where we *can* see, not indeed that two alternative totals are *equal* in value, but that they do not very greatly differ in value; and by his second class cases where, though we cannot see which is the greater, we also *cannot* be sure that the difference in value is not very great. Both these cases might be expressed by saying that the respective totals are "*as far as we can see, equal*;" since in both we cannot be sure that they are not equal: and yet there is a most important difference between the two, since in the one we are sure that the divergence from equality, if it exists, is not a great one, while in the other we are not sure but what it is a very great one. Cases of both these kinds do certainly occur; and it seems most probable that this is the distinction of which Mr. McTaggart was thinking. What are we to say of Mr. McTaggart's hedonic conclusion on this interpretation of his meaning?

I think we have to say that the objection, which, on any of the three interpretations, would have held against his judgment of the second case (his "third case"), will, on this interpretation, hold against *both*. *The two cases are now alike in this, that in both we cannot tell* but that the results of the two courses will be equal in value in all respects except amount of pleasure; and Mr. McTaggart lays it down as a universal rule that in all such cases we shall do well to prefer the course which gives the greater pleasure. This universal rule I think we may see to be certainly wrong.

The data we have to consider are these: We have two courses, one of which is certainly productive of more pleasure [354] than the other, whereas their results in other respects, though differing much in kind, are, so far as we can see, equal in value. It certainly seems plausible to conclude, as Mr. McTaggart does, that, assuming pleasure to be good, it is reasonable to choose the course which gives more pleasure. But this plausibility is certainly fallacious. For by the datum that the other results are, so far as we can see, equal in value, it is only meant that we *cannot* declare these totals with certainty to be unequal. And this being the case, the probability that they are *actually equal* is so small as to be negligible:[3] it is far more likely that the one is, in some one of the many possible degrees, greater or less than the other. The number of case, therefore, in which the course which gives greater pleasure is right, because the other results are equal, is so small as to be negligible, and in all other cases we are just as likely to be equally right in preferring the lesser pleasure. Now this certainly gives an infinitesimal probability that we shall be right to choose the course which gives the greater pleasure; but that this infinitesimal probability gives ground for a rational solution of such cases cannot be maintained, because there is *the same probability in favor of any other criterion whatsoever*. To take an instance, which Mr. McTaggart uses above (pp. 103–104): It will be just as rational to prefer a Home Education to a Public School, on the ground that it gives a decisive superiority in *culture*; or a Public School Education to the other, on the ground that it gives a decisive superiority in *genuineness*; as to prefer either on the ground that it gives a decisive superiority in pleasure. In short, upon the principle which

Mr. McTaggart here uses in favor of the hedonic criterion, it will always be *equally rational* to adopt either of two compatible courses, if only each is superior to the other *in some one respect*: that is to say, there will be *no rational solution* in such cases; the very principle which Mr. McTaggart uses in favor of the hedonic criterion is decisive against it. Let us ask ourselves the question: Am I to send my son to a Public School or to educate him at home? Mr. McTaggart [355] says we cannot here decide between the respective values obtained, other than pleasure; but if the principle we are now considering were true, we certainly could decide between them—we could decide rationally in favor of *either*. For Mr. McTaggart admits that the first course has a decisive superiority over the second in *one* of the many points involved—namely that it gives more "genuineness." Let us consider all the other points, *except* the two degrees of genuineness. Can we say that *in these other points* the home education is decisively the best? Not according to Mr. McTaggart; for this is still one of the questions—a comparison of sums of goods other than pleasure—"which it is impossible in most cases, if not in all, to decide." We have it then that of two courses, *equal, as far as we can see, in other respects*, one is decisively superior in the good of genuineness: *therefore*, Mr. McTaggart would be bound to say on his present principles, *choose that one*. But unfortunately by an exact parity of reasoning, we should also be bound to choose the home education. For this, according to Mr. McTaggart, has a decisive superiority in respect of *culture*. Let us now consider all results *except degree of culture*, including, of course, now, in each, its degree of genuineness. These two totals are also, in all probability, *as far as we can see equal*. Therefore of two totals, apparently equal in other respects, one is decisively superior in the good of culture: and we are bound to choose this one. Of course, we are not bound to agree with Mr. McTaggart (nor perhaps Mr. McTaggart to agree with himself) that, when we consider two sets of results in all except some one respect in which the one set has a decisive superiority, these other respects will be, as far as we can see, equal in value. The only point we require to make is that, *if* they are so, this decisive superiority in one respect is no ground for preferring the course which has it; since, if it were we should often have an equally good ground for preferring *either* course. The facts may be expressed in another way, which makes them seem sufficiently obvious as soon as it is pointed out. If of two totals, upon the relative values of which we cannot decide, there be added to one a greater, to the other a less, amount of pleasure, the two new totals thus [356] formed will still, in general, be totals, upon the relative values of which we cannot decide: we shall still be unable to say whether or not the one is greater than the other, and consequently unable to say which is the greater; so that we obviously shall have no ground for rational choice. That Mr. McTaggart must hold these two new totals to be *always* thus "as far as we can see, equal in value," follows from his contention that we can never determine the relative values of any amount of pleasure and any other good: for the one could only be certainly greater than the other, if the difference between the amount of pleasure contained in the one and that contained in the other were certainly greater than any possible difference in value between the two sets of remaining constituents. Mr. McTaggart cannot hold that this is *ever* the case. It may, however, be allowed, if we believe that a certain amount of pleasure can be seen to be greater than a certain amount of other goods, that it may sometimes be the case, in the last of the two cases we are now considering—namely where we *can* see that the difference between the total values of the two sets of other constituents is not very great. Mr. McTaggart has debarred himself from the right to hold that the distinction he makes between this and the other case has any bearing on the correctness of the hedonic criterion. But we may admit so much in his favor: That, where the difference in value between the other goods is very small, and that between the amounts of pleasure very large, it *may* be right to prefer the course which gives the greater pleasure. But such cases are certainly not very common: and how far short does the admission of them fall from the sweeping contention of Mr. McTaggart that, wherever we cannot see which set of remaining results has the greater value, we are entitled to judge the course which gives most pleasure the best!

I conclude, then, that Mr. McTaggart's attempt to show that the course which promises most pleasure is in most cases the right one has utterly broken down. On his own principles, it will *only* be the right one in the *first* of the three cases which he distinguishes—namely where we can also see that the other results of the pleasantest course are also better than those of [357] the other. And it is plain that there is little meaning in calling amount of pleasure a *criterion*, if it is only safe to follow it where we can also see directly that the total results are better. Of the other two cases, on which Mr. McTaggart must rely to make up his majority, I have tried to show that Mr. McTaggart's universal conclusion is simply fallacious. It can only be admitted that in a *subdivision* of the first of these, the course which gives the greater pleasure *may* be plainly the right. But here, too, it is idle to talk of amount of pleasure as a *criterion*, since in order to show that the pleasantest course is the best, we must, *in each individual case*, institute a comparison between the difference in amount of pleasure and the difference in amount of other goods.

It has, however, only been shown that the proposition: The course which gives most pleasure is, in general, the right one, cannot be sustained by the reasons which Mr. McTaggart gives for it. The peculiarity of Mr. McTaggart's attempt to prove it, consists in the fact that his proof, if sound, would hold, whatever view we took of the value of pleasure relatively to other things. My refutation of this proof shows that, unless we *can* estimate the value of pleasure relatively to other things, any rational choice is impossible in three out of the four classes into which Mr. McTaggart divides all practical cases. Mr. McTaggart holds that we can never form any estimate of the value of pleasure relatively to other things; and it seems to me to be demonstrated that, if this be so, no rational choice is open to us, in any case, where there is a balance of pleasure on one side, except in the first of Mr. McTaggart's cases—namely where there is also a balance of other goods on the same side. This first class of cases, as we saw, Mr. McTaggart must hold to be comparatively rare; and, therefore, we get the result that on his view a rational choice is in most cases impossible. But Mr. McTaggart may be wrong about the rarity of these cases also. Our decision upon the actual truth of the proposition that, in most cases, the pleasanter course is the best, must, it is now plain, depend (1) upon the view we take of the nature of most practical cases, (2) upon the view we take of the value of pleasure relatively to other things. The first of [358] these questions I propose to postpone: upon the second some light will be thrown by the discussion of Mr. McTaggart's most general proposition, namely: That it is *never* plain we ought to choose a course which will give less pleasure. To this discussion I shall now proceed. The proposition would certainly follow from what I have said I should call Mr. McTaggart's two main premises. These are (1) that pleasure is a good, and a greater quantity of pleasure always proportionally better than a less, (2) that no other good is ever certainly greater than the smallest obvious quantity of pleasure. The first of these premises was also involved in the proposition we have just been considering; and we shall see no great reason to quarrel with it. The second, on the other hand, is highly important, since, if Mr. McTaggart's view of practical cases is also correct, it would prove that in the majority of cases no rational choice is open to us. What are we to say of these two premises?

Now the first of them is part of what Mr. McTaggart has failed to prove by his treatment of the question of the Supreme Good.

Mr. McTaggart has given us no reason to think that pleasure is good at all. Even if the Absolute as a whole were very good (and this was not proved) and if also its goodness partly depended upon its containing pleasure, it would not follow that pleasure was good at all. For it is quite possible that a whole may be the better for containing a certain element, and yet that element itself possess no value whatever. And apart from the question of proof it does seem very probable that pleasure has no value at all; even although we admit that certain states of mind are the better for containing pleasure. And again, even if we admit that pleasure has some value (and it would be rash to deny it), it would not follow (as Mr. McTaggart assumes) that a greater quantity of pleasure was always also proportionally greater in value.

Nevertheless, even if this first assumption of Mr. McTaggart's, that a greater quantity of pleasure is always proportionally better than a less, is erroneous, the error does not seem very serious; but it does not seem serious, only because the error involved in his second assumption seems so enormous. So far [359] does it seem from being the case that no other good is ever certainly greater than the smallest quantity of pleasure, that the very greatest quantity of pleasure seems to have an almost imperceptible value compared to many other things. This second assumption of Mr. McTaggart's is the premise that seems most obviously open to question.

Whether it is or is not preposterous, must in the last resort be left to inspection. I may give an instance, which seems to me to show its absurdity as plainly as any other. It certainly seems to me that the state of mind of a person feeling, with great pleasure, that kind of love which Mr. McTaggart takes to exemplify the other element in his Absolute, is far more than twice as good as that of a drunkard who might be enjoying twice as much pleasure in the occupation of breaking crockery. The ultimate decision must, I say, depend upon the view we take of instances like these: but it may be useful to point out certain defects in the arguments which Mr. McTaggart uses to give plausibility to his view.

(1) It is not quite plain that Mr. McTaggart recognizes all the consequences which his view entails. What he says is (I choose the clearest statement, but the same view is also expressed on p. 124): The position that "a great change for the good in one element will counterbalance a moderate change for the bad in the other is theoretically indefensible. It implies that we have some means of knowing, *within very broad limits*, how much happiness will be more worth having than a given degree of development. And it is impossible to settle this" (p. 123). (The italics are mine.) Plainly this involves that no loss in other goods can be seen to overbalance any obvious gain in pleasure. But Mr. McTaggart does not apply the doctrine to his Supreme Good and say: Supposing the pleasure in the Absolute just perceptibly decreased, and the other element remaining the same, we cannot tell whether or not it would be superior to a world of persons enjoying that perceptibly greater pleasure but whose minds were otherwise solely occupied with the contemplation of dunghills. The argument with which, as we have seen, Mr. McTaggart might be tempted to rejoin, namely that the pleasure in his Absolute *could* not [360] be less than it is, and that the contemplation of dunghills *could* not give as much, is, as we have also seen, irrelevant.

(2) Mr. McTaggart does not recognize that he does admit the possibility of knowing, with regard to two goods as heterogeneous as pleasure and, say, love, that one is greater than the other. That he does so is obscured by the fact that he treats all other goods as if they were merely one, under the name "development of ideals." Yet it is obvious that when he says "one man's ideals may be lower than another's" he means not merely that the one man admires the same things, only less strongly or less often than the other, but that to admire one kind of thing is worse than to admire another. This being so, it seems unreasonably arbitrary to main-

tain that with regard to pleasure alone we can make no judgment of this kind. Pleasure itself is merely one among ideals; and there seems no greater difficulty in deciding that a man whose education has led him to regard mere pleasure as the Supreme Good, instead of so regarding, let us say, Mr. McTaggart's Absolute has suffered a deterioration, than in making the same judgment of a man whose education has led him to prefer "Philistinism" to "culture."

(3) Mr. McTaggart shows a considerable confusion as to the *grounds* of his contention that no other good is ever certainly greater than any amount of pleasure. I have just pointed out that he does not seem aware of his admission that we *can* compare the values of heterogeneous goods. In spite of this admission, he seems to rest his contention with regard to pleasure on the proposition that we *cannot*. And he actually states that we cannot in the most emphatic manner: it is "impossible," he says (p. 123), "to compare" *any* two "elements of the good with any hope of discovering which" is "the most desirable." This statement is certainly in flat contradiction with his admission that we can tell whether our ideals have or have not been developed; and yet it is solely to it that he appeals in support of the doctrine that pleasure cannot be compared with other goods: he only adds that pleasure and development exhibit "*the greatest* heterogeneity" which is, in itself, by no means apparent (p. 123). But the confusion to which [361] I wish to call attention here is that he refers to this doctrine that we cannot compare heterogeneous goods as something which "we saw above"; whereas the only thing which he has tried to show previously is something quite different. He must be referring to the long argument, in which he professes to show "that the idea of perfection cannot give us any criterion of moral action" (pp. 99–107). But all that he tries to show in this passage is that where we are considering *two complicated sums of goods*, it is "impossible in most cases, if not in all" (p. 101), to tell which is to be preferred.

With regard to two such sums (he gives as an instance "marriage" and "free love," p. 102) he obviously does try to make us see that we cannot be sure of their respective merits. But his very argument in favor of this contention, implies that with regard to certain *elements* of those sums we can make a very decided judgment. In order to see that this is so, we need only refer again to Mr. McTaggart's second instance—the comparative merits of Public Schools and home education (pp. 103–104). "Are we nearer to heaven," asks Mr. McTaggart, "if at this moment we buy genuineness with Philistinism, or buy culture with *Schwärmerei?*" That *this* question is, as Mr. McTaggart says, difficult to answer, may be admitted. But it is obvious that its difficulty depends upon the ease with which we can judge that other question—upon the ease with which we can judge that "culture" is better than "Philistinism," and "genuineness" than "*Schwärmerei.*" It is difficult only because, on each side, we have a thing comparatively good *bought with* another comparatively bad. The difficulty would not arise, unless it were obvious that a combination of "genuineness" with "culture" would be actually *more than twice as good as* a combination of the evils of "Philistinism" with those of "*Schwärmerei.*" When, therefore, Mr. McTaggart appeals to this passage in favor of the assertion that it is impossible to compare any two elements of the good with any hope of discovering which is the most desirable, it is plain that the facts to which he appeals show something quite different: they even imply the contradictory of his assertion. In this passage he only tries to show that [362] upon those *complicated* sums of goods which occur in *practical* cases it is very difficult to decide: whereas for his later point it is essential he should show of the single good, "any given amount of pleasure," that it is never certainly less in value than any other single good. For my part, it seems to me quite obvious that a lifetime of genuineness is certainly superior in value to the pleasure obtained by a moment's enjoyment of turtle-soup: and the point I am now making is that, whereas Mr. McTaggart seems to think he has shown that it is *not* certainly superior, he has said nothing which even tends to show this. That such judgments will not suffice, by themselves, to decide *practical* cases, must, of course, be admitted. But the question whether practical cases are soluble, is quite different from the question what data we have for deciding on their solubility; and we have evidence that, owing to a confusion of these two questions, Mr. McTaggart has arrived at a wrong conclusion on the latter. We cannot decide off-hand, as he does on his "fourth case" (p. 124), that, where a gain in pleasure is certainly accompanied by a loss in other goods, there is "no reasonable solution." We *may* be forced to the conclusion that there is no reasonable solution either in this or in Mr. McTaggart's second and third cases: but all three questions must be treated on the same principles, and we cannot decide this one on the ground that no pleasure is ever certainly less in value than any other good.

The same confusion between practical cases and our data for their solution is very strikingly exhibited by another characteristic of Mr. McTaggart's argument—a characteristic which is worth mentioning, because it also exhibits another weakness in Mr. McTaggart's hedonistic position. Mr. McTaggart obviously thinks that in practical cases of importance we often can decide which course will bring the most pleasure: the whole point of his argument is to show that pleasure is an applicable and correct criterion *of morality*, not only of those cases "in which we do not bring morality into the matter" (p. 111). But it is very noticeable that all the instances which he gives, as showing that we can estimate the relative value of pleasures, are taken from cases of the latter sort; whereas in [363] those problems "which are the real ethical difficulties of life" (p. 105), he does not attempt to show that it is plain which course would give the greater pleasure. He *fancies*, indeed, that why most independent thinkers have concluded in favor of marriage, is "because they take a more practical criterion.

If we estimate the gain or loss of happiness which would follow from the abolition of marriage, we may *perhaps* find excellent reasons for declining to make the change" (p. 103). But he does not give these excellent reasons; and that "most independent thinkers" have actually been led to their conclusion by the use of the hedonistic criterion may be confidently affirmed to be a *mere* fancy. Hedonistic arguments have, indeed, been frequently used with success to give plausibility to a conviction of which a thinker was already strongly convinced; but that an impartial consideration of the hedonistic evidence has *ever* sufficed, by itself, to produce a strong conviction on any question of importance it is by no means bold to deny. However that may be, Mr. McTaggart's argument in favor of the usefulness of pleasure as a criterion exhibits just the converse fallacy to that which appears in his arguments against the applicability of other goods. In the case of pleasure he only shows that we can *sometimes* decide that one sum of pleasure is greater than another; and then concludes, without further demonstration, that we can so decide about the highly complicated sums involved in practical problems. In the case of other goods he only tries to show that we cannot decide on the complicated sums involved in practice; and then concludes, without further demonstration, that we cannot decide that *any* one element of the good is preferable to another.

Mr. McTaggart has, therefore, given us no reason in support of his opinion that we cannot pronounce with certainty that any other good is greater than the smallest quantity of pleasure; and, accordingly, he has also failed to prove his most general practical proposition, namely that it is never plainly right to prefer a course which would give less pleasure: he has given us no reason to think that in his "fourth case," no reasonable solution would be possible, in any of Mr. McTaggart's three [364] last cases: we should only be able to decide which was our right course, when one course showed a decided superiority both in pleasure and in other goods; pleasure would be a correct criterion, only if in most cases a gain in pleasure coincided with a gain in other goods. But I have already said that this opinion appears to me not merely incorrect but preposterous; and I have given an instance which seems to me to make this self-evident. If, however, the opinion is incorrect, if we can estimate, within broad limits, the value of pleasure relatively to other goods, we have seen that a rational solution may be possible both in the second and the fourth of Mr. McTaggart's cases: our decision on them will depend on the value we assign to pleasure relatively to other goods. The assumption, therefore, that Mr. McTaggart's opinion is incorrect, calls for a reconsideration of practical cases, in which the question how much value pleasure has will probably not be unimportant. It is only by such a reconsideration that we can decide, whether, after all, pleasure is, in general, a correct criterion; and, if not, by what other principles we can guide our actions.

And, first of all, it appears to me, as I have already said, that the value even of very large amounts of pleasure is very small in comparison to that of other goods: for it may be questioned, without paradox, whether pleasure has any value at all. That such a doubt is not paradoxical may I think be made apparent, if we refer to a principle which Mr. McTaggart strangely neglects. Mr. McTaggart assumes that the value of a whole must always be the same as the sum of the values of its parts (*e.g.* p. 115)—a view which is, perhaps, the only one, in the whole range of philosophy, to which his own term "Atomism" can be justly applied as a term of abuse. If, on the contrary, we remember, what is certainly true, that the value of a whole may be very much greater than the sum of the values of its parts, it becomes plain that from the fact that the presence of pleasure very much heightens the value of certain wholes, we cannot infer that pleasure has any value at all. But it is only this proposition—that the subtraction of pleasure from certain wholes would very much impair their value—which it is paradoxical to deny. There is certainly a very general [365] tendency to think that the presence of pleasure in certain states of consciousness very much adds to their value; and from this fact it is commonly inferred, as by Mr. McTaggart, that *pleasure itself* has a very high value. Yet, if it be even possible that the value of a whole should differ from the sum of the values of its parts, the inference is utterly invalid. And can any other fact than this, that pleasure *often* adds greatly to the value of a whole, be urged in defense of the proposition that great pleasure has admittedly great value? On the contrary, the supporters of that proposition have notoriously great difficulty in reconciling their opinion with the verdict of Common Sense, that many states containing the most intense pleasure are nevertheless of little value, if not positively bad. There will, of course, be no such difficulty, if the principle, that the value of a whole may differ from the sum of the value of its parts, be admitted; but then also the contention that pleasure has very great value loses all its plausibility. The question must now be settled by the consideration whether the existence of pleasure, by itself, apart from any thing else whatever that we are able to distinguish from it, would even in the greatest quantities, have any great value; and it is certainly not paradoxical to deny this. On the contrary it seems self-evident that its value, if it have any, would be very small indeed.

Assuming, then, that the value of pleasure, even in large amounts, is very small indeed, we may proceed to our second question, and ask: Is it true that, in most practical cases, the course which gives most pleasure will also give most good on the whole? Is pleasure, after all, a correct criterion of morality? What is the nature of practical cases, in general?

I think the first answer that should be given to these questions is an admission of very thorough ignorance. Until the subject has been investigated far more conclusively than has ever yet been done, no conclusion should be asserted dogmatically. I shall confine myself to certain generalities, which seem to make against the conclusion that pleasure is the best available criterion.

In the first place, it seems to me that in most cases, where a man will actually ask himself with anxiety: "Which is the [366] right course?" it is impossible to ascertain, with any certainty, *either* which course will in the immediate future bring most good on the whole *or* which will bring most pleasure. On the first point, as we have seen, I have Mr. McTaggart with me; and on the second, as we have also seen, I have his remarkable failure to give any instance to the contrary. But this state of things (if it is the state of things) may well be due to the fact that such cases are only those in which Common Sense does not give a clear decision. It is, in general, only where this is the case, that a man will ask himself the question; and, if we assume that Common Sense morality has decided rightly upon most of the cases, where our ignorance allows a right judgment, it will follow that in the cases, which we cannot decide, the difference in value between the alternative results will probably not be very great. That Common Sense has generally decided rightly where it has decided, may, I think, be proved: and it may, at least, be fairly assumed here, since most moralists are agreed about it, at all events as regards the Common Sense of Christendom, and Mr. McTaggart is certainly no exception. It only, then, remains to ask whether, in the vast number of cases where Common Sense is clear, and in the few, in which perhaps a conclusion can be drawn by a philosophical examination of Common Sense, the course preferred will give most pleasure; and whether, therefore, in the few cases where we can perhaps see a balance of pleasure on one side and cannot see a balance of good, pleasure may be safely used as a criterion.

Now the question of the relation of the hedonic criterion to Common Sense has been very fully discussed by Professor Sidgwick, in the interest of the view, which Mr. McTaggart agrees with me in rejecting and the falsehood of which I have claimed to be self-evident, that pleasure is the sole good. It does not seem probable that a much better case for the agreement of hedonistic judgments with those of Common Sense could be made out, than Professor Sidgwick has given us; and it must be admitted that even on this case the verdict remains very problematical. But, assuming that Professor Sidgwick's verdict is correct, what exactly does it state? No more than [367] this: That in most cases there is no very manifest divergence between the course which would give most pleasure and that which is recommended by Common Sense. This conclusion is certainly problematical; but, if it were true, it would be sufficient for Professor Sidgwick's point: for it would show that Common Sense could not be seen, in a majority of cases, to *conflict* with hedonic judgments. But, even if it be true, is it sufficient to show that pleasure is a safe *criterion*, when admittedly pleasure is not only not the sole good but is one of the least among goods? This is quite a different question; and it seems to me that for this purpose Professor Sidgwick's conclusion is *not* sufficient. For it does not assert that in a majority of cases the hedonic judgments manifestly agree with those of Common Sense: on the contrary we may fairly assume that the number of cases in which the two do obviously agree is no greater than that in which they obviously disagree; or, in other words, that Mr. McTaggart's fourth class of cases is about equal in number to his first class. He cannot, therefore, argue that, since the pleasure-criterion is correct in a majority of the cases which are *clear*, it will be safe to use it in those which are uncertain; for Professor Sidgwick's conclusion does not maintain that it is correct even in a majority of the cases which are *clear*. We have then to consider by themselves the large number of cases, in which, for one reason or another, we cannot tell whether a course which gives most pleasure does or does not coincide with that which Common Sense declares to be best on the whole: it is only by adding these to the cases, where the two certainly coincide, that Professor Sidgwick gets, as a large majority among all cases, those in which there is no obvious disagreement between Hedonism and Common Sense. Now among these cases a large number will certainly be indeterminate for the reason that it is not plain which course gives a balance of pleasure; and these obviously cannot affect at all our judgment as to the correctness of the hedonic criterion. There remain only the cases, which, although they do present a balance of pleasure on one side, are unclear because Common Sense does not declare which is best on the whole. These are the cases which form Mr. McTaggart's [368] second and third class; and it is plain that the probability with regard to them is that the number of cases in which the hedonic course does, and in which it does not, coincide with that which is best on the whole will be equal in number. It was pointed out that in these cases there is, on Mr. McTaggart's principles, no rational solution, since, wherever one course shows a decisive superiority in one good (be it pleasure or any other), the other course will show a decisive superiority in some other. That there is, for this reason, no rational solution, must, I think, still be admitted; but, if we now take into account the fact that pleasure is a very slight good, I think it may be seen that pleasure is likely to be a *worse* criterion than many others. For if we use as our criterion a superiority in any good more valuable than pleasure, the chances that our choice will coincide with the course that is best on the whole will still be equal; but, in the cases where it does not coincide, the gravity of our error is likely to be considerably less, since we shall at any rate have secured a good of considerable value. Of course, it may be said that the course which shows a superiority in pleasure will generally also show a superiority in some more valuable good. But it cannot be assumed that this is always the case. And, for practical purposes, the important point to insist on is that, if pleasure be a comparatively small good, we cannot safely be satisfied that we have chosen a course, as good as we can see any to be, if we have chosen on the ground that it offers a balance of pleasure. For to adopt pleasure as a criterion, on the ground that it is as likely to be right as any other, means that in doubtful cases, where with great hesitation we decide that there is probably a superiority of pleasure on one side, we shall give the preference to that decision over an equally doubtful judgment that there is probably a superiority in other goods on the other side. The immense majority of cases are cases of such hesitating judgment; and, if pleasure be a small good, it is certain that to give this preference to the hesitating hedonic judgment will probably be wrong.

If this be so, then, if we must adopt any criterion at all, to adopt as such *any* considerable good will be more likely to lead [369] us right than to adopt pleasure. It may be said that of no other single good will there be so often a distinct superiority on one side as of pleasure. But, even if this be so, it will still be better to use different kinds of good as criteria in the different cases where they are applicable than to use pleasure in all. And finally it may well be doubted whether the calculation of pleasures does give us a definite result in more cases than the attempt to balance the total of goods on each side. That it does so is generally maintained on the plausible ground that to determine the effects of our actions on a single kind of good *must* be easier than to determine the effects on all together. But we have seen that Mr. McTaggart gives us no reason to think that the calculation of pleasure does in most cases give us a definite result; and against the *a priori* argument that such a calculation must be less complicated than the other, we have to urge the fact, which is generally neglected, that in this other we are dealing with quantities most of which exhibit a very decided difference in size. The greater *number* of the terms which we have to take into account may well be counterbalanced by the magnitude of their differences in respect of the relevant kind of quantity—namely quantity of intrinsic value. And, indeed, it seems, in practice, to be just as easy to decide that two whole sets of results are nearly equal in total value, as to decide that they are nearly equal in pleasure-value: and in practical cases, as has been said, such a judgment is all that we can hope for. In the vast majority of cases, cases in which we do not raise a question, Common Sense clearly has no doubt that the total of good on the one side is unquestionably greater than on the other; and the philosopher who argues that there is a superiority of pleasure on the same side cannot avoid bearing witness to the clearness of this judgment, and generally bears witness also to his own conviction that the judgment is correct. Mr. McTaggart himself does not fail to give indications of the ease with which he can judge totals of good other than pleasure: "The happiness a man gives is" he can see "generally more closely proportioned to the development of his ideals than is the happiness he enjoys" (p. 125). In any case, whether it be easier or not, it is by endeavoring to compare totals of [370] different goods and not of pleasure only, that men always have attacked and do attack their practical cases; and most men find it easy to see a decisive superiority on one side. They may, perhaps, be as often wrong as right; but, until a further philosophical investigation has settled the point, there is reason to think that, since the value of pleasure is small, when they are wrong, they are less wrong, than if they had taken pleasure for their guide.

NOTES

1. By John McTaggart Ellis McTaggart, M. A., Fellow and Lecturer of Trinity College, in Cambridge. Cambridge: At the University Press, 1901.

2. Mr. McTaggart himself admits that it occurs, p. 134.

3. So Mr. McTaggart himself admits, p. 126 note.

10

Kant's Idealism

"It has been hitherto assumed," says Kant,[1] that all our knowledge must conform to objects; but on this assumption all attempts to make out anything about those objects *a priori* by means of conceptions, in such a way as to enlarge our knowledge, came to nothing. Then let us try for once, whether we do not succeed better in the problems of Metaphysics, by assuming that objects must conform to our knowledge; an hypothesis, which is immediately more agreeable to the desired possibility of an *a priori* knowledge of them—a knowledge which can establish something with regard to objects, *before they are given to us*.[2] It is with this assumption as with the first ideas of Copernicus, who, when he found he could not advance in the explanation of the motions of the heavenly bodies, on the assumption that the whole host of stars revolved around the spectator, tried whether he could not succeed better, if he supposed the spectator to revolve and the stars to stand still. Now a similar experiment can be made in Metaphysics, so far as concerns the *Intuition* of objects. If our intuition were bound to conform to the nature of the objects, I do

Originally published in *Proceedings of the Aristotelian Society* n.s. 4 (1903–1904): 127–140.

not see how we can know anything *a priori* about that nature; but if the object (as presented to the senses) conforms to the nature of our intuitive faculty, I can very well imagine such a possibility. Since, however, I cannot stop short at these intuitions, if they are to be converted into knowledge, but must relate them as presentations to something or other as object and must determine this object by their means, I can again [128] either assume that the *conceptions*, by means of which I bring this determination to pass, also conform to the object, and then I am again in the same perplexity regarding the manner in which I can know anything about it *a priori*: or else I assume that the objects or (which is the same thing) our *experience*, in which alone they are known as given objects, conforms to these conceptions, and then I at once see an easier way out of my difficulty, since experience is itself such a kind of knowledge as to require the Understanding; and I must presuppose the rule of the Understanding *in myself*,[3] before objects are given me, that is, must presuppose it *a priori*—a rule which is expressed in *a priori* conceptions, to which accordingly all objects of experience must necessarily conform, and with which they must agree."

In this passage Kant gives a sufficiently clear account of one of the points in which his Idealism differs from the Idealism of Berkeley, with which he was so angry at having his own confused. And this point is the one to which, as he himself explains, he refers by calling his theory Transcendental Idealism. He means by that title that he attributes merely ideal existence, or existence in the mind, to certain entities which are not indeed *transcendent*, since they are not *objects*, but which are also not *parts* of experience or particular experiences, since they are, as he says, conditions of all possible experience. These entities are not *objects*—substantial individuals or things—but are merely "forms" in which the objects of experience are arranged: they are the forms of Intuition, Space and Time, and the forms of thought, conceptions of the Understanding or "categories," of which one instance is "causality." Kant's Idealism is Transcendental, and differs from Berkeley's in that, whereas Berkeley only maintained the "ideality," or merely mental existence of particular objects, Kant maintains the ideality of the forms in which these objects are arranged. Berkeley and others before Kant had not perceived the [129] necessity of distinguishing so clearly between sense-impressions, "the matter of knowledge," and the forms in which all such impressions are always arranged.

Kant, then, here gives us one point in which his Idealism differs from Berkeley's; he holds, what Berkeley did not expressly hold, that space and time and causality exist only in or for the mind. And he also gives us one of the reasons which lead him to think this particular view of his true. If, he says, we only saw that particular objects had geometrical properties, we could not possibly be entitled to assert that *all* objects would *always* have them. It is only if the mind is so constituted that, whenever anything is presented to it, it invests that thing with geometrical properties, that we can be entitled to assert that everything we shall ever experience will have those properties. In short, Kant offers his theory as an explanation of how we can know that certain things are true of *all* objects. If, he says, we know that the mind always attaches these predicates to everything presented to it, then we can know that everything presented will have these predicates. Therefore, he concludes, the only predicates which do attach to *all* things—formal predicates—are given to them by the mind.

Kant's Transcendental Idealism is thus connected with what was certainly a great discovery of his. He discovered that all mathematical propositions are what he calls "synthetic"—as he here says, that they "enlarge our knowledge." They do not merely tell us that a certain predicate is a part of that of which we predicate it: they tell us that A has the predicate B, although B is neither identical with A, nor a part of A; they are not identical nor analytic. Hume had convinced Kant that the proposition, "Every event has a cause," was not analytic; and, in thinking of this fact,

Kant discovered, what no one had clearly recognised before, that 2 + 2 = 4 was not analytic either. Hume had inferred that we had no reason whatever to believe that every event had a cause; but Kant thought it was obviously absurd to maintain this of 2 + 2 = 4: it was [130] absurd to say that we had no title to assert "2 + 2 are *always* 4"; to admit that 2 + 2 might sometimes make 4 and sometimes not. But, on the other hand, all previous philosophers, who had held that we did know *universal* propositions, had held that they were analytic; that it was only because they asserted "B is a part of A B," or "A" is identical with "A," that we could know them to be *always* true. Kant, therefore, saw an entirely new difficulty. He saw, in consequence of what Hume said, that 2 + 2 = 4 was synthetic; yet he was convinced (what Hume would have led him to deny) that 2 + 2 = 4 was *always* true—true of every case. In his own words, he recognised for the first time that there are "*a priori* synthetic propositions." He asked himself the question: How are synthetic *a priori* propositions possible? And Transcendental Idealism was his answer. They are possible only because Space, Time, and the categories are "ideal"—ways in which the mind arranges things.

I have thus represented Kant's Transcendental Idealism as an attempt to answer the question: How can we know *universal* synthetic propositions to be true? This is certainly a part of the meaning of the passage which I have quoted: Kant certainly does maintain this, whatever else he may maintain besides. And it is only this theory which I propose to consider. I may, perhaps, explain (since I have used ambiguous language) that I mean by a universal proposition, any proposition which asserts, either "All instances of A have the predicate B," or "Anything which has the predicate A has the predicate B." I may also add that I have no doubt whatever that the instances of such propositions which I have quoted, namely, all mathematical propositions and the proposition, "Every event has a cause," are, as Kant thought, synthetic.

I do not propose to argue that point. I regard it as an exceedingly important discovery of Kant's—a discovery which would, perhaps, by itself alone, entitle him to the rank usually assigned him among philosophers.

[131] My present business, however, is with Transcendental Idealism.

I propose to consider *both*, whether Transcendental Idealism gives a satisfactory answer to the question: How are synthetic propositions *a priori* possible? *and* whether Transcendental Idealism is true. And for this purpose, I will first try to re-state, in the simplest possible terms, with less reference to Kant's own language than I have hitherto used, precisely what the question is, to which I doubt whether Transcendental Idealism is a satisfactory answer. Kant, as I have said, may be trying to answer other questions as well; the meaning of his terms is much more complex than that of those which I shall use: but he certainly does pretend to have solved the difficulty I shall state—that was one of the difficulties in his mind—and I only propose to consider that part of his doctrine.

Well, then, we have the fact that we do make judgments of the following kind. We believe that: If there be *any* two groups of objects, of each of which it may be truly predicated that there are two objects in the group, then it may be truly predicated of the whole that it is a group of four objects: this proposition is *universal*, it concerns *all* groups of the kind named. And we have similar geometrical beliefs. We believe that: Of any objects of which we can truly predicate certain geometrical relations, we may also truly predicate some other different geometrical relation. Finally, we can at least think, whether we believe or not, that: Every event in time has been preceded at a certain interval by some other event, such that, whenever an event of precisely this second kind exists, an event of the first kind will exist after it at exactly the same distance in time: *i.e.*, every event has a cause.

These are all of them universal propositions, they all assert that a certain predicate, of what Kant calls a *formal* kind, attaches to *all* objects to which a certain other predicate attaches. And, [132] being universal, they are all independent of experience in the following sense: they all assert that certain predicates apply to things which we never have seen and never shall see—to things which nobody has even thought of: they say that certain predicates apply to *all* objects of a certain kind, whether actually experienced or not. This was Kant's difficulty. How can we know that certain predicates do attach to things which we have never experienced? How can we know that any universal proposition is true? And his answer is: Because the mind is such that it attaches these predicates to everything whatever which it ever experiences. This is the doctrine of Transcendental Idealism.

Now what I want first to point out is that Kant's question is ambiguous. He is asking, as if they were one, *two* quite different questions. *Two* questions are always asked, whenever we ask: How can we or do we *know* a thing? for the simple reason that knowledge is a complex concept. When we say we *know* a thing, we mean *both* that we believe it, that we have a certain mental attitude towards the proposition in question, and also we mean that the proposition is *true*. Hence, when we ask: How do you know that? we are asking both: (1) How do you come to believe it, what is the *cause* of your believing it? and (2), How do you know that what you believe is true? What title have you to say that your belief is knowledge and not *mere* belief? What evidence proves that the object of your belief is true?

Now it is evident that the second of these questions is far the more important; and it is evident also that Kant intended to answer this second question. He wished to explain the *validity* of universal propositions; not only how we could come to believe them, but how they could be valid. Only so, could he be contradicting Hume's sceptical conclusion. Hume asserted: We have no title to believe that every event has a cause; and Kant answers: We have a title; I can prove it *true* that every event has a cause.

[133] Kant, therefore, is trying to prove the validity of universal propositions—that we have a title to assert them. And he regards his Transcendental Idealism as giving this title. His argument is: Every object will have certain formal predicates, because mind always gives an object that form. I wish to point out two absolutely conclusive objection to this argument:—

(1) Kant says: From the fact that mind is so constituted as to give to every object a certain form, we can infer that every presented object will have that form. And this reasoning is perfectly valid; the conclusion does follow from the premiss. But the *first* objection which I have to make to the whole argument is this, namely, that the premiss itself is a universal proposition of exactly the same kind which it was proposed to *prove.* The premiss is: Mind *always* acts in a certain way upon, arranges in a certain manner, *everything* which is presented to it. That is to say, the only evidence which Kant offers to prove the validity of universal propositions is—merely another universal proposition. It is, then, perfectly certain that he has not done what he professed to do—given us a title to believe all universal propositions. There is *one* universal proposition, at least, which he has simply assumed, for which he has given no reason. If you ask him: How can you know that mind will *always* act in that manner? he has no answer to give. He simply assumes that *this* proposition is true, and that there is no need of evidence to prove it so. It is certain, on the contrary, that it needs evidence just as much as $2 + 2 = 4$; if we need a title to believe that $2 + 2 = 4$, we certainly need one to believe that mind always acts in a certain way on every presented object. I do not now say that this universal proposition of Kant's is untrue; I shall presently try to show that it is. My present point is only this perfectly certain one: that there is *one* universal proposition, at least, which Kant has given us no title to believe; that,

therefore, Kant has *not*, in his own words, "explained the possibility of *all* synthetic propositions *a priori*."

[134] But (2) there is a far more serious objection to Kant's argument. I have just said that a certain conclusion will follow from Kant's premiss, if once you assume that premiss to be true; and it is, I think, this fact—the fact that that conclusion does follow from the premiss, which gives to Kant's Transcendental Idealism whatever plausibility it possesses. But what is the conclusion which follows from the premiss? The premiss is: "Mind always gives a certain form to everything presented"; and the conclusion which follows from this is: "Everything presented will always have the formal predicates which mind gives to it." And what I have now to point out is that this conclusion, which *does* follow from Kant's assumption, is *not* the conclusion which Kant set out to prove. Let us remember what the universal propositions were, of which Kant was going to prove the possibility. One of them was: The total number of objects in any two groups, of two each, is 4. And *this* conclusion will *not* follow from Kant's premiss. What *will* follow is only this: Whenever we perceive two groups of 2, then the whole group has the predicate 4 given it by mind. That is to say, it does not entitle us to assert that *any* 2 groups of 2 make 4; but only that any two presented groups make 4 *at the time when they are presented*. Kant's premiss does not entitle him to any more than this: he has given us no reason whatever to think but that the moment 2 groups of 2 objects cease to be presented, precisely the very same objects in those same two groups, which had the total number 4 when presented, may have the total number 7 or 5 or a hundred billions. In other words, Kant's premiss does *not* prove that $2 + 2 = 4$ in every case: on the contrary, it allows that more often than not $2 + 2$ may make 5 or any other number. That is to say, Kant's Transcendental Idealism gives no answer to that scepticism, greater than Hume's, which he devised it to answer.

But, so far, I have given to Kant's argument the interpretation which is the most favourable for him in one respect: [135] I have assumed his principle to be that mind does really give to objects the formal predicates in question, so that when they are presented they really and truly have those predicates; I have allowed that, assuming his premiss, it would follow that 2 and 2 are *sometimes* 4; and this is certainly the *most* favourable interpretation possible: his premiss certainly will not entitle us to assert that 2 and 2 are always or even generally 4. But even this conclusion—that 2 and 2 are *sometimes* 4—will only follow if we assume him really to mean that mind *gives* these predicates to objects, so that, for the moment, they really belong to them: and I believe that this hypothesis was part of what was in Kant's mind. Yet I believe also that he would never for a moment have entertained such a belief, unless he had confused it with another, which is quite different and much more plausible. No one, I think, has ever definitely maintained the proposition, that mind actually *gives* properties to things: that, *e.g.*, it *makes* one thing the cause of another, or makes 2 and 2 = 4. What it *is* plausible to maintain is that the nature of our mind causes us to *think* that one thing is cause of another, and to *think* that 2 and 2 are 4. This, I think, is certainly *part* of what Kant meant by his Transcendental Idealism; though he confused it with the different theory that mind gave objects these properties. Indeed, I think it may be worth while to point out that this interpretation strictly follows from one doctrine of Kant's, the precise meaning of which has not received all the attention it deserves. Namely, Kant holds that we cannot know *at all* what properties belong to "Things in Themselves." What I wish to point out is that if we examine carefully the meaning of the statement, it merely amounts to this: That we never can know that a thing, *as it is in itself*, really has, even for a moment, any property whatever. It would follow, therefore, that in Kant's view, when I think "The fingers on this hand are five," I do not really know that those fingers, as they are in themselves, are five; and if I don't know that, the only alternative is that, in Kant's view, I merely [136] *think* them to be 5. A good deal of confusion has, I think, arisen from the failure to see that the only alternative to the admission that we do know things *as they are in themselves*, is the admission that we have no knowledge at all. We cannot escape this dilemma by contrasting with "Things-in-themselves" the "objects of experience": for, if we know anything about the objects of experience, then we know what properties the objects of experience have, *as they are in themselves*. Even to know what we think about them is to know a Thing-in-itself. For if we do know that we think a thing at all, then we know that our thought, *as it is in itself*, really is a thought of that thing. Thus, in so far as Kant denies any possible knowledge of "Things-in-themselves," there is reason to suppose that he does not really think that mind *gives* predicates to objects, so that even for a moment those objects really have their predicate: his theory is that we do not know what properties anything really has itself.

Let us then suppose his Transcendental Idealism to mean that the mind is so constituted as always to *make us think* that the objects presented to it have certain predicates. Can he infer from this premiss the validity of universal propositions? On the contrary, he cannot now infer that 2 and 2 are 4 even in any one instance: he can only infer that we shall always think them to be so. From the fact that we always think a thing it certainly does not follow that what we think is true.

I have, then, tried to show that on neither of two possible interpretations of Kant's Transcendental Idealism will it follow from that doctrine that universal propositions are valid: on the first, it will only follow that 2 and 2 are sometimes 4, on the second it will not follow that 2 and 2 are ever 4, but only that we always think so. And, before that, I pointed out that Kant's Transcendental Idealism was itself an universal proposition; and that, therefore, even if it proved the validity of any others (as we now see it doesn't), it does not prove the validity of all.

[137] I now propose to deal briefly with the question: Is this universal proposition itself—the proposition that the mind always attaches to things certain formal predicates, or makes us think that things have these predicates—itself true? And first of all: What reason has Kant to give for it? Here we find, curiously enough, that his chief reason is the assumed fact that other universal propositions are true: he infers that this must be true of the mind, from the assumed fact that mathematical propositions and the principle of causality are true. What he says is: They could not be true, *unless* mind contributed these predicates; we could have no title to assert that all things had causes, unless the mind gave them this predicate. Since, therefore, all things have causes, and 2 and 2 are always 4, the mind must give these predicates. This reasoning obviously will not prove Transcendental Idealism. From the mere fact that the number of objects in two groups of two is 4, we cannot infer that mind caused them to have that predicate; nor from that fact can we even infer that mind caused us to think that they were 4. There is, therefore, so far, no reason whatever to think Transcendental Idealism true; and I am not aware that Kant gives any other reason for it. He does not profess, by an empirical observation of the mind, to discover that it always does cause events to have effects or cause us to think that 2 and 2 are 4. Nor do I know of any facts tending to show that this is the case. It may be true that every mental event has some mental cause; and thus if Transcendental Idealism only asserted that our *belief* in universal propositions has some mental cause, Transcendental Idealism might possibly be true. But even this is quite doubtful; I have only to say, as against one form of the theory, that I can find no evidence that, when I apprehend that 2 and 2 are 4, that apprehension is any more due to the activity of my mind than when I see the colour of that tablecloth. I can appre-

hend that 2 and 2 are 4 as passively as I can apprehend anything. Transcendental Idealism may possibly be true if it [138] be understood as this comparatively unimportant psychological proposition; what is certain is that it does not explain the possibility of experience, if by that be meant that it gives us a title to assert universal propositions, and not merely that it asserts our belief in them to have some mental cause.

So much then for Kant's Idealism, so far as regards the point, in which, as I said, it differs obviously from that of Berkeley, namely, the contention that our knowledge of universal propositions is due to the constitution of our minds. This appears to me to be the only Idealistic contention for which Kant offers any arguments, and I have tried to show with regard to those arguments (1) that it will not explain the validity of universal propositions, *i.e.*, will not give us any ground for thinking them true, and (2) that it will not follow from their validity, and is at best merely a doubtful psychological assumption. But I have now to mention certain idealistic opinions, for which Kant gives no arguments, but which he certainly holds and which differ in no respect from those of Berkeley. Kant holds, namely, that spatial and temporal properties, that sounds and colours, and that causality exist only in the mind of him who is aware of them. He holds that space and time themselves are forms of consciousness, that sounds and colours are sensations, that causality is a conception. In all this he agrees with Berkeley; Berkeley also held that everything of which we are aware is an idea or a notion—a constituent part, that is, of our own minds. Kant himself has denied furiously that he does agree with Berkeley; he says he holds that we do know that objects really exist in space; and if he had held that, he certainly would not have agreed with Berkeley. But I shall try to show that he himself did not know what he held; that, at least, he certainly held that objects do not exist in space. It has often been pointed out that at one time Kant says his difference from Berkeley is that he asserts the existence of Things-in-themselves, while Berkeley denies it; and at another time says his difference is that he [139] asserts the existence of things in space, while Berkeley denies that. On the first point he certainly does not differ from Berkeley, since Berkeley also holds that there do exist things-in-themselves, though he says there are none except God and other minds. But that matter exists, Berkeley certainly does deny: and what I have now to show is that Kant denies it too.

Let us consider what is Kant's theory of experience. He holds that objects of experience, *e.g.*, chairs and tables, consist of the "matter of sensation," colours, sounds, and other qualities, arranged in the "forms" of space and time, and connected by the categories or forms of understanding. With regard to the first of these entities, sensations, he never suggests for a moment that he means by them anything but mental facts: on the contrary, he repeatedly insists that what he is talking about is *presentations* (Vorstellungen), *i.e.*, when he says "blue," he means *the consciousness of blue*; when he says "hard," he means *the sensation of hardness*. It is, then, these mental, purely subjective, elements, out of which, according to him, when they are arranged in space and time, matter and all material objects are *composed*. When we perceive an object in space, what we perceive, according to him, is merely some sensations of our own arranged in space and time and connected with other things by the categories. That is to say, the *subjects* of what I have called his formal predicates are exclusively our own sensations: when I say that there are 4 chairs there, he understands me to say that I have 4 groups of sensations—it is to my sensations that the predicate 4 attaches. It is plain, then, that the matter of sensation is, according to him, merely in my mind. But it is equally plain that time and space and the categories are so too: his great discovery is, he often says, that the former are ways in which the subject is affected, and that the latter are ways in which it acts. If, then, he did maintain that matter really existed, other than as a part of mind, he would be maintaining that [140] out of three subjective things, things in my mind, there was somehow composed one thing that was objective, *not* in my mind. But he never does maintain this: what he does maintain is that to say that sensations have spatial predicates and are connected by the categories, is *the same thing* as to say that they exist objectively. And, if this be understood, it is plain why he thought he disagreed with Berkeley. If to say that matter exists is simply equivalent to saying that the categories do apply to it, he does hold that matter exists. But the fact is that the two statements are *not* equivalent: I can see quite plainly that when I think that chair exists, what I think is *not* that certain sensations of mine are connected by the categories. What I do think is that certain *objects* of sensations do really exist in a real space and really are causes and effects of other things. Whether what I think is true is another question: what is certain is that if we ask whether matter exists, we are asking this question; we are not asking whether certain sensations of ours are connected by the categories. And one other thing is certain too, namely, that colours and sounds are *not* sensations; that space and time are *not* forms of sense; that causality is *not* a thought. All these things are things *of* which we are aware, things *of* which we are conscious; they are in no sense parts of consciousness. Kant's Idealism, therefore, in so far as it asserts that matter is composed of mental elements, is certainly false. In so far as it asserts this, it differs in no respect from Berkeley's, and both are false. Whether or not Kant's further contention, in which he also agrees with Berkeley, is also false—namely, that what we really do mean by matter, something *not* composed of mental elements, does not exist—this, as I say, is quite another question.

NOTES

1. Preface to Second Edition of *Critique of Pure Reason.*
2. My italics.
3. My italics.

Index